Medieval warfare

Medieval warfare

H W KOCH

CRESCENT BOOKS
NEW YORK

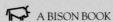 A BISON BOOK

This 1983 edition is published by Crescent Books,
distributed by Crown Publishers, Inc.

Printed in Hong Kong

Library of Congress Cataloging in Publication Data

Koch, H. W. (Hannsjoachim Wolfgang), 1933–
     Medieval Warfare.

     Reprint. Originally published: London : Bison Books,
c1978.
     Includes index.
     1. Military art and science – History. 2. Military
history, Medieval. 3. Middle Ages. I. Title.
[U37.K62 1983]   355′.009′02   82-17231
ISBN 0-517-39938-5

h g f e d c b a

Previous page. *The capture of Ascalon, 1099 (*Chroniques
d'Outremer, *fifteenth century).*

Below. *The Hundred Years' War: infantry scaling the walls of an
enemy encampment (*Chroniques de Charles VII, *fifteenth
century).*

Alexander the Great (356B.C.–323B.C.) besieges the city of Tyre, 322B.C.
Miniature from a French ms illustrating the history of Alexander the Great.

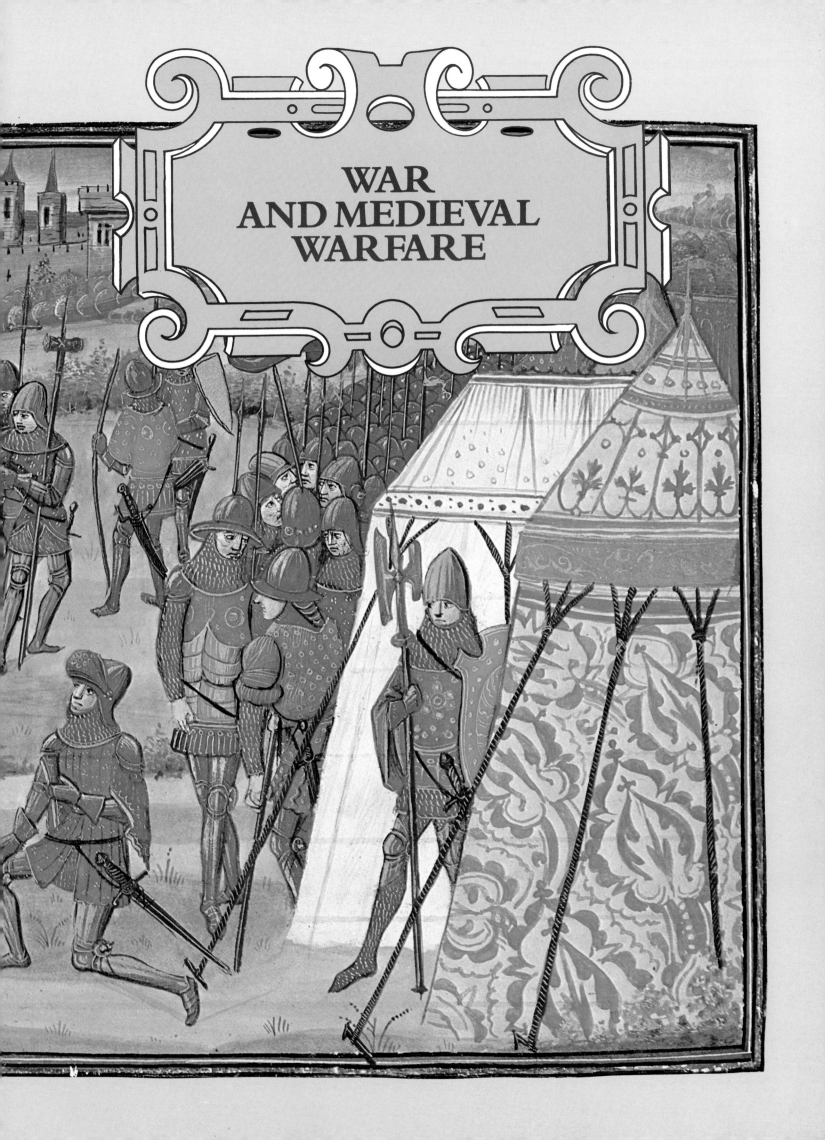

WAR
AND MEDIEVAL
WARFARE

Throughout history the most dominant expression of conflicts between tribes, states, and civilizations has been war. There is no civilization, no empire, no state whose roots do not go down deeply into soil drenched with the blood of the victor and the vanquished. The very fact that the Mediterranean culture was Roman and not Carthaginian is the outcome of war. That France remained Frankish and did not become Islamic is the result of war. Wars and battles have been so fundamentally important that they have shaped our world for centuries. Historical understanding also includes the understanding of war.

Naturally there is a difference between a fight over contested territory and a confrontation between two different cultures. Wars between different cultures are conflicts over principles, over questions of faith, involving the complete displacement of either one or the other of the antagonists. Such was the expansion of Islam that within a few centuries half the then-known world was subjected to its rule. In the Islamic conception there was only the Territory of Peace subject to Allah and his prophet Mohammed. Outside that territory there was the Territory of War settled by infidels, territory which one day would inevitably be conquered and transformed and integrated into the Territory of Peace.

History has shown that when two different societies clash it is by no means certain that the socially and materially more advanced will be the victor. The history of antiquity is rich with examples of that kind. Very often a relatively highly advanced society ventured forth to conquest only to find that its resources were very quickly drained to an unreplenishable extent. It depended upon a leader or leadership elite which when removed caused the collapse of the entire edifice of expansive ambitions. In ancient Greece the thoughts of the philosophers had always been confined by the Greek city-state. The very idea of expansionism was alien. It was Alexander the Great and his

idea of world empire which represented the breaking down of the old barriers between Greeks and Barbarians leading towards an all-embracing universalism. Socrates had already preached the mission of Greece as the conquering nation and the civilizer of the Barbarians. Alexander represented the Pan-Hellenistic movement, but within a few short years he had transcended that attitude and in its place had put the imperial aim of creating a New Order of Peace based on the intellectual and cultural premises of Greek society. He ignored the advice of his teacher Aristotle who emphasized that the native born Greek should at all times take precedence over the assimilated Barbarian. Carried by the conviction that he was a prince of peace, Alexander endeavored to wield into one state all those willing to accept his laws before which everyone was equal. Alexander's premature death brought about the disintegration of his vision. What remained was his idea, the idea of 'Empire.'

The synthesis of the genius of Greece with that of Latium came when Rome ultimately took up the idea of Empire. Of immensely greater political ability than its eastern neighbors, Rome had established its predominance over Italy by the third century B.C. A century later it took its first steps towards world power: Carthage and Africa became Roman provinces. Greece was reduced to a protectorate of the province of Macedonia, and eventually Corinth and the rest of Greece fell under Roman dominance. By the time Caesar's adopted son Augustus took power, the Roman Republic had been transformed into the Roman Empire. The Roman Emperors became 'Fathers of Mankind.' Public offices were no longer the privileges of native

The Roman Empire showing the disposition of the Roman dioceses and Barbarian tribes under Diocletian (245–513). His period of office was troubled by the waves of Barbarian invasions which finally overwhelmed the Roman Empire in the fifth century. Rome was sacked on two occasions, the first was in 410 by the Visigoths and the second in 455 by the Vandals.

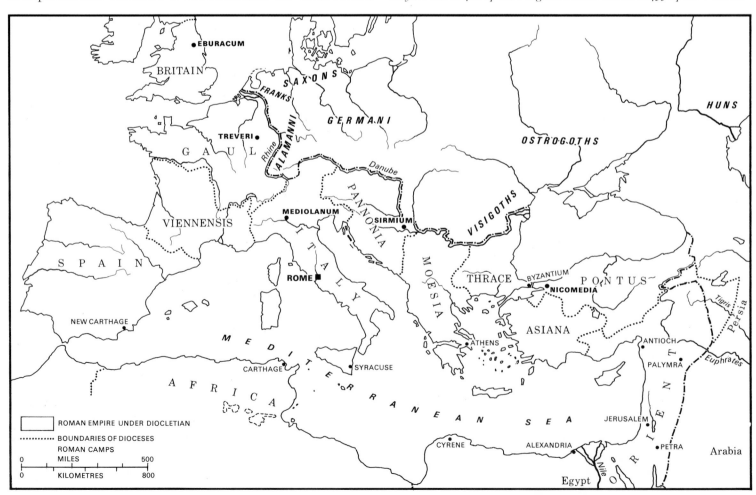

citizens of Rome; they were accessible to all subjects of the empire.

Yet at the height of its achievement the seed of decay and destruction of the Empire had already been sown. The Empire was not large enough, yet at the same time, it was too large. It did not embrace and civilize the Barbarians on its frontiers who could not therefore participate in its honors and privileges. By the time these exemptions were remedied it was too late. The decaying Roman Empire lacked the organizational forces necessary to integrate the Barbarians.

It was in the protracted military conflict between the decaying Empire and the Barbarians that many characteristic elements of medieval warfare were forged. These elements—the typical weapons, tactics, organization, command structures and so on—did not, to be sure, come into being in any systematic way. Some were primarily of Graeco-Roman origin; some derived from the Barbarians; some resulted from a fusion of the ideas of the two cultures; and some were inventions owing little to the past.

This book is intended to be no more than an outline of the history of warfare in the Middle Ages. Nevertheless the author has been confronted with one major problem which applies both to specialist reports and to general works. How does one define the Middle Ages? When do they begin and when do they end?

At this point one could enter into endless pedantic discussions to which there would be no final correct solution but several equally correct but diametrically opposed answers. For greater ease and convenience, I have chosen to interpret the question in my own way and rephrase it for the purpose of this volume: Why begin with Arminius and the Romans and end with Gustavus Adolphus and Wallenstein? Why begin at an age before what is now called the Middle Ages and end well after they have passed? To *these* questions I have answers.

A history of warfare should not simply be about battles—how soldiers conduct them and how they behave in them. If that were what warfare was about then there would be only minor differences between Thermopylae and Stalingrad or between Cannae and Blenheim. This writer is conservative enough to believe that basic human character has been more or less the same throughout the ages and will remain so. But this cannot be said about his environment and more importantly about the reciprocal processes of man's adapting to it and his adapting it to meet his needs and purposes.

A history of warfare should not only concern the heroism, indifference or cowardice of individuals or armies but should discuss the societies which reared them, the social and economic framework within which they operated, and the changes within that framework that affected and transformed the methods of conducting war. Hence this book begins with an early confrontation between different forms of social and economic organization and methods of industrial production, a confrontation in fact between the Germanic tribes and the Roman legions. It ends with a society at war, a war that began with a military organization that can be traced back to the Middle Ages. Wallenstein's army was the first standing army to bear the characteristics associated with the modern armies of today.

History as it occurs 'in the field' is not ordered or structured. It is only the minds of historians who introduce order and discipline into the disorder, using such 'measured' means as chronological divisions and periodization. But these divisions and the attaching of labels to particular periods are rarely correct and never precise. That is no fault of the historians but of history itself. Continuation and overlapping of events and ideas within and between periods obscure their precise definition. For ex-

Medieval miniature illuminating the 'C' of the Emperor Charlemagne (742–814) who, during his lifetime, stemmed the tide of the later Barbarian Invasions in Europe (William of Tyre ms).

ample, nationalism is frequently described as a by-product of the French Revolution and of the nineteenth century. Yet, are not many of the characteristics of '*nationalism*' now observable in societies which identify themselves not with a '*nation*' but with a city, a religious faith or ideology, or, for that matter, with a color of skin?

The limitations of both chronology and of applying labels to periods are evident within the text of this book. Labels are necessary, but nevertheless, we must always be aware of the auxiliary role they play within the historian's conceptual and methodological apparatus; we must be aware of their intrinsic tenuousness and the *flow* of events. The period between the Battles of Adrianople and Agincourt in which cavalry dominated foot soldiers was not suddenly pre-empted by one in which infantry gained ascendency. Adrianople, Courtrai, Agincourt and so on are simply milestones marking the process of change—they are not turning-points themselves. Although there is a chapter entitled 'Renaissance Trends,' for instance, the reader will discover that this period was still dominated by the traditional medieval methods of warfare, although the geographic environment of the area examined was, in fact, loaded against these methods. But he will also find the new beside the old, sometimes together, sometimes in opposition and that it was not always the new which conquered or replaced the old.

In other words, there are few if any clear-cut divisions; the history of medieval warfare reflects, as all history, continuous flux. The object of this exercise is to present an overview of European *society* at war at given points in its development, points which illustrate significant societal alterations more than the obvious short-term or even long-term consequences of any particular battle or war.

In any case, it is not possible to understand medieval warfare without first knowing something of its antecedents. The story must necessarily begin with the long bitter struggle between Rome and the Barbarian tribes of western Europe.

Barbarian warriors of Europe and their weapons.

THE ROMAN EMPIRE AND THE RISE OF THE BARBARIANS

The principal forces with which the Romans had to contend were the Germanic tribes to the north, tribes which on the surface were vastly inferior in their political, social, economic and military organization. The Germans did not comprise a single political and social unit at the beginning of the year 1 A.D. but were divided into various tribes, each settling within an area of one hundred square miles. Because of the danger of hostile invasions, the marches of these territories were left uninhabited, the population concentrating itself in the interior. Some twenty Germanic peoples lived between the rivers Rhine and Elbe as well as the Main to the south in an area covered predominantly by woods and swamps. The approximate density of the population, living from subsistence agriculture, amounted to 250 per square mile. The size of the individual tribes varied from 25,000 to 40,000, which would mean that each of them could muster 6000 to 10,000 warriors.

Their social structure also explains their early vulnerability to attacks by the Roman legions. Each people divided itself arbitrarily into large family units, *geschlechter* (kinships). (Towns and cities to which family members could have migrated and intermingled did not exist at this time.) These family units were also called *hundreds*, because they either comprised a hundred families or a hundred warriors. The hundred which included family members ranged in numbers from 400 to 1000 and lived on a territory of a few square miles in a village which was situated according to the suitability of the immediate environment. Women and men unfit as warriors carried on what little agriculture there was.

In times of war the members of the hundred formed one troop of warriors. The German word *dorf* (or *thorpe* in the Nordic countries) connotes such a warrior community. The thorpe was also a form of assembly; troop is its direct derivative.

Hence, the Germanic tribal community consisted of villages or settlements, the territory it covered was called a *gau* and its basic military unit was the hundred. Each community had its elected head, the *ealdorman* or *hunno*.

The *hunno's* official function was twofold; he was the head of the village community and the leader in war. Although the post was not hereditary, evidence exists showing that the custom of electing the sons of *hunnos* in succession was widespread. Since the leader in war also had the privilege of getting a larger share of the booty than the other members, the riches accumulated by the leaders allowed them to have servants and to rally the bravest around them who would defend their lord unto death. From these families the popular assembly of the people, the *thing*, would elect its leader, the *first*, a term which in German became the *fürst*, or the prince, whose functions also included holding courts throughout the *gau* to administer justice.

What stands out from all this is that the Germanic peoples were rather few in number; yet all the chroniclers from Tacitus onwards tell us about the fierce bravery of the Germans and their military effectiveness. Considering their small numbers individual bravery would have amounted to little if there had not been an efficiently functioning military structure. Unlike the Romans, the Germans knew nothing of military discipline. Among the Germanic tribes the cement which held them together was provided by the organic ties within a village, a hundred, or for that matter within an entire tribe.

Of course the effort and the bravery of the individual were essential but of value only when exercised within a coherent tactical body, and that body was the hundred composed of men related to one another by ties of blood. There is no evidence to show that the hundreds ever carried out military exercises. They displayed none of the drill of the Roman legions, but their inner

Left. *The Teutoburger Battles.*

Below. *Captured Germanic woman: detail from Trajan's Column.*

cohesion, based upon the certainty of being able to rely fully on those around you, was superior to that shown by the Romans. A Roman force when defeated usually scattered. A Germanic force in similar straits usually remained intact because it was an organic body. The *hunno* had the advantage of commanding a 'natural' force rather than the artificial one of his Roman counterpart. By the military standards of Rome, the Germans were a rabble, and from a Roman perspective rightly so, but as the Romans were to experience time and time again, this 'rabble' was efficient. The Romans eventually came to realize that the Germans confronted them with a different type of military organization explicable only against the background of their social and political construction.

Tacitus provided us with a description of the way in which the Germans fought on foot. He portrayed them as tactical bodies which were as deep as they were wide—in other words front and rear and both flanks are equally strong: 400 men, 20 deep and 20 wide, or 10,000 men, 100 deep and 100 wide. Naturally the most exposed positions of such a formation would be the warriors at the flanks of the first line, because they were threatened by their opponent from the front as well as from the side. This square was the basic tactical formation of the Germans, in the same way as the phalanx was the original tactical formation of the Romans. In an attack the phalanx had the advantage of bringing more weapons to bear than the square and had greater maneuverability for its wings. The weakness of the Roman phalanx was the vulnerability of its flanks especially when attacked by cavalry, and cavalry was one of the strengths of the Germans. To show equal strength in all directions the Germans preferred deep formations.

These two different tactical approaches have their origins in technological development. The Germans possessed relatively little protective armor and few metal weapons. Consequently the Germans placed their best armed men in the front ranks to protect those less well armed in the center of the square. Another advantage which the Germanic square had over the phalanx was that it was tactically more mobile and it could more easily adjust to its geographical surroundings than the linear formation, much in the same way as the Napoleonic divisional column proved superior to the linear tactics of the eighteenth century.

Tacitus described the arms of the Germans as follows: 'Only few possess a sword or a spear with a metal head. As a rule they carry spears capped with a short and narrow metal point; the weapon is so handy that it can be used to spike as well as to throw. Cavalry carries only shield and spear. Those on foot also carry missiles (stones or stone balls catapulted by a hand sling.) The Germans enter battle bare chested or, at the most are clad with a light cover which hinders them little in their movement. Far removed from them is any idea to shine in the splendor of their weapons. Only their shields are painted in glaring colors. Only very few possess armor, hardly anyone a metal or leather helmet.

Their horses are distinguished neither by their beauty nor by their speed. Nor are they in contrast to us, trained to carry out maneuvers of many kinds. The Germanic cavalry rides either straight forward or with one movement to the right—a circular movement so that no one remains behind.

The main strength of the Germans are their foot troops; for that reason they fight in mixed formations in which the foot troops, because of their physical dexterity, are required to adjust to the movements of the horsemen. For that purpose the quickest young men are selected and put at the point where the cavalry has its place.

To leave one's place as long as one pushes forward again is not interpreted as a sign of fear but one of clever calculation. They salvage their wounded and dead even under the most unfavorable of battle conditions. The loss of one's shield is considered as a particularly great disgrace; he who does is not allowed to participate in a religious

celebration or in the *thing*. Therefore many a one who has come back from war in good health, has taken the rope to put an end to his disgrace . . .'

The shield was made of wood or wickerwork covered with leather. Such headgear as there was, was made of leather or fur. The long spear had to be used with both hands, which of course did not allow its bearer to carry a shield. This in turn led to the gradual adoption of armor taken either directly from the Romans on the battlefield or made from leather. In addition it was the task of those carrying smaller weapons like hand axes to protect the spear-carrying warrior with their shield. Something that has hitherto found no adequate explanation is why the Germans who had used the bow and arrow in the Bronze Age did not continue to use that weapon. The bow and arrow did not reappear until the third century.

After the Romans had captured Gaul, their main motive for trying to make inroads into the heartland of Germany seems to have been to secure their provinces from the attacks of the Barbarians. It was not the kind of countryside which looked particularly inviting, nor did it prove suitable for Roman-style battles. A rough climate, seemingly endless forests, dangerous swampy regions were hardly worthy of conquest.

Securing Gaul by subduing nearby Germanic tribes posed the major problem of securing supplies. Caesar could afford his campaign in Gaul, for supplies were plentiful there. However, supplying large armies in the German interior was another matter, lacking as it did any network of communications other than its rivers. Drusus's first attempt was abortive; he had to give up and return to base. In his next attempt he decided to

Above. *Mounted Germanic warrior carrying a simple round shield: detail from Trajan's Column.*

Left: *German envoys before Emperor Trajan 113A.D: detail from Trajan's Column.*

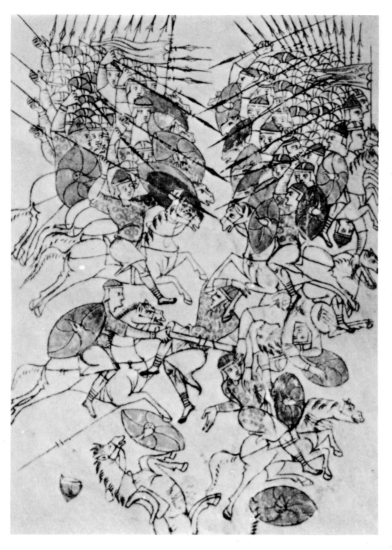

Tenth-century portrayal of the Hunnish invasions.

utilize the existing waterways. He built a canal from the Rhine to the Yssel which gave him access to the North Sea coast via the Zuider Zee. He also used the river Lippe which in the spring is navigable right up to its source. He moved along the Lippe upwards into Westphalia, and at the point where the river was no longer navigable he built a Castle at Aliso which was to be a supply rather than a fortified base from which the interior of Germany was to be subjected to Roman rule. Roman expeditions ventured into the interior where they were relatively well-received by the German tribal chiefs. To some the Romans appeared as welcome allies in their own tribal conflicts, particularly against the ambitions of the chief of the Markomani, Marbod, who had established his rule in Bohemia and was now extending it to the lower Elbe. However, the moment when the Roman commander in the region, Quintilius Varus, attempted to establish Roman supremacy, the Germans annihilated his three legions and their auxiliary forces in a three-day battle in the Teutoburger Forest in 9 A.D.

Neither precise date nor location of the battle is totally verified by historical evidence. The traditional version of the Germans luring the Roman Legions into the forest is no more than a fable. What is certain is that the legions of Varus marched during the autumn, accompanied by their entire train. This indicates that Roman forces had been operating in the German interior during the summer months and were now returning to their winter quarters on the Rhine or at Aliso. Had Varus set out to quell a rising by the Germans he would hardly have set out with all his baggage. The unsuspecting Varus believed himself to be among friends. After all, the leader of the Germanic tribe

of the Cheruscans, Arminius, had himself been in Rome as a hostage; he received part of his education there, and had been made a Roman knight. However, resenting attempts to establish Roman overlordship Arminius headed a conspiracy against the Romans and ambushed them.

The Roman force consisted of three legions, six cohorts of auxiliaries, and three troops of cavalry; estimates of their total strength vary between 12,000 and 18,000 combatants plus 12,000 more making up the train. As soon as the first battle cries of the Germans could be heard at the head of the column which extended about 2·5 miles, the vanguard halted near present day Herford. A suitable place was chosen, hastily fortified and surrounded by a stockade and moat. As the column arrived it assembled inside the stockade. The thought must have occurred to Varus to return to his original summer camp which was well-fortified, offering better protection than this makeshift fortification. But he was bound to have been short of food supplies, and the way back was unlikely to be less dangerous than the way ahead. Apart from that there was every likelihood that the castle was in German hands already. Varus was forced to jettison all his surplus luggage as well as his wagons. On the next day, in a better formation than before he marched out with the aim of reaching Aliso at least. Although the territory was an open field, the harassing attacks by the Germans seemed weak, with little cavalry to support them. But Arminius held his horsemen back, not wishing to expose them to the Romans. On that day the Romans covered ground slowly, and progress was slowed down even further when towards the end of the day they again entered the forests. As they approached the dark Doerren Gorge they found that the Germans had blocked its exit and occupied its heights. To get out of the canyon they had to attack up-hill. Outflanking movements were impossible and even the weak attacks by the Germans had been sufficient to cause serious losses. The Romans were forced to camp, exposed to the incessant attacks which the Germans maintained throughout the night. All this was made worse by the onset of violent fall storms and rains which transformed the soil into a quagmire in which it was even more difficult to fight on the next day, let alone make headway. Roman attacks against the Germans repeatedly came to a halt, while the lightly equipped Germans could attack and withdraw at will. Failing to storm the pass the Romans were now firmly locked in the Doerren Gorge without any hope of escape; morale disintegrated. Varus and a number of his officers committed suicide and the bearer of the Roman eagle jumped into a swamp to ensure that Rome's insignia

Frankish warrior grave from the period of the Great Migrations. Warriors were usually buried with all their military equipment.

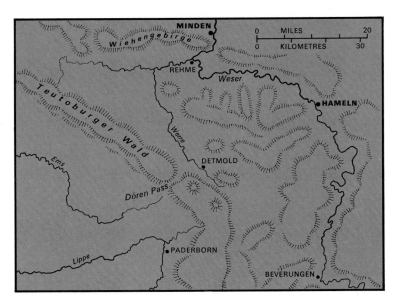

Battle of Teutoburger Forest.

would not fall into German hands. The remainder surrendered except for a few, primarily cavalry, who managed to escape and make their way to Aliso where they were besieged. Successful strategy rendered them able to break out and get back to Roman lines along the Rhine. The Germans, now fearing that a strong Roman force would come to avenge their comrades, withdrew back into the interior.

In fact the Romans were in no position to mete out retribution. Tiberius hurried to the Rhine to ensure the security of the frontier of Gaul and to restore the badly mauled army. The contested succession to Emperor Augustus in Rome made Tiberius's presence there more important than launching a major military venture in Germany.

Once established on the Roman throne his adopted son, Germanicus, undertook two major campaigns. Whether in fact he achieved two victories over the Germans is subject to speculation. Some authorities relegate it into the realm of deliberate myth-making on Germanicus's part for his own political ends.

Be that as it may, Arminius evaded an open battle, since he realized that the Roman forces were superior to his own. Instead he fought a war of attrition, for which the land was ideally suited, while the Romans faced the ever-present danger of having their lines of supply to the Rhine cut. Nevertheless it was quite within the military capacity of the Romans to subject Germany. Purely defensive war can lead to negotiations but never to victory. Among the Germanic tribes opinions began to divide sharply. Arminius's father-in-law, Segestes, led the Roman party which planned and carried out the murder of Arminius. Nor was Tiberius in an enviable position. The concentration of Roman legions in Germany under Germanicus could bring about the same situation as that of Caesar and his legions in Gaul.

What the Battle of Teutoburger Forest clearly indicated was that the conquest of Germany would be slow, bloody and expensive, and could be carried out only by an extremely able general furnished with extensive powers. These very powers could become a threat to the Emperor in Rome. Nor was it advisable for the Emperor to leave Rome for an extensive campaign lasting for years. The Battle of Teutoburger Forest and its following skirmishes under Tiberius and Germanicus were 'little more than an apology for a final retreat to the Rhine, which henceforth was to remain the northeastern frontier of Latin civilization.' Or as Sir Edward Creasy put it, 'Had Arminius been supine or unsuccessful . . .

this island would never have borne the name of England.'

During the halcyon years of the Roman Empire, which came to an end with the death of Marcus Aurelius in 180 A.D., the flow of Germanic peoples into the border territories of the Empire was steady and therefore controllable. Each successive tribe which asked for permission to live within the confines of the Empire was required not merely to obey the dictates of the Emperor but to be prepared to defend the Rhine-Danube boundary in case of a border incursion on the part of fellow Germans living across the frontier. This system not only worked well from a military point of view. It had the effect of 'civilizing' resident as well as non-resident Germanic tribes, transforming a nomadic and warrior race into a pastoral one.

The period between 232 and 552 A.D. marks the transition from Roman to Medieval forms of war. The struggle between the Germanic tribes and the Roman Empire was drawing to a close. So was the Roman Empire.

In military terms battles now showed the supremacy of the cavalry over the infantry. One of the causes of Rome's final collapse was the sudden invasion of eastern Europe by the Huns, a new race of horsemen, formidable in number, rapid in their movements, and masters of the bow and arrow. They encountered the Goths, a Nordic Germanic tribe which by the beginning of the third century had left Sweden and spread from Pomerania to the Carpathians and from there to the Black Sea. (This movement was part of the Great Migrations in the course of which Franks, Allemani and Burgundians moved into the lands between the Harz mountains and Danube and when the Allemani began to move further westwards, they posed an

Sixth-century Allemanic helmet but of southeast European origin which probably came to the Allemani by means of the battlefield.

The Fury of the Goths (Painting by Paul Ivanovitz).

immediate threat to Gaul. In August 357 A.D. Emperor Julian met them in battle near Strasbourg and defeated them.)

The people most immediately affected by the pressure of the Huns were the Goths. It is not possible to tell why they obtained the names Ostrogoths and Visigoths respectively. Probably the terms originated only after the Goths had settled near the Black Sea where their settlements spread from the River Don to the mouth of the Danube and the southwestern hills of the Carpathians. The Romans were quick to recognize both the danger as well as the potential usefulness. Under Emperor Severus Alexander (222–235) the Goths were paid handsome subsidies to defend the frontier and otherwise maintain peace. This relationship was only of short duration. With ever-increasing frequency the Goths, in particular the Ostrogoths, raided eastern and southeastern border provinces of the Roman Empire. However, these raids turned into a major invasion, not because the Goths had realized the endemic weakness of the Roman Empire, but because they were badly pressed by the Huns who defeated them at the Dnieper in 374 A.D. forcing them to seek refuge south of the Danube. Here they built up an extensive Empire from a center in the Hungarian plain. Eventually, the Hunnish threat reached such proportions that the Roman Empire lost control of its western provinces. Menaced by the Huns, both Roman armies and the Germanic tribes added the bow to the weapons of the foot soldier and placed a renewed emphasis on the rapid mobility of their cavalry. Fear of the Hun caused the Ostrogoths, the Franks and the Romans to become allies. In 450 A.D. together they faced the Huns on the plain of Châlons and victory was won over the Huns, not by superior tactics but by Theodoric's heavy horsemen who simply rode them down.

The Huns had been stopped and turned back, and the self-confidence of the Germanic tribes, especially that of the Ostrogoths, had been immensely strengthened. More than ever before, they now posed a threat to the collapsing Roman Empire.

For more than three centuries Romans had drawn German auxiliaries into their armies and thereby initiated a process which inducted Germans and other tribes into the Roman army. One could hardly speak of a *Roman* army any more. The Roman army of the fifth century was not the same as it had been under Tiberius and Germanicus. The German mercenaries, paid in money and in kind had increased their demands over the centuries. The land grants they received at the frontier for their own agricultural pursuits were in themselves not dangerous as long as the Empire was strong enough to keep these frontier forces at its most exposed and vulnerable spots. In that role the mercenaries played a part vital to the security of the Empire. But when the Barbarians, recognizing the weakness at the center, demanded the ownership of land not just its use, the danger became imminent that the Empire would be barbarized.

In Italy a rising of Germanic mercenaries under Odoaker had successfully taken place. Emperor Zeno, of East Rome, anxious to regain West Rome and to remove the Ostrogoths from his immediate vicinity, presented the Ostrogoth king, Theodoric, with Italy, a present which had to be conquered first. Theodoric's task was to vanquish Odoaker and to settle the Ostrogoths in Italy. Whether or not Theodoric or Odoaker won was immaterial, either way Byzantium was bound to gain by losing at least one enemy or a potential one. Theodoric, accompanied by his host of warriors and their families, won.

It must be noted that the Great Migrations had transformed some of the tribal institutions profoundly. Five centuries before, most of them lived in settlements, each family community in its village under its *hunno* or *ealderman*, a collection of family units held together by tribal ties. The *fürst* and his institutional apparatus was simple and served its purpose. Migrations of the scale that took place in the first few centuries A.D., and the campaigns associated with them, required power to be more centralized. Furthermore to preserve continuity and its resulting tribal security, the holding of supreme power became hereditary. Out of this situation grew the concept of kingship. Whenever an entire Germanic people entered the service of the Emperor in Rome or Byzantium, a Germanic prince was simultaneously made a Roman general and became the link between his people and the Emperor. Gaiseric, King of the Vandals, ruled North Africa, on behalf of the Emperor but he soon rejected Roman overlordship, and felt strong enough to claim sovereignty for himself.

On the other hand the Frankish Empire, in contrast to the Vandals and the Goths who were conquering *peoples*, was created by a conquering *king*. The family of the Merovingians under Clovis managed by sheer ability to gather numerous Germanic peoples, and with them conquer large parts of Gaul and thus establish Frankish rule. The elective principle could not operate with such vast numbers. The crown became hereditary, though never uncontested. But in spite of several civil wars, the institution of the centralizing office of the crown remained.

Inevitably the same causes that lay at the root of Germanic kingship led to a transformation of the military structure of the Germanic tribes. Military hosts of a size between 10,000 and 30,000 men require a more sophisticated structure than the hundred of old. It was not possible for the prince or the king to issue his orders to a hundred or more *hunni*. Additional ranks of

Hilt of a Frankish sword.

command had to be created, institutions of command that functioned efficiently. Furthermore, in the past while still settled, a primitive form of agrarian communism served the needs of the hundred and the families. During the Great Migrations this was no longer possible. Thus the Great Migrations were also vast campaigns of plunder. When the Germans stormed Gaul they pillaged and plundered the towns. In consequence the spacious Roman urban planning gave way to reconstructed towns, whose buildings and streets were narrow to provide better defense, whose outskirts were surrounded by thick walls and watch-towers: they were the first of the medieval cities.

But looting and pillaging did not resolve the problem of supplies for armies and their dependants on the move. No people could afford to live hand to mouth. Storage places had to be established to hold supplies for future needs, and these had to

Conquest of the Cantabrian by the Visigoth King Leovigildo. (Panel from the ivory reliquary of San Millan de la Cogolla, eleventh century).

Statue of Charlemagne (742–814) King of the Franks and Roman Emperor.

be administered. Thus the *hunni* needed subalterns who would collect, distribute and store the gains.

Nor could the king alone govern at the top without an intermediary between him and the *hunni*. He delegated his authority to his counts, who on his behalf administered strictly defined territories.

Evidence for the new structure of the military hierarchy has come down to us from the Visigoths, but it can safely be assumed to have applied with some variations to the other German tribes of the time as well. The military structure began with a leader of a maximum of 10,000 men; the next unit was 500 strong and so on down to the hundred, which was divided into groups of ten. The vital core within this structure, however, was still represented by the hundred which, from an organizational point of view, was just large enough to cope with supply problems.

Having stressed the origin of the Germanic monarchy and the hereditary principle, it would be a mistake to assume that once established it remained unchanged. For instance when Theodoric died without issue, he *appointed* the young son of his sister as his heir. She was to act as regent until the boy had grown up to assume his responsibilities. But her son Athalaric died while still an adolescent. His mother Amalsuntha was unequal to the task that confronted her when Byzantium decided to reconquer Italy from the Goths, so the Ostrogoths reverted to the *elective* principle. The heroic Vittigis, Totila (who in his personality represented the rare synthesis between Gothic simplicity and courage and Latin culture) and the depressive Teia were all elected by the Ostrogoths.

The bulk of the Ostrogoths were warriors, but among the Franks the warrior represented only one part of a rather more numerous people. Even among them, once the Carolingian Empire had disintegrated, the elective principle returned, though in a different form. The German kings of the Middle Ages were formally elected by the most important of their magnates, the electors.

During the Great Migrations kingship was still too narrowly based to create a dynasty that could rest upon its ancestors. The kings emerged from the strongest families, renowned for their fame in battle. Fame in practical terms was reflected by the material gains they had made. At a lower level the same applied to the *hunni*, who in the process of evolution became the Germanic warrior nobility.

The strongest concept of kingship existed among the Vandals. Originally located between the rivers Elbe and Vistula they gradually moved south. Pressed by bad harvests and consequent starvation they moved on, ultimately invading Spain in 409. In 429 they crossed the Straits of Gibraltar into North Africa, the

granary of the Roman Empire, which was divided into six Imperial provinces which the Vandals conquered one by one. In 442 the Romans and the Vandals under King Gaiseric made peace. Though of short duration—the Vandals invaded Italy and sacked Rome—West Rome was no longer in a position which would have allowed it even to consider the reconquest of the lost provinces. Under the Emperors Leo and Zeno of Byzantium major campaigns were launched against them led by several generals the last of whom, Belisarius, was ultimately successful in conquering the Vandals. After the death of Gaiseric the Vandals politically disintegrated and became easy victims. The last King of the Vandals, Gelimer, is known for little more than surrendering to the forces of Byzantium. The kingdom of the Vandals had experienced a meteoric rise but had disappeared with equal speed. Their hostility towards the Ostrogoths had deprived them of a vital ally. They could not match the resources of Byzantium alone.

Not all German tribes were affected by the Great Migrations. The Markomani (the ancestors of the Bavarians), the Allemani and the Franks traveled only relatively short distances or simply spilled over into neighboring regions. Frequently the newcomers established large landholdings whose native populations accepted the protection of the Germanic *hunno*. In return they rendered services on the land. The situation of the Britons when overcome by the invasions of the Anglo-Saxons was very similar. The native population was subjected and, in time, absorbed. From the *hunni* or *ealdorman* emerged the Anglo-Saxon nobility, the earls. By contrast, the Franks although establishing large estates, produced no nobility during that early period. The Merovingians ensured that they ruled by way of their counts alone. The traditional institution of the *hunno* declined in significance to that of a mere village administrator.

The fact that West Rome had fallen, does not mean that the Barbarians who had brought this about were actually aware of it. When Theodoric set out for Italy in 488, he did so as the representative of the Emperor of East Rome. In numbers the Ostrogoths were approximately 200,000 strong including their families. Odoaker and his men were first encountered on the banks of the Isonzo River, but they were thrown back and the Goths made the crossing. On 30 September 489 they conquered Verona. Odoaker then withdrew to Ravenna, in those days like Venice, a water city. From there he counterattacked recapturing Milan and Cremona and beseiging Theodoric in Pavia. Only with the aid of the Visigoths could Theodoric return to the offensive, once again beating Odoaker and pushing him back behind the walls of Ravenna. The population at large supported Theodoric, a support shown by a peninsula-wide conspiracy which with one blow removed all supporters of Odoaker in Italy. For three years, until 493, Odoaker defended himself in Ravenna. After having been promised his personal security, that of his family and the maintenance of his royal dignity, he surrendered in February 493. Soon after Theodoric's entry into Ravenna he held a banquet at the Palace Leuretum. Odoaker was guest of honor. Theodoric killed him on that occasion with his own hand, and Odoaker's followers met the same fate.

Theodoric, already King of the Goths, by virtue of his conquest, had proclaimed himself King of the Italians as well, a step which crossed the intentions of Emperor Zeno. But as yet Zeno was in no position to retaliate. The Gothic rule in Italy was characterized by the dualism between the Romans and the Italians of the provinces on the one hand and the Ostrogoths on the other. While the former retained their institutional and administrative apparatus directed as it was towards Byzantium, Theodoric, with a few exceptions, excluded the native population from his army. His reign in Italy was determined by his relationships with Byzantium in the east and the Frankish king-dom in the north. But he was unable to convince Zeno that he was not simply another Odoaker any more than he could convince the Frankish King Clovis that he was not set upon further conquest. Nor was his position improved by the re-establishment of cordial relationships between the Papacy in Rome and the Emperor. Jointly they decided to persecute the heretics within the Christian faith, believers in the Arian 'heresy' to which the Goths adhered. Before the matter came to a head Theodoric died suddenly in 526. At that time his empire included Italy, Sicily, Dalmatia, Noricum, Pannonia, Tyrol, Grisons, southern Germany as far north as Ulm, and Provence—an empire too large for the Goths to sustain.

This became clear very quickly after his death when Justinian of Byzantium took the first steps to reconquer Italy. The expe-dition was to be led by Belisarius, who had already distin-guished himself against the Persians. As his first objective he reconquered North Africa from the Vandals, a natural launch-ing point and supply base for an invasion of Italy. In 535 Belisarius landed in Sicily, and most cities opened their gates to his forces; the reconciliation between Church and Empire bore its fruits. In May 536 he crossed the Straits of Messina and took Naples. At that point the Goths elected Vittigis as their King. To avert any threat from the north Vittigis ceded Provence to the Franks and, trusting as he was, he left Rome to the care of Pope Silverius who promptly opened its gates to Belisarius. For three years Vittigis laid siege to Rome. It was 'the grave of the Gothic

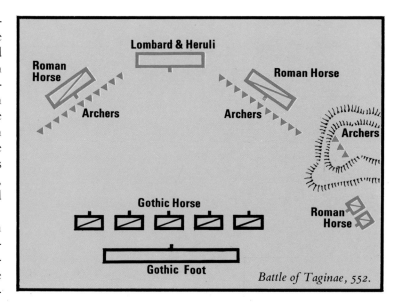

Battle of Taginae, 552.

Hippic phalange formation (Byzantine military treatise, eleventh century).

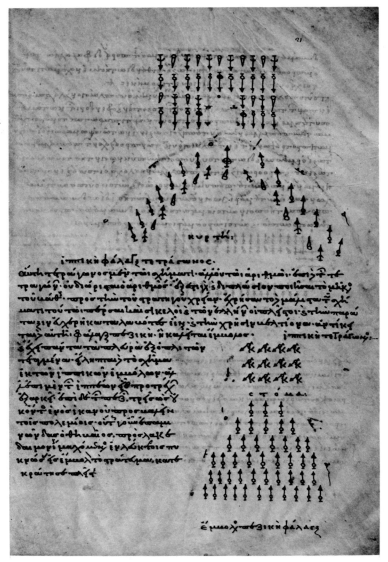

monarchy in Italy,' dug by 'the deadly dews of the Campagna.' Starvation and pestilence ravaged throughout Italy, decimating natives, Goths and Byzantine invaders alike. Only the Byzan-tines had no shortage of manpower. Other Germanic tribes such as the Franks who made inroads into Italy at the time did so for their own aggrandizement and not to assist the Goths in any way. Vittigis retreated to Ravenna where he was besieged by Belisarius. In order to put an end to the blood-letting Vittigis offered Belisarius the Gothic crown. He accepted, entered the city, took Vittigis prisoner and sent him and some of his as-sociates to Constantinople. However, Justinian became sus-picious that Belisarius might become another Theodoric, and recalled him to Constantinople. When he left Italy the Goths had been reduced to holding a single city, Pavia. However, in 542 Totila was elected King ('quite the noblest flower that bloomed upon the Ostrogothic stem'), and he recovered the whole of central southern Italy, except Rome and a few other fortresses in a rapid campaign. After he had taken Naples, Totila laid siege to Rome. Belisarius was sent back to Italy.

Rome was taken by Totila in December 546. The Byzantine forces were left holding only four fortresses in Italy. Belisarius returned again to Constantinople and was replaced by Justinian's Court Chamberlain, Narses, a man who conducted his generalship less with flamboyance than with the precision of a mathematician. In the meantime Totila had taken Sicily again and manned 300 ships to control the Adriatic. By the spring of 552 Narses had mobilized his forces fully, composed mainly of Barbarian contingents, Huns, Lombards, Persians and others. Finding his way south blocked by Teia and his Gothic warriors at Verona, he outflanked them by marching close to the Ad-riatic coast, reaching Ravenna safely. When Totila received the news in the vicinity of Rome, he took almost his entire army, crossed Tuscany, and established his base at the village of Taginae, the present day Tadino.

The two armies prepared themselves for battle. Narses's dis-position show his superior generalship. He immediately rec-ognized the tactical significance of a small hill to the left of his flank which he occupied with archers. He dismounted his Lom-bards and formed them across the Flaminian Way and on each of the flanks of the phalanx he placed 4000 Roman foot archers with cavalry behind them. His calculation was accurate. Totila had ranged his cavalry in front of his infantry intending to win with a single charge. He advanced directly into the trap Narses had set for him. The Gothic cavalry failed to break Narses's center and instead was rapidly depleted by the archery and the spears of Narses's warriors. Spears and bows proved decisive

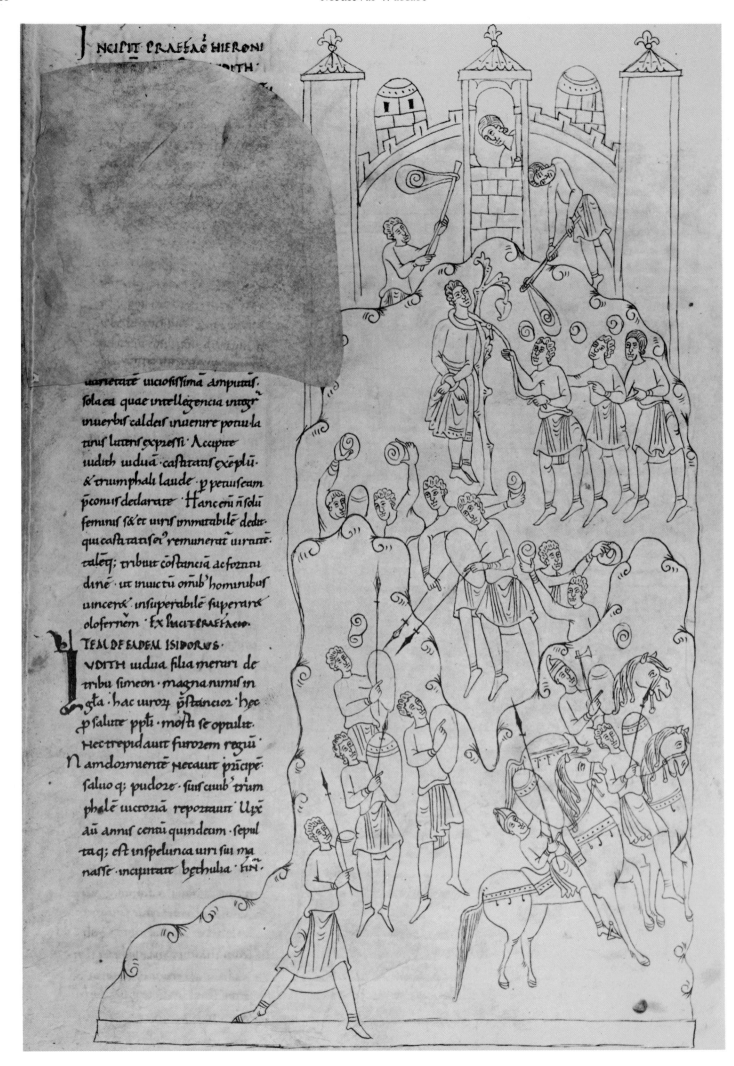

against Totila's cavalry attack (as it was to prove, centuries later, at Crécy). Some 6000 Goths were killed, among them Totila.

After the death of Totila the Goths elected Teia as their new King. The role he played was in accord with his doom-laden character. At the foot of Vesuvius he defended himself for two months and was finally slain in battle at Mount Lettere. The moment of capitulation of the Goths had come. They were to leave Italy and settle in any Barbarian kingdom of their choice. The greatest Barbarian empire hitherto established in Europe had come to an end. The last of the warriors of the Ostrogoths, carrying the body of their dead King upon their spears, trudged down the slopes into history.

Their brothers, the Visigoths, held out for a few centuries longer, into the first decade of the eighth century. Within the course of three and a half centuries they had traveled through Sweden, east-central Europe, the eastern shores of the Black Sea, to the Balkans and Greece, then moved up the Dalmatian coast into Illyria, turned round into Italy marching south, until nearly at its tip they turned back along the Mediterranean coast until they had reached Spain by the middle of the fifth century. During the middle of the fourth century they were converted to Christianity, the work of Bishop Wulfila, who translated the Bible into Gothic. Like so many other German tribes they entered Italy not to despoil it but to ask for land grants in Venetia and Dalmatia as well as grain and subsidies, in return for which they offered their military services. Rome, already in its final agonies, refused. Alaric, the King of the Visigoths, was not in a position nor did he intend to replace the Roman Empire with one of the Visigoths for he was far too weak. Like the Vandals, the Visigoths tried to cross over to Africa. But a storm wrecked their boats in the Straits of Messina twice and they could not assemble another fleet. Still, the Romans were impressed and intimidated. Since the days of Hannibal no Barbarian tribe had penetrated their peninsula so far south. The sudden death of Alaric cut these ventures short. He perished after a fever and his warriors buried him with his weapons and personal treasures in a grave in the River Busento near Cosenza. For that purpose they temporarily diverted the river restoring it to its original path once the King had been put to rest. Then they moved along the coast to create their kingdom at Toulouse which lasted almost ninety years and from which they were expelled by the Franks. Withdrawing into Spain, they re-established themselves again at Toledo, expanding throughout the Iberian peninsula (with the exception of its northwest corner which was held by the Suebs) and reaching north beyond the Pyrenees into Aquitaine. Like the Ostrogoths they had become Arian Christians, but submitted to Catholic conversion by the end of the sixth century until they were finally pushed back by the Islamic invasions. By then Romans and Visigoths had mixed to provide the nucleus from which the knighthood of Castile arose.

The Visigoths' problem was similar to that of the Ostrogoths', they held an area too large to be effectively defended. Militarily and socially they were made up of a warrior nobility which, after the last strong king was slaughtered, did not produce another king capable of containing the centrifugal forces at work within their society.

The Visigoths like most of their contemporaries fought on horseback, carrying round shields, swords and daggers. They wore defensive armor; even the mail shirt was not unknown. The provincial levies, raised by the Visigoths much against the will of those who had to serve, carried whatever they had, usually crude weapons and represented the unarmed foot sol-

diery. One craft in which the Visigoths excelled was in the building and use of missile-throwing devices, stone-throwing machines and fire arrows.

The period of the Great Migrations and the decline of Rome saw a considerable change in military tactics. The early Germanic tribes such as the Cheruscans could hardly maintain the same tactics and style of combat in an environment so different from the Teutonic forests. Cavalry moved to the fore, as both the Battles of Strasbourg and Adrianople showed.

'Hitherto infantry normally had been the decisive arm, and when they relied upon shock weapons, they had little to fear from cavalry as long as they maintained their order. But the increasing use of missiles carried with it an unavoidable loosening and disordering of the ranks. The old shield-wall began to be replaced by a firing line, and because archers and slingers cannot easily combine shield with bow or sling, and as the range of these weapons is strictly limited, and, further still, because they are all but useless in wet weather, opportunity for the cavalry charge steadily increased. The problem was how to combine missile-power with security against cavalry . . .' (Fuller).

The Ostrogoths excelled in their use of cavalry, fighting with lance and sword but not with bow and arrow. That, among other things, proved their undoing at Taginae. Archers on foot, as individuals, could not afford to take on horsemen, but protected by their own cavalry, fortification or favorable terrain they could be highly effective.

The effectiveness of the infantry depended on their tactical order. The wild bravery of the old Germanic tribes was of little use when facing Roman forces in open field. However, the old Germanic square formation would have been worth maintaining had it been able to adjust itself to new weapons such as archery. The Byzantine foot soldiery made this adjustment. They were mainly Germanic auxiliaries, but the use of bow and arrow had to be imposed from above. Furthermore, the old Germanic square battle formation was an organic unit, a family organization. With the Great Migrations this bond was seriously weakened, if not altogether dissolved. Outside its social context the Germanic square lost the qualities which it once had possessed. The tendency moved towards the individualization of combat, the maximization of individual effort by putting the warrior on a horse, without giving up the facility to fight on foot should the occasion arise.

If warfare was changing, Europe had changed. The Roman Empire had all but disappeared. On its debris settled a series of Germanic kingdoms in Italy, Germany, Gaul, Spain and Britain. Yet the influence of Rome remained, for the Barbarians had been exposed to and affected by it over centuries. The Barbarian war-band ethos weakened and discipline as a prerequisite to any ordered and settled life made itself felt. The glory that had been Rome continued to exercise its magnetic force to the extent that its heirs had nothing better to do than to try to perpetuate it by emulating it. And beyond the fringes of the old Empire and the new rulers, new hosts of Barbarians lurked ready to seize their chance at invasion. And most important, the institutional framework of the Empire, shaky as it may have been towards its end, underwent a rejuvenating experience at the hands of the Roman Catholic Church.

Left. *Foot soldiers carrying shields, lances and slings (eleventh century).*

Right. *Weapons of a Germanic warrior (Southwest Germany, third century).*

Danish ships invading England.

THE CHALLENGE
FROM
THE EAST

The Islamic Invasion

The spread of the Islam during the eighth century was a factor of profound importance for the consequences it had both upon the Roman Empire as well as for the Germanic tribes in central and western Europe. After the collapse of West Rome, the Barbarians who had shattered it were in varying degrees absorbed by its culture and traditions, ultimately claiming continuity and direct succession of their kingdoms from the Imperial past.

What erupted during this process of absorption was the Islamic expansion which came quite unexpectedly. From the depths of the Arabian Peninsula rose a tidal wave which transformed not only North Africa but Europe. It originated in an area with which the Roman Empire had had little contact. For the protection of Syria against the nomadic Bedouin tribes it had constructed a wall much in the way in which Hadrian's wall was built in Britain as protection against the raids of the Picts. But Syria is in no way comparable with the English North, the Danube and the Rhine. The Roman Empire had never considered its outermost southeastern frontier as highly vulnerable. Its legions were concentrated in the north and west. The southeast was of importance only in so far as it was a trade route over which spices and rare cloths were imported into the Empire. That changed in 613 A.D. when Mohammed, a hitherto unknown native trader of the city of Mecca, began to preach a new revelation. He claimed to have experienced divine visitations and demanded the destruction of all idols on pain of eternal damnation. Archangel Gabriel had revealed to him to submit only to one God—a demand in opposition to the polytheistic faith of his Arab contemporaries—but at first his gospel fell on deaf ears. In fact he was compelled to leave Mecca in 622. As he moved on he mixed Arab aspirations with Jewish and Christian beliefs, and ears became more receptive to his message. Though in parts not dissimilar to other Oriental religions, Mohammed's gospel suited the warlike tendencies of nomadic tribes. For their livelihood Mohammed and his followers constantly preyed on the caravans of his Meccan relations; a religious war was in the making.

Islam connotes submission and implies brotherhood among all Muslims, since differences among humans are of so significance before Allah, the one true and everlasting God. This message was driven home emphatically in the lines of the Koran. Combative religious fervor was heightened by the promise of a paradise into which all those would be accepted who died in battle against the infidel. The alternative to that paradise was scorching hell.

Three years after leaving Mecca Mohammed was ready to fight all infidels, Jews, Christians and other heathens. He did this so successfully that in 630 he re-entered Mecca as the uncontested leader of a new faith. Two years later he died and his father-in-law Abu Bakr took over the direction of the movement, calling himself the successor, the Caliph.

Little note of that was taken in Constantinople, which was much more preoccupied with the activities of the Germanic tribes than with anything else. Also the struggle with the Persians had left both East Romans and Persians in a state of exhaustion. Syria, Palestine and Egypt had been restored to Byzantium. Emperor Heraclius could now think of resuming the policy of Justinian aiming at the restoration of the position of East Rome in the west where the Longobards held vital parts of Italy while the Visigoths had deprived Rome of its last positions in Spain. East Rome was not given that chance. The simultaneous Arab invasions into Europe and Asia took place at a speed comparable only to those of Attila and, later, Genghis Khan. However, the Arab conquests were of relative permanence.

Compared with the Germanic tribes who over centuries fought at the fringes of the Empire until they penetrated it, the Arabs with one blow captured mighty positions. In 634 they conquered the Byzantine fortress of Bothra; a year later Damascus fell into their hands; in 636 the whole of Syria was theirs. Another year later Jerusalem opened its gates to them, while at the same time they conquered Mesopotamia. This was followed by an attack upon Egypt, and Alexandria was taken in 641. This was followed by the conquest of Cyrenaica and advance parties of Arabs penetrated as far as Tunisia.

Obviously the Arabs gained much by the surprise element of their attack, its sudden and unexpected impact and by the way in which they managed to sustain that impact. Quick on horses and camels, both products of an environment which could

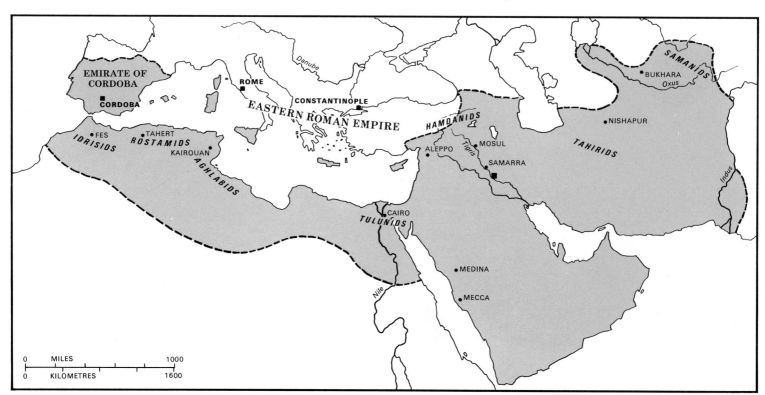

Right. *Viking warriors: detail from the Oseberg Tapestry.*

Left: *The spread of Islam.*

make do with little for a long time—a characteristic which of course applies to their riders too—armed with lance, sword, bow and arrow, they were unencumbered in their movement by the kind of baggage trains which Roman armies, or for that matter the Germanic tribes, carried with them.

The question has been put why the Arabs were, unlike the Germans, not absorbed into the fabric of Roman culture. The answer is that they were in possession of a spiritual power, the Islamic faith. Theirs was not a quest for new lands, for territorial expansion, but the submission of the world as they knew it to Allah. That submission did not necessarily mean the conversion of the conquered, but simply obedience to God and his prophet Mohammed. Religion and national faith are one and the same thing. Every Muslim is a servant of Allah. The conquered are their subjects compelled to pay taxes but stand outside the community of the faithful. The wall between faithful and infidel is almost unsurmountable. By comparison the Germans had nothing else to do than to try to put themselves in the service of the conquered and adapt their style of life to theirs. The Koran says that if it had been Allah's will he would have

made of mankind one people. Therefore there was no need to carry on missionary activities. The faith of the infidel was not attacked but simply ignored.

The Germans in the provinces of the Roman Empire were Romanized; not the Arabs. Their conquest of the Mediterranean put an end to the *mare nostrum* of the Empire. The Mediterranean world no longer represented one entity, but was divided into a Christian sphere in the north and the Muslim sphere in the south. Latin civilization was extinguished in northern Africa.

However, their main objective throughout their conquest was the citadel of the infidel empire, Constantinople. As early as 655 the first attempt took place. Besides being good horsemen the Arabs had been excellent sailors and they decisively defeated the Byzantine fleet. Only internal dissension among the Muslim leaders forced the abandonment of the conquest of Constantinople. They returned to that project thirteen years later, but not with the sense of purpose the first attempt had displayed, partly because Muslim endeavors elsewhere took priority. In the west the Atlantic coast was reached and by 711 Spain had

Left. *Carved roundel from the church door, Valpjófsstaòir c 1200. One of the finest examples of carving of the Viking period depicting the popular medieval legend of the knight, the lion and the dragon.*

Right. *A Saxon axeman.*

been overrun, while in the east the Arabs had penetrated into the Punjab and in central Asia they reached the frontiers of China.

In 715 Caliph Suleiman set into motion again the conquest of Constantinople. His first move was to send two armies into Rumania. These operations did not yield any concrete results. On the other hand, the overall situation was dangerous enough for Emperor Leo to withdraw to Constantinople, where he immediately replenished the stores and arsenals of the capital, had the fortifications repaired and engines of war mounted on them. From land Constantinople was virtually unassailable; it could not be taken by storm. It could only be blockaded by closing the Bosporus as well as the Dardanelles. Hence sea power was crucial and Emperor Leo's fleet was inferior to that of the Muslims. Caliph Suleiman's brother Maslama decided to surround the city by advancing on land and on sea. While Maslama commanded the land forces, Suleiman was in charge of the naval operations. The precise numbers of Muslim forces involved cannot be stated with any degree of reliability. The claim that the army was 80,000 strong while the fleet contained 1800 vessels with another 80,000 men aboard is very doubtful. Nevertheless in other parts of Egypt and Africa further vessels were made ready for action. Maslama appeared before the outer walls of Constantinople on 15 August 717 and attempted a land attack at once. In the face of the skills of the Byzantine engineers

and their missile equipment, the attack had to be abandoned. Maslama prepared to blockade the city. He encamped outside the walls, fortifying it strongly, and instructed the fleet to divide into two squadrons, one to cut off supplies coming from the Aegean, the other to move through the Bosporus to cut off the city from the Black Sea. All seemed to go well until the second squadron, approaching the Bosporus, was brought into some confusion by strong currents. Emperor Leo immediately recognized his advantage, sailed out with his galleys, and poured Greek fire—a mixture of sulphur quicklime and naphtha which ignites immediately when whetted—on them destroying approximately 20 Muslim ships and capturing several others. The action proved decisive. The Muslims made no further attempts upon the Straits until the following year when an Egyptian squadron under cover of darkness closed it. In the meantime, however, the blockading Muslim land forces had undergone a severe winter which depleted their numbers seriously. Leo, in another surprise attack, scattered the Egyptian naval force, and followed it up with a successful attack upon the Muslim forces opposite the Bosporus. Meanwhile his Bulgarian ally Tervel and his army gave battle to Maslama. In the vicinity of Adrianople some 23,000 Muslims are alleged to have been killed. Maslama and his forces had to abandon their blockade. Leo's victory had stemmed the Muslim tide; the Byzantine

Empire was shored up for another seven centuries. Had Constantinople been captured, it is safe to assume that the Muslims would have taken the route into Europe as they were to do later on, and as the Muslims who had swept north up the Iberian peninsula were doing.

From Spain they entered Aquitaine in 712; in 719 they occupied Narbonne and in 721 they laid siege to Toulouse. Defeated there by Duke Eudo of Aquitaine, they returned to the region in 725 occupying Carcassonne and Nîmes, moving into Burgundy which they thoroughly ravaged and penetrating as far north as the Vosges mountains.

By that time the Frankish house of the Merovingians was in a state of decline, actual power passing into the hands of the Mayors of the Palace. In that role the Mayors were able to acquire large territorial possessions for themselves: Pipin II, the father of Charles Martel (the Hammer), had made himself lord of the territory between the Loire and the Meuse and of Aquitaine. In that position, of course, he was a threat to Eudo who, as far as his territories were concerned, feared the Franks as much as the Arabs. When Eudo, in the turmoil caused by the Islamic invasion, declared himself independent from Frankish overlordship, Charles Martel marched against him, defeated him and pacified the territory.

Eudo, to secure his southern flank, entered into alliance with a Muslim Berber chieftain, whose daughter he married. The Muslim Governor of Spain, Abd-ar-Rahman, greatly disapproved of this action, defeated the Berber chieftain and sent Eudo's wife to the Caliph's harem in Damascus. He then decided to invade Aquitaine. Crossing the Pyrenees in the northwest, he entered Gascony spreading terror throughout the territories. At Bordeaux Eudo met him in battle but was utterly defeated; Bordeaux was taken, sacked and burned. From there the Muslims marched in the direction of Tours. As one monkish chronicler put it:

'Then Abd-ar-Rahman pursued after Count Eudo, and while he strives to spoil and burn the holy shrine at Tours, he encounters the chief of the Austrasian Franks Charles (Martel), a man of war from his youth, to whom Eudo had sent warning. There for nearly seven days they strive intensively, and at last they set themselves in battle array; and the nations of the north standing firm as a wall, and impenetrable as a zone of ice, utterly slay the Arabs with the edge of the sword.'

The account is scanty, probably in part because very little is known of the Muslim's military organization, except that most of them were Moors and were mounted. Unlike in North Africa they do not seem to have used bow and arrow but depended upon their swords and lances. Armor was scarce.

About the Franks one is better informed. They relied mainly on their infantry made up of the personal troops of Charles, which had to be kept busy at all times for plunder was the only pay they got. To these came local levies, generally of ill-equipped men. It was a very primitive army compared with that of the Goths; discipline seemed to have been entirely absent, and the only thing that kept it together was the availability of food. Once food was scarce the army dissolved. Among the Franks horses seem to have been used for purposes of transportation only. But the Frankish warriors wore armor and fought with swords, daggers, spears and axes.

The Muslims had not anticipated the arrival of Charles Martel and his forces. After a few days of maneuver and counter-maneuver, the Muslims decided to bring their offensive strength into play. They opened with a cavalry charge that made the earth tremble. Charles had drawn up his host in a solid phalanx which repelled charge after charge. Abd-ar-Rahman was killed, and the onset of night ended the battle. When the Franks expected a renewed attack in the morning, they noticed the Muslims had disappeared. They fled south leaving their plunder behind them. That they refrained for some time from renewing their attacks north of Pyrenees has little to do with the defeat they suffered, but rather more with substantial internal divisions among the Islamic peoples. For Charles Martel, however, this victory elevated him to a position of pre-eminence that allowed him to transform a tribal state into the Frankish Empire.

Three years later the Muslims were back again. In 735 the Arabs conquered Arles, once again invaded Aquitaine and ventured as far north as Lyons. Charles Martel returned, wrested Avignon from them, but failed to expel them from Narbonne, a city which only in 759 was captured from the Muslims by the son of Charles Martel, Pipin. The Islamic invasion resulted in developments which in their significance equaled the event which caused their origin. For centuries the center of Europe had been the Mediterranean. It was the connecting link between the countries of antiquity. Hellenic and Latin civilization gave that region its imprint. Later on even a common religion was a further force of integration. The invasion of the Germanic Barbarians certainly shook the structure of the Empire, toppled its political apex in West Rome, but did not destroy the structure of the Empire, let alone its culture. The Barbarians had nothing to put in its place. They were only too eager to adapt all that which they recognized was superior to their own culture. Nor did they possess an idea with which to counter the concept of Roman universalism. Their invasions caused serious tremors, but in time they were assimilated; there is nothing to show otherwise.

Under the sudden impact of the Islamic invasions the cultural, economic and social unity of the region was broken. The link that had connected east and west across the sea was severed. Byzantium was thrown back upon its own resources to main-

Emperor Otto I the Great (912–973).

no longer forthcoming. In the light of this development the Church was compelled to look for another power capable of filling the void left by East Rome. The alternative was found in the strongest of the successor kingdoms, that of the Franks.

The Frankish tribes which had been brought under a form of unity by Clovis were, in spite of their contact with the Roman Empire, among those considered to be the least civilized by Roman standards. By contrast with the Gothic tribes their weapons and tactics during the sixth century bore a greater resemblance to the arms with which Arminius encountered the Romans than to anything used in southern Europe.

'The arms of the Franks are very crude; they wear neither mail-shirt nor greaves and their legs are only protected by strips of linen or leather. They have hardly any horsemen, but their foot soldiery are bold and well-practiced in war. They bear swords and shields, but never use sling or bow. Their missiles are axes and barbed javelins. These last are not very long; they can be used either to cast or to stab. The iron of the head runs so far down the stave that very little of the wood remains unprotected. In battle they hurl these javelins, and if they strike an enemy the barbs are so firmly fixed in his body that it is impossible for the enemy to draw the weapon out. If it strikes a shield, it is impossible for enemy to get rid of it by cutting off its head, for the iron runs too far down the shaft. At this moment the Frank rushes in, places his foot on the butt as it trails on the ground, and so, pulling the shield downwards, cleaves his uncovered adversary through the head, or pierces his breast with a second spear.'

The throwing axe, the *francisca*, was another favorite Frankish weapon. It was a single-bladed axe with a heavy head which in shape and function was not dissimilar to the tomahawk of the North American Indian. Added to it were, of course, shield, sword and dagger. These weapons, though primitive, nevertheless show an important difference from the Germanic weapons a few centuries before. The amount of metal used in them allows two conclusions; firstly, that iron ore, or metals in general must have been more accessible then; secondly, that some degree of industrial processing must have been achieved.

Their weapons were indigenous products, they owed nothing to Roman examples. A strong conservative attitude among the Franks is betrayed by the fact that once they did adopt weapons and armory other than their own, they tended to hold on to them, even though they had become obsolete elsewhere. In their conquest of Gaul they were quick to utilize the available manpower reservoir and enrolled Gallic levies under their own banners. For the Franks this was easier because under the Merovingians, the traditional Germanic unit, the hundred, based upon blood ties, had ceased to play its function. However, among both Ostrogoths and Visigoths as well as among the Vandals it continued almost to their very end so that these tribes had been rather less able to integrate military levies from outside than the Franks. In terms of Frankish policy in Gaul this meant that the native Gauls were quickly assimilated into Frankish society until all distinctions were blurred. Even Frankish names were adopted. Again this contrasts starkly with the dualism existing in Italy between the Ostrogoths on the one hand and the Romans and native provincial population on the other.

The tactics of their foot soldiery continued for some time to adhere to the old Germanic square, often mistakenly described as a great disorderly mass of unarmored infantry fighting in dense column formations. Only during the course of the sixth century did they show any signs of Roman influence. Slowly armor made its appearance and so did horses, but as the Battle of Tours indicates horsemanship had not made any great headway by the middle of the eighth century. They were a means of transport for the King, his friends and officials, and were only very slowly adopted by the lower ranks. But innovations, even

tain her position in the east. Her claim to represent the Roman Empire as a whole could no longer be upheld, and gradually it transformed itself into a Greek state. Meanwhile the Bulgarians, Serbs and Croats spread the Slavic influence southwards on their route into the Balkans. Constantinople had its hands tied defending itself in the east without wishing to face similar burdens in the west, whether on the Italian peninsula, along the Danube or the Rhine, let alone Gaul and Spain. Byzantium had contracted to an area limited by the Illyrian coast in the west and by the upper Euphrates in the east. From now on it spent most of its energy defending itself against the onslaught from the east and south. In fact Byzantium was separated from the developments in the west.

If it can be said that Byzantium was forced back on its own resources, the same applies to the West. At first this looked like a separation from its cultural roots, from the intellectual inspiration which Europe had derived from them. Of course Muslim settlement in Spain brought the West nearer to the Orient, but intellectually the Arab world had little to offer to the West at that time. Indeed, Islam had no desire to offer anything. Western Europe was isolated from the rest of the world. The Mediterranean, that vital artery of commerce, was almost closed. Western Europe also had to rely on its own resources.

Yet there remained one institutional link: the Roman Catholic Church. Orientated as it had been at first towards Byzantium which could offer secular protection, that protection was when used at the top, could cause adverse comment. In the sixth century one bishop among the Franks was chided because when riding into battle he wore armor plate across his chest instead of the sign of the heavenly cross. By the middle of the seventh century, however, breast plates had come into general use among the Franks. Their helmets were rather different from those of the Romans and have been described as 'a morion-shaped round-topped head-piece, peaked and open in front, but rounded and falling low at the back, so as to cover the nape of the neck.' Those for the common soldiery were made of leather. Metal ones were to be found among the Frankish commanders. The shield was not made of iron but of wood, only the edges were bound with iron.

The use of cavalry was underdeveloped among the Merovingians due to their horses which, compared with those of the Muslims, were cart-horses; any battle between Arab and Frankish cavalry would have courted a major disaster for the latter. The Merovingians had discouraged the growth of a nobility within their ranks, preferring to delegate administrative and military duties in their provinces to counts or dukes directly appointed by them—probably in anticipation of that problem that was to dominate most of the kingdoms of the Middle Ages, that of the 'overmighty subject.' The King's appointee upon his

command rallied the Frankish forces of his province as well as all freemen among the Gauls. To be the King's administrator as well as one of the military commanders entailed honor but relatively low material rewards. While elsewhere large estates developed, the Frankish Kings let land out only in small parcels on a possessory not a proprietary basis, another device to contain the power of what was in essence a nobility of service, not one of birth. Large landholdings became common among the Franks only when the last economic consequences of the Islamic invasions had worked themselves throughout Europe. And whenever such checks as the Merovingian Kings introduced to maintain power in their hands on occasions did not curb the ambitions of a subject and his family, they had no scruples about slaughtering the potential rival, as well as his entire family.

Since Frankish soldiers did not receive any pay, they had to live off the land in times of war, irrespective of whether or not the territory crossed was that of a friend. As the Merovingian dynasty declined, its counts were prone to take greater liberties, question the King's commands, and in the end did pretty much as they liked. Only the Arab threat forged them together again into a community of interest, and when the Merovingians were replaced by their mayors, the reins were pulled tightly together again. Out of the confusion of conflicting and rivaling competencies a firm military and administrative hierarchy was forged. This trend began under Charles Martel, his son Pipin the Short, and was finally completed by Charlemagne.

Anglo-Saxon psalter illustrating Viking ships invading the shores of Britain.

The European periphery: Vikings and Magyars

Relations, especially those of a hostile nature between the Franks and the Norsemen, date back to the sixth century when Theudebert of Ripuaria slew Hygelac the Dane in combat. Hygelac was the brother of Beowulf. This appears to be the earliest recorded encounter between Franks and Vikings. Apparently thereafter the Vikings were too busy fighting one another to have much time for the world to the south. Late Merovingian Franconia offered few attractions. But once the reputation of Charlemagne echoed through Europe, its sounds were heard in the fjords of the north. When he had conquered the Saxons the influence of the Franks also moved nearer. The leader of the Saxons, Widukind, found refuge in Jutland. If he told them his side of the story the tale must have been terrible enough. When he had finally returned to Saxony and accepted Christian baptism, the potential danger of Franks to the Scandinavian north was bound to have increased.

The term Viking does not indicate a tribe but rather an activity. An adventurer who took to the sea was said to go *i viking*. The term, like that of Norsemen, is simply one of convenience and includes not only Danes and Norwegians but also many other adventurous folk who joined them on their expeditions and became part of their society. There are no adequate explanations to the questions who they originally were or what caused them to take to their boats and pillage the British Isles and the European mainland. Overpopulation may have been one reason, overpopulation of those areas of Denmark and Norway which allowed a subsistence agrarian economy. Nordic saga has it that approximately one century before Christ a chief by the name of Odin ruled over a city in Asia:

'The Roman Emperors were going far and wide over the world, beating down all peoples in battle; because of the unrest many lords fled from their lands. When Odin looked into the future and worked

France during the period 451–732.

magic, he knew that his offspring would dwell and till in the northern parts of the earth.'

Odin, endowed with supernatural powers, then led his people into the lands of the north to rule over the country and the men he found there. Although a saga, considering the area from which the Norsemen are supposed to have migrated, it is probable that their wanderings across Asia into northern Europe were part of the first stirrings of the Great Migrations. Once in their new homelands they developed considerable skills in woodcraft and metal work. Soon these lands became too small for large families, because among the Norsemen polygamy was commonplace. The economic pinch probably coincided with what we now might call a technological advance in the Norsemen's ship-building in which they first ventured along their own coasts and then across the seas, to Ireland, England and the Frankish Empire.

Of course sagas may supply us with indications on the basis of which one can speculate, but they are not evidence. Moreover they were not put to paper before the twelfth century. The account of the raids of the Norsemen have been handed down to us by the chroniclers, that is to say by their victims; the Norsemen themselves left no written records. The only concrete evidence left by them is of an archeological nature, such as the fourth-century vessel discovered at Nydham in Denmark. This shows a very low-sided ship equipped only for rowing, long, light and undecked. Its overall length was 76 feet, rowed by 14 pairs of oarsmen. It is more than doubtful that with a boat of this kind the treacherous waters of the North Sea could have been braved. But when, at the beginning of the eighth century the sail was introduced, the Norsemen lengthened and deepened the hulls of their boats, strengthening their structure all around. One such authentic surviving example is the Gokstad ship found near Oslo towards the end of the last century. Although still equipped with oars, it was primarily a sailing vessel. That was the kind of boat with which the Vikings made their assault upon Europe, and in perhaps their most daring expedition under the leadership of Leif Ericson they ventured across the Atlantic and set foot upon the New World five centuries before Columbus.

In their early raids upon Ireland, England and the Frankish Empire they appeared to have been very primitively armed, no better than the Germanic tribes when they first collided with the Romans. Such helmets and mailshirts they had seem to have been obtained from their slain victims or by trade. Therefore the majority of the raiders in the late eighth century were wholly unmailed. Within a span of half a century this had changed profoundly. From their enemies they had not merely captured arms, armor and equipment superior to their own, but also the skills of making it themselves. By the middle of the ninth century all Norsemen warriors wore mailshirts, based very much on the Frankish model. Even their shields were at first copies of those of the Franks. The shape of shield such as we find on the Bayeux tapestry is a product of the late ninth or early tenth century.

Archeological discoveries show the weapons of the Norsemen to have been double-bladed short swords with a small hand-grip and devoid of a cross-guard. In the course of their struggles with the Franks they adopted longer blades. Their spears were very similar to those of the Frank; only their axes were very heavy instruments, with a long wooden shaft which required both hands for its use. The axe was of course more than a weapon; it was a tool necessary for the repair and construction of their ships, to fell trees for encampment, purposes for which the small Frankish axe was unsuitable. In their skill of using the

Viking–type helmet worn by the sixth warrior on the first wagon (early Icelandic ms).

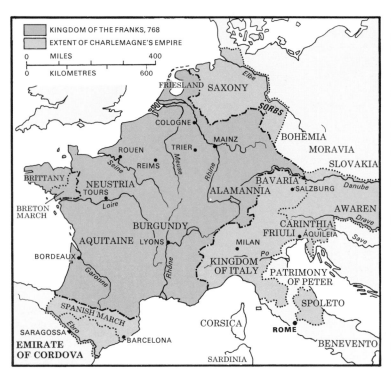

The French Kingdom in 768.

bow they were never matched by any of their adversaries, with the exception of Muslims on the southern shores of the Iberian peninsula.

When the Norsemen first appeared on their plundering expeditions, they operated on the basis of hit–and–run raids. At that time they could still be dealt with because the raids were individual ventures with very few boats involved. This changed during the ninth century when their massed fleets appeared on the shores of Ireland, England and the Frankish Empire. Then the boats were left under strong guards at their point of anchorage, while the bulk of the Norsemen made their way inland. In Ireland resistance to them was ferocious but lacking in organized leadership. England was also vulnerable because of its political divisions. In the Frankish Empire the Norsemen's impact was limited as long as Charlemagne reigned. But one monk records what is alleged to have been Charlemagne's reaction

when in the year of his coronation as Emperor of the Romans he was having a meal at the shores of the Mediterranean and Viking boats were sighted. He writes:

'When the Norsemen heard that Charles was there, they vanished in marvelously swift flight. Rising from his table, the most just and devout Charles stood looking from the window, while tears ran down and no one dared speak to him. Then he explained his tears to his nobles in these words: "I do not fear that these worthless scamps will do any harm to me. No, I am sad at heart thinking that while I live they dare intrude upon this shore, and I am torn by a great sorrow foreseeing what evil they will do to my descendants."'

If the account of this chronicler is to be believed, and there is nothing that would speak against it, Charlemagne had good reason to be anxious about the future, and his fears were more than vindicated.

After what might be called their phase of hit–and–run raids, the Norsemen turned to the next phase: full major invasions of the three major areas of their previous operations. That phase was marked by the changing character of the invasions. No longer did the Norsemen come simply to plunder; they came to settle. This is true of Ireland where they created and administered cities. It is true of England which they penetrated and, as already seen, it is true of the Frankish Empire. It was the last great migration of Nordic peoples before the sixteenth century, a migration which threatened the very survival of Europe's romanesque civilization.

Like the Franks, so the Anglo-Saxons at first were in despair of how to meet the new threat when it appeared on such a massive scale. They were prepared for any threat on land, but not one coming from the sea. When the Viking boats appeared in mass on the coast and rivers leading to London or York, each boat disembarking 40 warriors created havoc. While the Norsemen quickly rounded up all the horses they could lay their hands on and transformed themselves into mounted infantry, no defense mechanism existed to check or delay the rapidity of their movements.

The main objects of attack were monasteries and churches which were both holders of wealth as well as centers of the medieval culture that was developing on the ruins of Roman civilization. They were the repositories of the art and literature

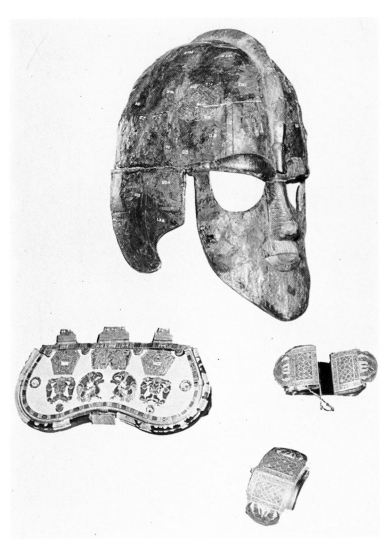

Above. *Treasures from the royal long-ship excavated at Sutton Hoo, c 650.*
Left. *The Storming of Ipswich by the Danes (Painting by Lorentz Ipplich).*

of the period. Commerce already in a state of stagnation since the Muslim invasions came to an almost complete halt when the Norsemen fell upon Europe.

They approached the lands to be despoiled from two major routes. The Norwegians chose the northern route over which quite a number of them had migrated to the Shetlands and the Orkneys and where they established their settlements. From there they made their way along the east and west coasts of Scotland as far as Lincolnshire in the east and down to the Isle of Man and to Ireland in the west. Ireland was a particularly rewarding area because it had escaped the impact of the Barbarian invasions. The climate was genial and Irish monasteries were filled with an abundance of wealth. Ireland was first attacked in 795, but from 850 onwards began a systematic campaign of conquest. As of 850 A.D. the Norsemen stayed permanently in Ulster; in 853 King Olaf founded his Dublin kingdom, and coastal colonies were established at Wexford, Waterford and Limerick. For 150 years the Norsemen exercised supremacy over Ireland and their power was not broken until the Anglo-Norman conquest in the reign of Henry II. The Isle of Man was not surrendered until 1266, the Shetlands till 1462 and the Orkneys until 1468.

The Danes preferred the southern route. Sailing directly from their own shores they were brought into immediate contact with east and southeast England, with the Low Countries and, once through the Channel, with Brittany, the Bay of Biscay and the Strait of Gibraltar from which they ravaged the coasts of the Mediterranean even capturing Sicily in a later phase. The Swedes, on the other hand, concentrated their efforts in the Baltic, entered Russia, which was the name they had given to it and opened up a southerly route as far as Constantinople.

The Anglo-Saxon Chronicle registers the first raids upon England. In 787 it records:

'In this year King Beorthoric took to wife Eadburh, daughter of King Offa; and in his days came for the first time three ships from the Norwegians from Hoerthland: these were the first ships of the Danes to come to England.'

As far as the chronicler is concerned there is no distinction between Danes and Norwegians, but they were most probably Danes.

Again in 793 it records:

'In this year terrible portents appeared over Northumbria, and miserably frightened the inhabitants: there were exceptional flashes of lightning, and fiery dragons were seen flying in the air. A great famine soon followed these signs; and a little after that in the same year on 8 January the harrying of the heathen miserably destroyed God's church in Lindisfarne by rapine and slaughter . . .'

King Egbert of Wessex fought them successfully in a pitched battle at Hingston Down in 838, but two years later they sacked London and again pillaged Lincolnshire and Northumbria. From 850 the period of systematic conquest began. More than 350 Viking ships did not return home after they had looted Canterbury, but their warriors wintered on the Isle of Thanet. It was the beginning of their permanent settlement. Fifteen years later the so-called 'great Army' of the Norsemen landed in East Anglia, and a year later in 866 they moved on to York. Northumbria, divided by political feuds, could offer no resistance. Then in 870 the great Army turned south towards Wessex, establishing its base at Reading, from which it could control the Thames and receive its supplies and strike at the capital of Wessex, Winchester.

The King of Wessex they faced was Alfred the Great. A deeply devout man as well as a very brave one, he decided to resist. But having no military organization worthy of the name, he tried to win time by negotiating with the Danes. He agreed to pay tribute providing the Danes evacuated Wessex. With that he won five valuable years in which to reorganize his forces.

The Danes had the advantage of being professional warriors prepared to fight all the year round. Against that Alfred had the old Anglo-Saxon *fyrd*, which by the ninth century was no longer a host of tribal freeman. As in the Frankish Empire, the feudal system was making its appearance; military service became connected with land-ownership, and even prior to Alfred's succession the nucleus of the *fyrd* was a small group of experienced soldiers, which on Alfred's instruction were constituted as a mobile infantry, to meet the Danes on their own ground. The mounted men were made up of the King's own close followers, his retainers, and those of the ealdormen, as well as from the heads of the shires, the thanes. He provided them with incentives, greater landholdings and turned them into a specifically military class whose expertise was rewarded with greater privileges. In Alfred's own words his society was composed of those who prayed, those who fought, and those who worked.

In contrast to the Franks Alfred recognized the importance of sea-power and initiated the construction of a fleet of long ships which in design and performance proved superior to those of the Danes. What Alfred's sailors lacked were the skills and the experience of the Danes and that could not be obtained in the short span of time available to them.

At strategically important points in Wessex, particularly on

Right. *Unearthed at Gokstad, Norway, this ship is one of the most remarkable finds dating from the Viking period. It was originally defended by a line of 32 wooden shields along each gunwhale. Painted yellow or black alternatively, the shields were reinforced at the center by an iron boss and overlapped to form a scale-like protection for 16 oarsmen.*

Below right. *Frankish warrior of the Carolingian period portrayed in carved ebony.*

its frontiers in the south and on the Thames, he built fortified strongholds, putting the responsibility for their maintenance upon the local people who had to provide the soldiers as well as the provisions. When the five years were up Alfred refused to pay further tribute and the Danes resumed their attacks. The first came in 876 from the west. After almost two years of inconclusive engagements, the Danes under their leader Guthrum struck a surprise blow which scattered Alfred's forces; Alfred himself had to seek refuge in the Athelney fens. But within a very short time he managed to reassemble his forces once again and defeat Guthrum at Edington in 878. As a result Guthrum agreed to be baptized, and eight years later a further agreement was concluded which delimited the Scandinavian settlers' territory in East Anglia and Mercia. The success of his policy is demonstrated best when one looks at the outcome of another Danish invasion between 892–896, this time coming from France. On three occasions the Danes traversed the country into West Mercia, expecting support from their countrymen. The majority, however, remained on their settlements. The Danes left without having achieved anything.

With his victory Alfred achieved more than just the supremacy of the Wessex dynasty among the Anglo-Saxon kingdoms. It was of European significance. What would have happened to the seedlings of Europe's medieval civilization had the Norsemen established their rule in the British Isles and used them as a base for their operations against the European mainland is not very difficult to imagine.

For England their threat had been banished, for subsequent Norse enterprises remained limited in scale and effect. What remained was an enduring horror and fear of them. In 1014 Olaf of Norway with his men helped the fugitive King Ethelred to return to England and take London from its Danish captors. The chronicler tells us:

'The Viking leader took his ships under London Bridge and wound cables round the stakes which supported the bridge, and taking the cables, they rowed all the ships downstream as hard as ever they could. The stakes were dragged along the bottom until they were loosed under the bridge . . . and the bridge came crashing down, and many fell into the river. . . . Now when the citizens saw that the River Thames was won, so that they could no longer prevent the ships from pressing up inland, they were stricken with terror at the advance of the ships and gave up the city.'

And most likely they would pray as did the French who had introduced this line to the litany of the Church, 'From the fury of the Norsemen, God deliver us.'

Under the combined threat from the Norsemen and the Magyars, Europe in the ninth century underwent several important military changes. In the Frankish Empire and its successor kingdoms the traditional levies of foot soldiery were quite useless in meeting a threat such as that posed by the Norsemen. They were clumsy and slow to assemble and move, and in combat were no match for the warriors of the north. They lacked the professionalism and experience which their enemies combined. The military aspect of nascent feudalism now began to gain in importance. The system of vassalage already developing during the eighth century provided the means of creating a class of military experts. At first they were people among the retinue of the monarch, but through subinfeudation the king's personal vassals would acquire knights of their own. Frankish counts and vassals at the Court of Charlemagne were expected to appear mounted. Their own retainers were equally expected to be mounted. It was the beginning of a period of over 400 years in which the cavalry dominated the field and its quality decided the battle. True, after the death of Louis the Pious, Frankish knights, in spite of their mounted levies, did not seem to have fared particularly well against the Norsemen, but it was a military failure at the root of which was the political instability of the late Carolingian period. To what effective use cavalry could be put to use against Barbarian raiders on horseback was to be demonstrated in Germany where, with the election of the Saxon Duke Henry I as King of Germany, stability returned and grew under his son Emperor Otto I, called 'the Great.'

The rise of cavalry meant in the final analysis that the defending forces could keep up with the Vikings in speed. It was more likely to break a Viking shield wall than ill-equipped levies on foot. The feudal pyramid running from the king downwards to his vassals and counts could produce a large number of knights well-equipped in arms and in training all year round, sustained in the end by the economic basis of the feudal system, the land.

Another transformation that was further accelerated by the invasions of the Barbarians from the north and east was the fortification of the towns and larger settlements. It was not a development that had its origins during that period. As already mentioned, in the provinces of the former Roman Empire it was a direct response to the devastation caused by the tribes of the Great Migrations. Previously spaciously laid-out towns and settlements were reconstructed as narrow, walled cities that could be defended. What was new was the building of castles as a specific defense requirement. Alfred the Great's burghs fulfilled the same function as the *burg* to King Henry I, who erected a whole series of them to defend his eastern frontier. King Odo in his Edict of Pitres of 866 which recognized the all-importance of cavalry, also laid down a policy of the construction of fortifications. When the great Viking siege of Paris took place, the city was already fortified. To the surprise of the Franks the Vikings constructed siege machinery such as towers and missile-throwing machines. They were good in adapting what they had seen elsewhere. What they did not know was how to use it effectively. Hence they settled for a tribute and left. The further rise of fortification, the growing dominance of cavalry, and the decline of infantry are the features that mark military development in the ninth century.

In the eastern part of the former Frankish Empire the threat of the Slavs and Magyars was added to the threat of the Norsemen. There, the old tribal duchies of Saxony, Bavaria, Swabia, Franconia and Lorraine combined and elected one of their own, Duke Henry of Saxony, as King of Germany. His election marks the origin of the German state.

This new kingdom, however, was weaker when compared to its Carolingian predecessor, because Henry had to recognize the dukedoms as independent, autonomous political units. He or any of his successors might replace a duke, but he could not eliminate the dukedom by dividing it among others. Such a precedent would have alarmed all the other dukes. The successors of Charlemagne, although they had acquiesced to it by necessity, did not look favorably upon the development in which their vassals acquired their own vassals, and in this way, their own military force. But needing the military force badly there was nothing else they could do.

This, of course, now also happened under Henry I. But since he was the product of his vassals, it was in their common interest to maximize their military force to the fullest extent which the feudal system allowed. In a later period the problems inherent in the feudal system came to the fore when the King's policy was not shared by one or more of his major vassals. Because as German King, even though from Otto the Great's day onward every King until Charles V acquired the Imperial crown, he was no more than a *primus inter pares* among his vassals. Since the feudal system implies also the delegation of authority downwards, in terms of offices and functions, and as these were inheritable, vassals acquired a quasi-sovereignty. This applied to the military sector as it did to that of the administration, and of course military and administrative functions were more often than not combined in one person. In the military sector feudalism in Germany and France offered the opportunity of personal aggrandizement, of keeping any size of military force a duke was capable of raising and supplying.

In 919, the year of Henry's election, none of that was felt. He had his power in Saxony firmly established and then went on to strengthen the military system as he found it. In one of the first gatherings with fellow dukes and bishops, a campaign was decided upon and every prince swore solemnly that he would come with all his men, a custom lasting well into the thirteenth century. The number of knights each vassal brought was up to him. The Carolingians had tried to establish fixed numbers for each vassal and had failed. Henry did not even try. Consequently one is in the dark about the precise numbers involved in each campaign, and this holds true for most of the campaign contingents of the Middle Ages.

Henry's main pre-occupation was with the Magyars, who first made themselves heard when they came from Hungary and invaded Bavaria's eastern marches, present day Austria, in 862. From the beginning of the tenth century onwards they regularly invaded Germany coming, like the Huns, on swift ponies, interested more in booty rather than combat.

Their attacks were made by small, widely spread-out bands, and like the Vikings in their first phase, they disappeared as quickly as they had come. Rapidity of movement was their major asset. Henry upon his accession to the throne realized that he was not yet sufficiently prepared to meet them, and therefore in 924 concluded a pact with them in which he promised them the payment of an annual tribute. Then he began to consolidate his military position. First, like Alfred the Great, he built his castles along the frontier, constructed by the population of the region, of which every ninth man was to live in the castle. Cities like Merseburg, Nordhausen, Quedlinburg and Goslar owe their existence to Henry's program of castle-building. As in centuries to come when the British sent their criminals to colonies, Henry sent his convicts to build castles. Finally in 933 when the Magyars once again attacked Thuringia Henry met them with his forces at the River Unstrut. The Magyars suddenly confronted with the German might took to their heels.

The battle on the Unstrut did not end the Magyar threat. After Henry's death they resumed their attacks in 954 with a major invasion, followed by a second one in 955. Again numbers are unknown, but chroniclers report that they had never been seen in such numbers before. They crossed Bavaria and laid siege to Augsburg at the River Lech. Henry's successor, his son, Otto, moved rapidly with his forces from Saxony, an army amounting to approximately 7000 men, almost all of them mounted knights, coming from Saxony, Bavaria, Swabia, Franconia and Bohemia. When Otto and his host approached the Magyars broke camp, the main body engaging Otto, while a smaller detachment, outflanking the German forces, turned up in the rear of the Swabians and slaughtered them. The Franconians under Duke Conrad came to their relief. Otto and the Bavarians, who had contained the Magyars so far, ordered a general charge. The Magyars on horses much smaller than those of the Germans, most of them without armor, discharged a volley of arrows before they were overtaken and slain. But Otto's forces had suffered heavily as well. Duke Conrad was killed the moment he lifted his helmet to get some air.

For two days Otto's forces pursued the Magyars capturing several of their leaders whom they promptly hanged. After the Battle of the Lechfeld the Magyar danger had been banished forever.

English ivory casket from the eighth century, presented by A W Franks and known as the Franks' Casket. The scene is reputed to depict the doom of Jerusalem.

THE EUROPEAN RESPONSE 'FEUDALISM'

Medieval man knew nothing of 'feudalism.' He only experienced it and was part of it. As a term it was invented for the convenience of historians and sociologists describing similar arrangements made by society in Europe and elsewhere in response to a changed economic and social environment. It was a response to economic and military necessities, involving large-scale social repercussions.

The Islamic invasions had thrown Western Europe back on its own resources in more than one sense. They had disrupted the traditional network of commerce. Specie became rare. The only source of wealth was land. But it would be an over-simplification to cite the Islamic invasions as the sole factor responsible for the origin of feudal society. It is marked by three characteristics, all of which show that other factors were at work as well.

Firstly there is the particularist characteristic. The states which succeeded the Roman Empire were, generally speaking, decentralized. Each state or territory was made up of several imperfectly integrated components, a process in which the old tribal ties still played a very great part. This resulted in a division of power between the King and his counts, a division based not on functional criteria, but on those of a territorial and tribal nature. The early medieval state was not a centralized unitary state but a kind of personal union under the King, whose office was the bracket holding it together; hence the bracket was as strong or as weak as the King who represented it.

Secondly, in the absence of an institutional apparatus, personal relationships were instrumental in the exercise of power. Thus feudalism was a system of personal rule, the only means available to govern a great empire (such as the Carolingian) based on a subsistence economy, underdeveloped communications, a state lacking as yet the necessary institutions which would have made greater centralization possible. The feudal state was a patrimonial state, patrimony exercised by the King and from him downwards by his lords.

Thirdly, there is the hierarchic characteristic, a result of the close connection between Church and monarchy, a connection based on the acceptance that all power derives from and is delegated by the Lord, handed out on loan to those who exercise it at the various levels. It is very much the opposite of the idea of the sovereign prince or the sovereign people, all power deriving either from the prince or the people. During the greatest days of the Papacy this culminated in the Papal claim that the Papacy alone represented the supreme authority for all Christendom.

The Carolingian Empire (751 A.D. to 987 A.D. in France and to 911 A.D. in Germany) represented a synthesis of Roman and Germanic traditions. The Germanic tradition is reflected in the personal character of the political and military leadership; the Roman tradition is found in institutions such as the Church which operated within the administrative framework inherited from the Empire. The early counts received a written commission, but they stood directly under the King.

Even during the Merovingian period (approximately 500 A.D. to 751 A.D.) changes took place, transformations which were signposts towards that kind of feudalism which blossomed out fully in the post-Carolingian period. The old Frankish army, made up of the King's close associates and the local levies they raised, made way for a professional caste of warriors on horse. Once the stirrup came into widespread use among the Franks during the second half of the eighth century, the horse was no longer solely a means of transport. It could now be used for fighting. 'Speed could be converted into shock. Spears need no longer be thrown but could be couched as lances and rammed home.' This new caste established itself under the King by means of a private treaty, combining personal and legal aspects, namely vassalage and benefice.

Vassalage represented the fusion of Roman and Germanic concepts. The Germanic concept of military service was voluntary, a concept diluted by the Gallic custom of compulsory participation and the Roman idea of a private soldier. Since the eighth century the Franks based military service on the principle of mutual loyalty and mutual obligations. In return for service the lord guaranteed the livelihood of his vassal as a member of his household or by giving to him a piece of land in fief. The land grant was the benefice, or fief. Originally fief meant the possession of livestock. The holder of the fief had the livestock on his fief at his disposal as well as the proceeds of the land. However, in the early phase of the feudal period he did not possess it—something that was to change later on. But this socio-economic relationship capsulated another threefold re-

Receiving and weighing coin, 1130–74. The figures are probably copied from an earlier ms.

Scenes from life in Anglo-saxon Britain (Trinity College Cambridge ms, 1130–74).

lationship characteristic of the feudal age: military specialization, land tenure and mutually binding personal obligation.

In the Merovingian kingdom not only the King but some of his lords had vassals as well. In other words, in its final phase enough military specialists were held by the King's vassals to constitute private armies. Charles Martel successfully curbed this development, but dire necessity made subinfeudation indispensable to raise the military forces necessary to wage war against the invading Muslims.

Vassalage replaced the Germanic relationship between prince and subject based on the family unit. Indeed by becoming a vassal, he implicitly renounced protection by his kinsfolk. Instead he accepted it from a more powerful lord. It is significant, however, that the vassal relationship did not reduce the status of the vassal as a free man but elevate it, for it was an honor to serve with the lord.

These changes did more than merely produce a caste of professional warriors. They affected the peasant as well. The settled peasant was no longer the man who looked after mobile livestock, he also turned to the arable soil. The very nature of this occupation tied him to the soil. He could no longer perform military services without seriously affecting his agricultural function and thus his output. And, it must be remembered that next to the plague, food-shortage was the major fear of medieval society. But the peasant too was in need of protection. The village community was no longer in a position to give it. Consequently many peasants by the act of commendation voluntarily sought the protection of a lord, who in return ultimately became their master and proprietor of their land. It was the beginning of the Germanic peasant's road from the position of a freeman to that of a dependant or even a serf. The medieval military specialist, the knight, could not till the soil of his benefice, but the peasants whom he protected could and, depending on circumstances, he could enlarge his property holdings at their expense.

The King was the fountain of justice, but size of territory and the nature of the lines of communication within his kingdom made it impossible for him to administer it. Therefore another feature of the feudal system was the granting of judicial power and authority to the vassals, to secular as well as ecclesiastical princes, which further increased the vassal's social and political position. To landed property, offices were added as fiefs in Germany and France with long-term attendant consequences: excessive particularism in the former, exaggerated regionalism in the latter.

Three factors then characterize medieval feudalism. The military factor produced a highly-trained and specialized warrior caste, knights, tied to their lord by bonds of loyalty and mutual obligations. Secondly, the socio-economic factor brought forth an agrarian economy on a basis which insured the income of the warrior caste. Thirdly, the factor of lordship opened to members of that caste the possibility of exerting considerable influence in affairs of state, or for that matter, as in Germany, to turn their own lands into semi-autonomous principalities, which more often than not acted against the interests of the central power as long as that power was lacking the political and technical means to centralize.

Feudalism was a stage in the development of human society, the product of many factors, but it did not affect all segments of human society in the same way and with equal intensity. In Europe it was most prominent and reached its highest forms in the successor states of the Carolingian Empire—Germany, France and parts of Italy and Spain—states which had their origin not in the direct transition from tribal unit to state, but by having been exposed to close contact with a disintegrating empire and its culture and by having passed through an intermediary stage of assimilating and integrating those traditions. Outside that area the formation of states took place without the feudal system developing intensely, if at all. The Nordic states as well as Poland and Hungary showed little if any feudal structure, but developed from tribal associations into states. Their warrior caste was not of feudal origin. Military service was generally obligatory.

England, perhaps, is a special case. The formation of its early kingdoms took place on Romanized soil, but considering the relatively short duration of Roman occupation, and the almost complete rupture of its connections with the world of Rome after the Romans had left, Roman influence was minimal. Compared with the Frankish Empire it represented a geographically manageable unit. Until the Angevin Kings, there were no signs of wishing to expand beyond the natural frontiers of the island. The disproportion between the task and the means to master it was much narrower there than in the Frankish Empire or its successors. Of course this does not mean that feudal elements did not exist in England, but they operated within certain limits, of which geography was one. A professional warrior caste developed in England as elsewhere, the thane holding five hides of land, but it was socially more open to members from other strata of society, such as merchants. It had its countervailing power in the continuing traditional institutions of Germanic origin such as the county, shire, and the hundred, which in England survived much longer than anywhere else in Europe, the usefulness of which the Normans were quick to recognize and to adapt for their own purpose. Yet even before the arrival of the Normans a relaxation of the old ties of kinship was noticeable. For the peasant to seek the protection of a lord is one indication. Village communities, or communities of kin among the Anglo-Saxons had the right to object to the sale of their land from time immemorial. Only the King with the agreement of the *witan*, an assembly made up of the nobility of birth and of men of wealth, created to check or advise the king, could turn such land into *bokland*, that is an inheritable possession. Thus after the Norman conquest, William the Conqueror by the right of conquest was able to claim supreme ownership of all the land of the realm and carry his

principle into practice that all land was the King's to grant as and when he saw fit. Although England was to experience the aberrations of the feudal system, their destructive effects were far more limited than elsewhere.

All this was very much in its infancy at the beginning of the Carolingian Empire. What is important though, is that by the time of Charlemagne's accession to the throne (800 A.D.) the feudal system had sufficiently developed to have established a caste of professional warriors, a military body permanently in being to meet the manifold threats. Their equipment was fairly expensive, and the existing evidence showing just how expensive it was, is indicative of the absence of the cash nexus, because its cost was measured in cows:

Helmet	6 cows
Coat of mail	12 cows
Sword with scabbard . . .	7 cows
Leg armor	6 cows
Lance with shield . . .	2 cows
Horse	12 cows

Forty-five cows were hardly inexpensive. Furthermore for a longer campaign a knight needed to take with him spare horses and in addition to the supplies which he had to provide from his own resources, he required the cart and horse to pull them as well as the driver. Considering the sweep and extent of Charlemagne's campaigns, their cost must have been extraordinary.

Below. *The Royal body guard of King Alfonso III, El Magno of Asturias (866–c 909), with swords, lances and shields* (Liber Testamentorum Regium, Oviedo Cathedral).

Right. *An example of early armor showing mail shirts and conical helmets. The illustration depicts David fighting Goliath and the Philistines (Bible of San Isidore de Lleo, 1162).*

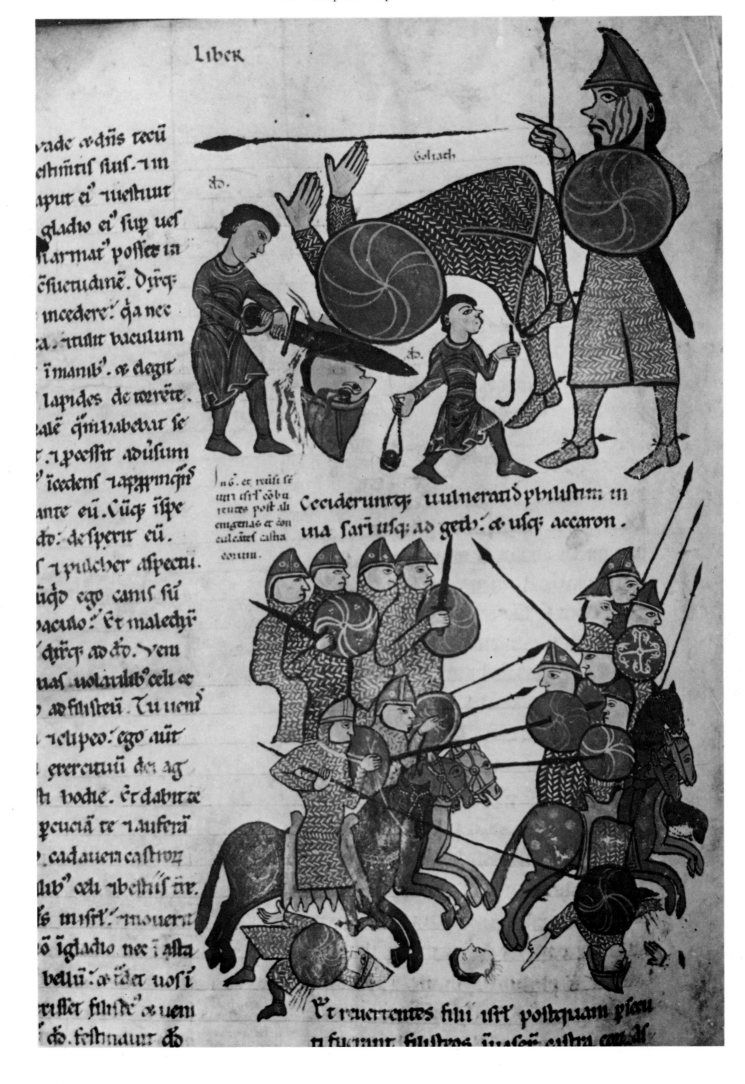

But the decisive turn which was to determine most of Charlemagne's policy had already been taken by his father Pipin. During his reign the Anglo-Saxon missionaries had begun their campaign to convert the Germans east of the Rhine to Christianity; their leader and outstanding representative was St Boniface, the Englishman from Devonshire who was to become the Apostle of the Germans. Pipin lent the missionaries his full support, because, religious reasons apart, the conversion of the Frisians, Saxons, Thuringians and Bavarians, all of them neighbors of the Franks, would make them less dangerous and easier to incorporate into the Frankish kingdom. St Boniface in that way became the direct link between the Carolingians and the Papacy. The Pope and Pipin needed one another. Pipin was *de facto* King of the Franks, but in a time when the royal title was of divine origin he was in need of having it confirmed *de jure* by the supreme spiritual authority in Christendom. The Pope, on the other hand, was about to break with Byzantium, whose form of Christianity in the light of Catholic orthodoxy was developing into heresy. Furthermore the Longobards to the northeast were increasingly making inroads on papal territory. The Papacy was in need of a secular protector, and who was better suited for that role than the Franks? With the Pope's sanction Pipin was formally crowned King among his assembly of notables. This arrangement of expediency became a fateful connection, determining the course of European history for almost 700 years. When Charlemagne came to the throne the problem of the conversion of the German heathens had not been fully solved. The Saxons presented another major obstruction. Nor was the relationship between the Papacy and the Longobards an easy one. Their conquest by Charlemagne bore no relationship to any concrete interests of the Frankish kingdom. Charlemagne carried it out for the Pope. The Papacy, after its break with Byzantium, and longing for the restoration of the old Roman Imperial Crown, crowned Charlemagne Emperor of the Romans on Christmas Day 800. The Papacy had become the supreme ecclesiastical and political arbiter in Christendom.

More relevant to Frankish interests were the renewed invasions of the Muslims across the Pyrenees. From that struggle was to emerge the famous *Chanson de Roland*, one of the great epics of the Middle Ages. Equally important was Charlemagne's campaign against the heathen Saxons between 779 and 804. The annexation of the Saxon territory was a strategic necessity for the security of the Empire which pushed its frontiers eastward to the Rivers Elbe and Saale. To the east were the Slavs and south of them the Avars, a people of nomadic character who originated in Mongolia. The Saxons had been converted at the point of the sword; 10,000 of their nobles were decapitated on the banks of the River Aller near Verden, but the Avars were completely exterminated. The Slavs were relieved, for the Avars had established a reign of terror over them. The fact that Charlemagne's campaigns were extensive is unfortunately not matched by any major field battles which would give us a true picture of the fighting and the tactics deployed. In the wars against the Saxons, lasting for over 33 years, only two actual battles took place, of which only the place names have been left to posterity, such as Detmold.

Although this would suggest that the Franks were formidably armed, evidence describing the equipment of Charlemagne's forces is very scarce. One commander calling his levy together required that every horseman was to be equipped with shield, lance, dagger, bow and arrows—a rather curious assembly of weapons, since the shield and the lance were bound to get in the way of the bow and arrow in action. The Carolingian knights appear to have used both sword and lance in close combat. The knights were professional warriors, but again there is no evidence to indicate that they subjected themselves to systematic tactical exercises.

When Charlemagne died in 814 he was succeeded by his sole surviving son Louis the Pious. As Louis had three sons the question arose of how the Empire should be divided among Lothair, Louis the German and Pipin, and how in fact an empire could be divided that had one imperial crown. With whom of the three should the imperial dignity rest? Primogeniture did not exist among the Franks. This resulted even during Louis's lifetime in fraternal struggles which rent the empire asunder. The Treaty of Verdun of 843, dividing the empire into three equal shares, was a compromise solution, eliminating in practice the idea of imperial unity. The imperial crown and the center part from Frisia to Italy went to Lothair. Louis the German received Germany, and Charles the Bald, the son of Pipin, France. After Lothair's death the struggle over the inheritance broke out anew until in 911 the last of the east Frankish line of Carolingians died. During that internecine strife the last remnants of the Merovingian administrative institutions, the counties, became feudalized and fiefs were distributed between the various supporters of the contesting parties.

The Empire's weakness coincided with the onslaught of the Norsemen. From 834 onwards they systematically devastated the coast from Frisia to the Gironde, destroying such cities as Nantes, Rouen and Bordeaux. After 855 they advanced up the Elbe, the Seine and the Loire. Taking to horses they erupted into the Auvergne; Amiens, Paris and Orleans were burned. They attacked Spain and Morocco and burned Pisa. In the north they sacked London and advanced to Bedford and York. At the same time Arab corsairs based on Corsica and Sardinia, stormed the towns of Sicily and Calabria, and then ravaged Campagnia and Tuscany. Even Rome was not safe from them.

One of the reasons why these Barbarians from the periphery of Europe could operate almost unopposed—only the Irish are reputed to have put up a stiff fight against the Norsemen—is what one may call the European civil war over the succession to the Carolingian Empire and the Imperial Crown. As long as the Emperor constituted the generally recognized authority, he was in a position to rally together such forces as were needed to meet a particular threat. But once that central authority had been eclipsed and the Kings became dependent on the good will of their counts, bishops and vassals, the picture changed. Only from the vicinity of the area directly under the control of the King could forces be mustered. Nothing or little came from remoter regions unless they themselves were affected by foreign invasion.

The Norsemen, coming from Denmark and Norway, represented a movement whose causes are analogous to that of the Great Migrations. They came from areas which because of their size and climatic conditions could not feed or sustain them at the level of many of the countries in their vicinity. Their total force was considerably smaller than the other Germanic tribes which had preceded them. What made them so terrifying to a society which had moved up several rungs on the ladder of civilization was the confrontation with the original, almost primeval warrior type which many of their forefathers had been when they settled in central and western Europe.

In England the Norse threat welded the Anglo-Saxon states together. In the Frankish Empire after Louis the Pious until 911 the organized will to unite was lacking. Nor was the Frankish military organization prepared and equipped for a threat coming from the sea and up the rivers. The Empire of Charlemagne had never possessed any naval force. Attempts to build one were made but so half-heartedly that four years before Charlemagne's death the Norsemen could invade Frisia, burn and plunder it, and sail off in their boats again before a Frankish force could be assembled. Under Louis the Pious nothing at all was done to secure the seas and the shores of the Empire. The possession of a fleet and their skills in handling it gave the Norsemen advantages which a military organization built exclusively for the purposes of land warfare could not match. The initiative lay with the invader who could appear at any point on the coast or in any river mouth, and the damage was done before countermeasures could be enacted. Attempts were made to turn the peasants into militia, but the feudal system had estranged them sufficiently from the craft of war to render them useless. They were slaughtered as quickly as their livestock. It was more advisable for them to take to their heels, and most of them did.

Thus the Norsemen could make their way down the Rhine, burn Aix-la-Chapelle, make their way down to Koblenz, and then up the Moselle to Trier. The Empire was paralyzed by their appearance and by its preoccupation with the wars for succession under the later Carolingians. Yet even the temporary unification of the Carolingian Empire, under Charles III, when one might have expected a concentrated effort to meet the danger, made no difference.

Charles III was hardly a warrior, and even less a hero. He preferred negotiation, and concluded a treaty with the Norsemen in which their leader, Godfrey, accepted baptism and married a Carolingian princess. In addition, payment in gold and silver was made to them and land was allocated to him and his men in Frisia. When the Norsemen laid siege to Paris Charles appeared with his entire army on the north bank of the Seine and occupied Montmartre. The Norsemen withdrew to the south bank where they remained. Charles avoided battle, concluded a new treaty paying ransom for Paris, and allocated Burgundy to the Norsemen as winter quarters. The disgust among the Frankish nobility was so great that they dethroned Charles.

When Charles had been deposed the western Franks had chosen Odo to be the defender of Paris. As Duke of the Franks he ruled the territory between the Seine and the Loire. But rivalry among the western Franks soon erupted again, the dissenters crowning Charles the Simple. The Norsemen took due advantage. For the rest of the ninth century they devastated the countryside between the Loire and the Rhine. Charles the Simple also preferred compromise to pitched battle; in 911 Jarl Rollo was given permission to settle his warriors and their families in the Caux area. But warlike habits did not die easily. The pursuits of an agricultural life were hardly tempting when the riches of churches, abbeys and monasteries lay at the Norsemen's threshold. They continued their raids in Brittany, Artois and other areas. In the end Rollo claimed the Orne and then the Cotentin peninsula. Normandy was in the making, although the Normans had yet to be absorbed into the feudal system, something which was never fully accomplished. A century later William the Conqueror, recognizing the strengths but even more so the weaknesses of feudal society, set out on the last voyage of major conquest with men of Norse decent and imposed his own version upon England, rather more efficiently practiced there than on the European mainland.

Infantry and cavalry with swords, spears, bow and arrow, and small round shields (Mozarabic ms, tenth century).

SIEGE TECHNIQUES

By strict definition a siege is a passive operation in which the besieging army surrounds a place, cuts it off from communications and supply, and waits for starvation or the lack of water or ammunition to compel the occupants to surrender. Given sufficient patience, this system cannot fail, and starvation and deprivation have played a significant part in sieges from the earliest recorded times up to the present century. Patience, though, is generally a scarce commodity with armies, particularly medieval armies who were inclined to lose interest around harvest time, and it became customary to hurry the process along by making demonstrations and attacks in order to demoralize the garrison and bring about a faster capitulation.

The castle, though, was specifically designed to keep out

Above. Landsknecht *using early bridge-crossing equipment. Note the hooks to catch on the far wall.*

Right. *Fourteenth-century siege.*

Above. *Collapsible drawbridge used for defense (Bellifortis, Conrad Kyeser's treatise on warfare, 1405).*

Left. *Instruments for storming a town (Renatus, 1529).*

Above. *Archers assault a city
(William of Tyre ms, 1250–60).*

Below. *Tower in use, covered in
wet hides to prevent the use of fire
as a countermeasure.*

unwanted visitors, and therefore to overcome the defenses required application of special skills and tactics. The architecture of fortification is based on the principle of placing a series of obstacles in the way of the attacker so that the winning of each obstacle involves a fight and gives the defenders the chance to reduce the number of attackers. Thus a typical castle defense would show firstly a deep and generally water-filled ditch to be crossed, backed by a precipitous wall, so close to the ditch as to afford little or no space for an attack to gain a foothold between the two. The wall would be surmounted by an *allure*, or walkway, from which bowmen could shoot down, protected by raised sections of parapet (*merlons*) alternating with lower sections (*embrasures*), the result being the familiar *battlements*. Towers protruding from the wall allowed the defenders a view of the foot of the wall and its front face, so that attackers managing to reach the wall could be taken by fire from their flanks.

Behind the wall would be an open area, the *outer bailey*, within which a second line of ditch and wall would protect the *inner bailey*. Inside this would be the *keep*, an immensely strong tower, difficult of access and well-protected. This acted both as the final defensive position and as a reserve from which troops could emerge to beat off attacks.

With all this to be overcome, certain techniques became standard. As a first step, it was usual to make a direct assault on

the outer ditch and wall, using brushwood and earth to fill the ditch allowing it to be crossed and ladders to scale the wall; this usually failed, but upon occasion a demoralized or somnolent garrison would be surprised, so it was always worth trying. But after that failed, more formal measures came into play. The first stage was always to extend the besieging lines until the place was completely surrounded to prevent escape or reinforcement. At the same time the surrounding countryside was scoured for all available foodstuff, to sustain the besiegers and to ensure that there was no chance for a party to sneak out of the castle at night and return with a few head of cattle. In fact when a siege threatened, an astute garrison would immediately go out and bring in all they could find, for their own benefit and to deny supplies to the attackers; more than one siege failed because the garrison's supplies held out while the besiegers starved because of the absence of supplies in the locality.

In order to deal with the wall, there were two options – go over it or go through it. To go *over* meant the construction of *beffroys* or towers on wheels which, after the ditch had been filled in, could be pushed across to the wall. The tower carried a number of platforms connected with leaders and filled with soldiers; on reaching the wall those on the topmost platform leapt across and engaged in hand-to-hand combat with the wall's defenders while the troops on the lower platforms raced up the ladders to join in the fray. If the attack was a success, a party would descend the inside of the wall and open the gates to allow the main body of the attacking army to enter.

The answer to the tower attack was to wreck it before it got close enough; pitch and oil could be flung at it, the men and horses propelling it shot by bowmen, and then torches flung from the wall, or fire-arrows, would ignite the structure.

To go *through* the wall meant bringing it down or making a hole in it. The earliest method was the battering ram, an iron-shod balk of timber suspended from a wheeled frame by chains and impelled back and forth by men. As walls became thicker the ram became less important, though it was still effective

Above left. Methods of self-defense using turtle-type shield (Bellifortis, Conrad Kyeser's military treatise, 1405).

Left. Miners: the wall has been underpinned and kindling is now being carried in.

Below. *A walled city under siege.*

against gates. Defenders could try to render it ineffective by lowering bales of wool or straw to absorb the ram's blow, or by snaring its head by chains and then dragging it away from the wall. However, the easiest method was to attack the men who were operating it, by stones and boiling water (never oil as it was too expensive and scarce) dropped from above and by arrows and spears fired into the mass of men. This defense, in turn, was defeated by the adoption of the *testudo* or *tortoise* a pentroof on a mobile frame which could be pushed over the ram and its workers.

More effective than the ram was the mine, and mining eventually became the most practiced method of attack, since once miners got to work the collapse of the castle was simply a question of time. The initial difficulty was to obtain a lodgment or foothold against the wall, and to achieve this end another tortoise was used, often put in place under cover of darkness and with some form of decoy attack or demonstration taking place against another face of the wall to draw the attention of the defenders. Once the tortoise was in place the miners went to work, digging away the earth beneath the wall and supporting the masonry of the wall with wooden props. Once a sufficient length of wall had been undermined, the cavity was packed with brushwood and a fire started. The props would then burn through and the unsupported length of wall would collapse.

Antidotes to mining attacks were few; the initial construction of the wall could be designed with mining in view, the lower part being given a considerable 'batter' or outward slope which widened the foot of the wall and presented a more formidable task for the miner. Another constructional technique was to

Left. *Trebuchet.*

Below left. *A beffroy or tower in use.*

Below. *Trebuchet.*

vant il ont fait le fai
rement si lor dist: Sig
nor les voes mercis v

Above. *Assault on a tower (*Le Roman de Lancelot du Lac et La Mort du Roi Arthur, *early fourteenth century).*

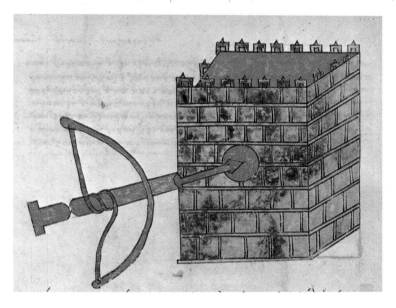

Left. *War machine (Byzantine military treatise, eleventh century).*

Above. *'Turtle' defense machine on wheels to protect soldiers about to attack (Byzantine military treatise, eleventh century).*

make towers and wall corners rounded instead of angular, since this gave the wall better cohesion. But the best defense was countermining, digging a shaft from inside the fortress to enter the mine chamber. Through this shaft a party of defenders could then rush in the hope of overpowering the miners, and subsequently fill in the mine chamber. Or, if this was thought too hazardous, the shaft could be used to introduce floodwater or fire and smoke. Unfortunately countermining was a two-edged sword and frequently did no more than assist the miners by removing even more of the wall's support and, in the worst case, could either hasten the collapse or, if the defenders lost the fight, left the shaft open for the mining party to effect an entrance into the place.

The third line of attack was by the use of *engines*, machines for throwing missiles. Three basic types existed; the *Ballista* which fired javelins or large arrows, and the *Mangonel* and *Trebuchet* which launched stones and other solid objects. The ballista employed a heavy framework to support the javelin; behind this a flexible strip of timber was hauled back by a windlass and then released, to fly back and strike the javelin to drive it forward. The effect of this weapon was quite surprising; at Marseilles, in 49 B.C., twelve-foot iron-tipped spears were fired from a ballista to pass through four rows of shields before striking the earth beyond.

The mangonel was a long wooden arm with a spoon-shaped end, mounted in a heavy framework. The foot of the arm was lashed to a cross-beam, the lashing giving the required degree of spring to the arm's action; it was also supplemented in many cases by a cross-bar of flexible timber attached to the arm by ropes in the manner of a bow. The arm was hauled back by the usual windlass, a stone placed on the spoon, and the arm released so as to fly forward flinging the stone a considerable distance into the air. Boulders of one or two hundred pounds weight were commonly used, and the impact of one of these on a wall was immense; a series of well-aimed shots could soon batter a

Below. *Mobile tower for attacking fortress (Byzantine military treatise, eleventh century).*

Right. *Elevated castle for maritime attack (Vigevano's military treatise, fourteenth century).*

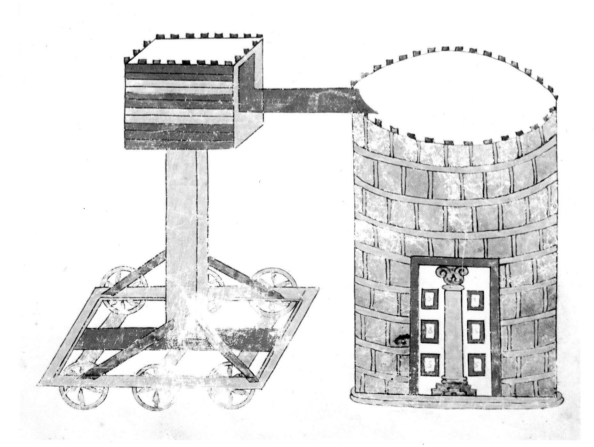

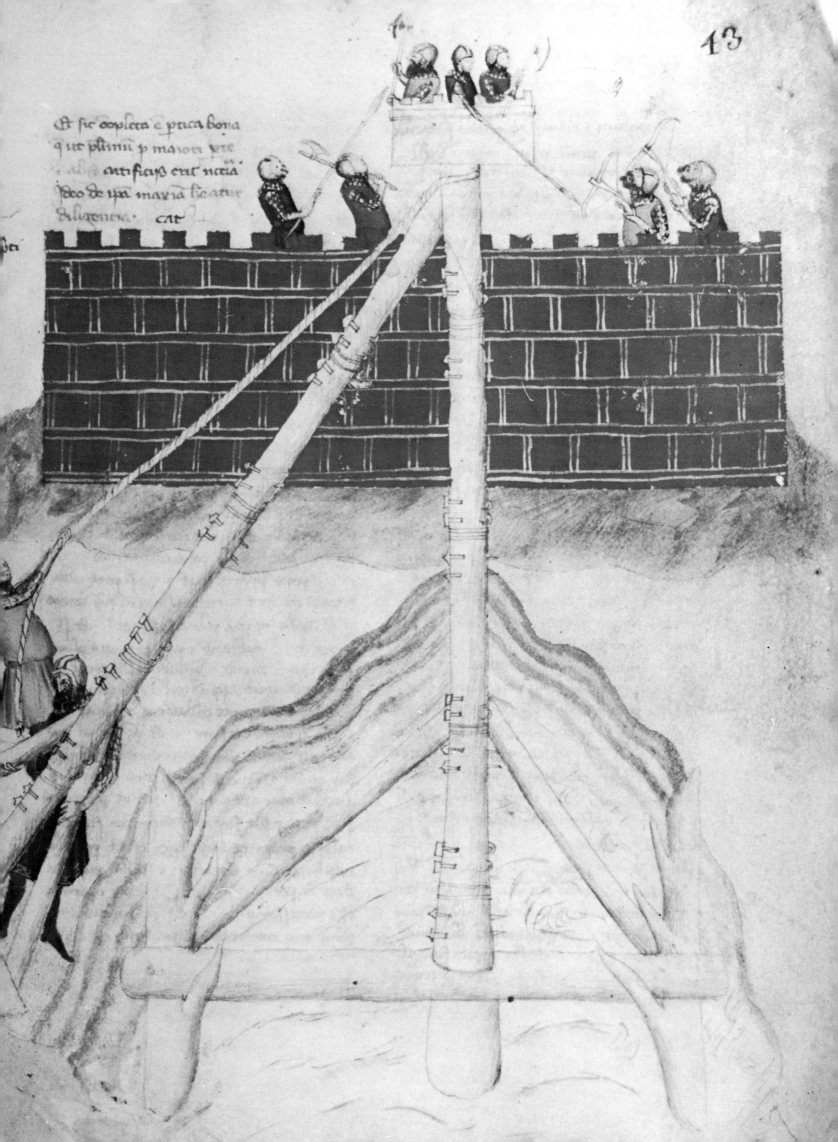

Left. *Mangonel: siege artillery for projecting heavy stones.*

Below. *Siege of a German town: foot soldiers and cavalry storm through the town gates.*

Below right. *A small catapult operated by a springlike action powered by twisted fiber.*

Bottom right. *Trebuchet.*

hole in the upper part of a wall, leaving a breach which could then be assaulted by foot soldiers. In addition to this direct assault the mangonel could also be used to bombard the interior of the place, the huge stones smashing the buildings beneath and causing casualties. To promote disease and despondency within the walls, it was common practice to launch dead animals, corpses and even prisoners across the wall from the magonel.

The largest of the machines was the trebuchet, or slinging machine. This used a long, whippy arm with a counterweight on one end and a leather sling on the other. The arm was hauled down and the sling filled with a stone (or stones) on release, the arm was propelled up by the effect of the enormous counterweight until it struck a cross-beam and stopped suddenly which allowed the sling to fly forward and launch the stone.

But when all the engines and devices were taken into account, the fact remained that no fortress was stronger than the garrison inside it, and the majority of sieges succeeded as much from the effects of starvation and isolation as from mechanical assault. It was not until the sixteenth century that cannons became powerful enough to make much of an impression on masonry. With the arrival of artillery the whole process of siegecraft had to be completely revised.

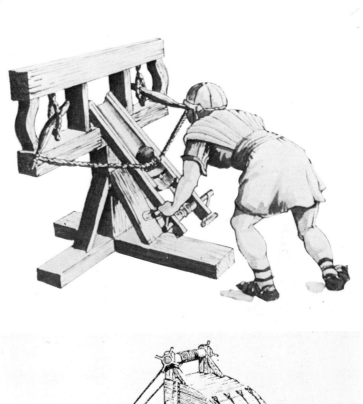

The Battle of Stamford Bridge fought in 1066 is here depicted with armor and heraldry of the thirteenth century. This scene is found in the Chronica Majorca compiled in about 1250 (Cambridge University Library ms).

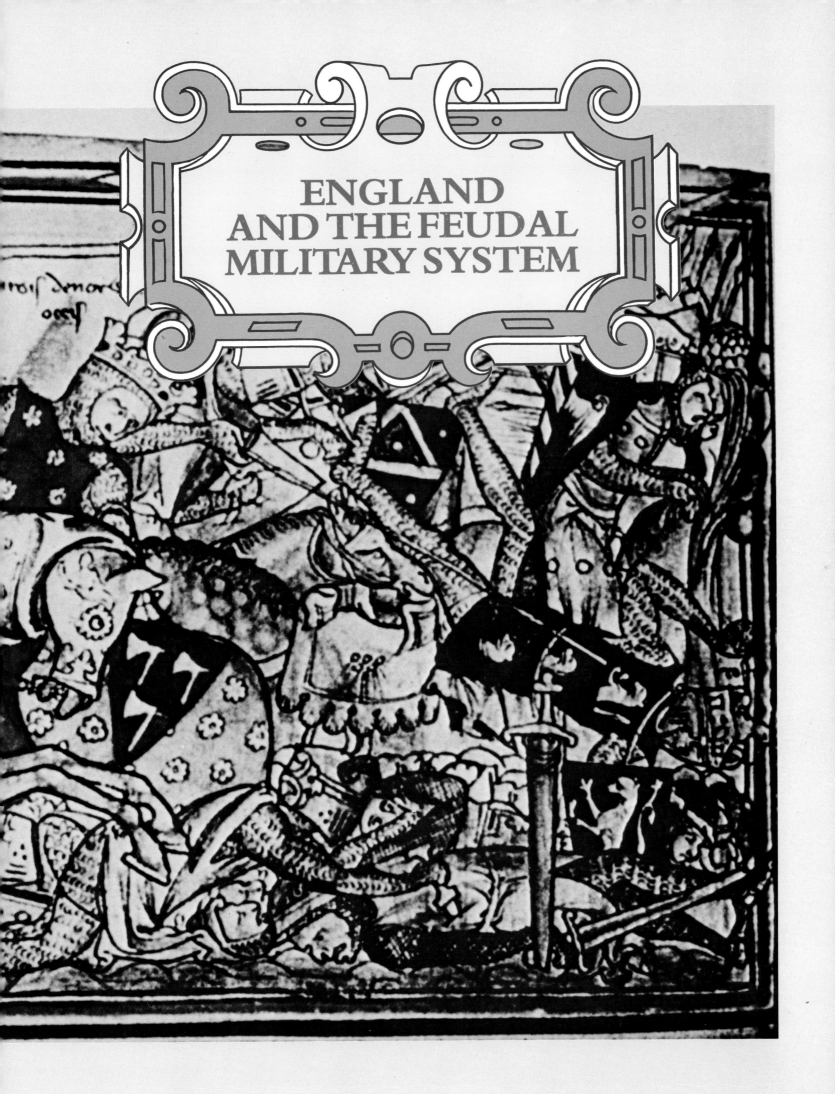

ENGLAND AND THE FEUDAL MILITARY SYSTEM

Had not Arlette, the daughter of the tanner of Falaise, captured the passions of Duke Robert of Normandy, there would not have been the offspring William of Normandy (1028–87) and history might have taken a different turn. William was one of the contestants for the English throne after the death of King Edward the Confessor (1004–66). Harold, one of the other two claimants, established himself on the throne first, but allegedly bound by an act of homage, through which he became the vassal of William of Normandy, he had also promised to support William in obtaining the Crown of England, a promise which by his own succession he had broken. Harold claimed the oath was invalid because he had taken it under constraint.

William now decided to reverse the decision. His political preparation included submitting his claims to the Pope for decision. After due examination by the Pope and his Cardinals William's claim was upheld, and a banner was sent to William from the Holy See, consecrated and blessed for the invasion of England. Its conquest became something like a crusade. William's army contained the chivalry of continental Europe of which the Normans considered themselves the elite. The spring and summer of 1066 was full of the sounds of busy preparation in Normandy, Picardy and Brittany. King Harold could not fail to see the threat. He was making preparations to meet it when a

Norwegian invasion in the north under King Harold Hardrada landed on the Yorkshire coast, and made its way towards York routing all opposition. The entire region from the Tyne to the Humber submitted to him. Within four days Harold and his army reached Yorkshire and took the Norwegians by surprise. In the Battle of Stamford Bridge the outcome was long in the balance. The English forces were unable to break up the phalanx of the Norwegians until Harold decided upon a stratagem. His English troops pretended to flee and when the Norwegians set after them in pursuit, English formations, held in reserve, burst among them. It was more than a battle; it was a massacre in which the Norwegian King and the flower of his nobility perished.

Many of Harold's best men were lost too, but the most important consequence of the Norwegian invasion and Harold's rush to the north was that William and his host gained an unopposed landing on the Sussex coast. His army when gathered on the English shore is calculated to have amounted to 7000 knights, and 2000 foot soldiers, though it seems that many knights must have fought on foot, since it would have been impossible to arrange transport for so many horses. At first William was delayed by unfavorable winds; it was not till the approach of the equinox that the wind changed from northwest to west and gave William the opportunity to set sail for Eng-

Left. *The Normans prepare their fleet for the channel crossing* (The Bayeux Tapestry: *this famous tapestry was probably embroidered in England in the eleventh century*).

Below. *Welsh archer (Chapter House Liber A, thirteenth century).*

land. But the wind turned into a gale and many boats were wrecked and lost, causing another short postponement until, with a southerly breeze, the last and final attempt could be made. On 29 September 1066 they landed in Pevensey Bay, between the Castle of Pevensey and Hastings.

Harold was still at York rejoicing over his victory when news of the Norman invasion came. Decimated by battle he hastened immediately southwards to London where he put in a rest period of six days. Then he moved on to meet his foe, who was busily establishing his base. Norman chroniclers describe the preparations on his landing with graphic vigor:

'It (his ship) was called the Mora, and was the gift of his duchess, Matilda. On the head of the ship in the front, which mariners call the prow, there was a brazen child bearing an arrow with a bended bow. His face was turned towards England, and thither he looked, as though he was about to shoot. The breeze came soft and sweet, and the sea was smooth for their landing. The ships ran on dry land, and each ranged by the other's side. There you might see the good sailors, the sergeants and squires sally forth and unload the ships; cast the anchors, haul the ropes, bear out shields and saddles, and land the war-horses and palfreys. The archers came forth, and touched land first, each with his bow strung, and with his quiver full of arrows, slung at his side. All were shaven and shorn; and all clad in short garments, ready to attack, to shoot, to wheel about and skirmish; and they scoured the whole shore but found not an armed man there. After the archers had thus gone forth, the knights landed all armed, with their hauberks on, their shields slung at their necks, and their helmets laced. They formed together on the shore, each armed, and mounted on his war horse: all had their swords girded on, and rode forward into the country with their lances raised. Then the carpenters landed, who had great axes in their hands, and planes and axes hung at their sides. They took counsel together, and sought for a good spot to place a castle on. They had brought with them in the fleet, three wooden castles from Normandy, in pieces, all ready for framing together, and they took the materials of one of these out of the ships, all shaped and pierced to receive the pins which they had brought cut and ready in large barrels; and before evening had set in, they had finished a good fort on the English ground and there they placed their stores. All then ate and drunk enough, and were right glad that they were ashore.

When Duke William himself landed, as he stepped on the shore, he slipped and fell forward upon his two hands. Forthwith all raised a loud cry of distress. "An evil sign," said they, "is here." But he cried but lustily, "See! my lords; by the splendor of God, I have taken possession of England with both my hands. It is now mine; and what is mine is yours."

The next day they marched along the seashore to Hastings. Near that place the Duke fortified a camp and set up two other wooden castles. The foragers, and those looking out for booty, seized all the clothing and provisions they could find, lest what had been brought by the ships should fail them. And the English were to be seen fleeing before them, driving off their cattle, and quitting their houses. Many took shelter in burying places, and even there they were in grievous alarm.'

The main difference between the two armies was that the English army comprised in its majority foot soldiers while many of the Normans were mounted. This emerges clearly from documented sources and the Bayeux Tapestry. For Harold this had one important consequence, he could not afford to meet his enemy on a plain; the mounted knights would have broken them apart. King Harold therefore chose his position on a broad height, surmounted by Battle Abbey, which declined very steeply to the rear making it invulnerable to a mounted attack from behind, while allowing foot soldiery to slip down and take to the adjacent forests in case of a withdrawal or defeat. According to all accounts the Normans were superior in the use of their archery. Most of Harold's army were equipped with

From 0900 hours until evening the English shield-wall withstood the Norman attack at Hastings. Then a ruse by the Norman cavalry made them break their ranks and they were eventually routed and roundly defeated (The Bayeux Tapestry).

swords, spears, battle-axes and the like; most of them were professional warriors and not troops made out of local levies such as the *fyrd*.

After prior fruitless negotiations between William and Harold, on Saturday 14 October, the Normans moved into attack—horsemen, their squires and archers together. As they approached the heights on which Harold was encamped, Norman archers moved to the fore and let loose a hail of arrows, but they were clearly at a disadvantage against the Anglo-Saxons who were throwing their missiles from above; one point in favor of the Normans was that their bows had further range. This was followed by an attack from the mounted knights together with knights on foot, an attack which was slow as it had to be carried out uphill. It was repelled and the Normans were chased back. Partly they turned back because they failed to get through the undergrowth covering the approach quickly enough, but also perhaps because they thought that turning back might tempt the English from their lofty perch. However, their strength lay in their defensive position, but this very strength was also their weakness. No battle can be decided by fighting solely from the defensive. If this was the intention then the Normans succeeded in the same way as Harold had succeeded by his stratagem at Stamford Bridge. As the Chronicler tells us:

'The Normans saw that the English defended themselves well, and were so strong in their position that they could do little against them. So they consulted together privily, and arranged to draw off, and pretend to flee, till the English should pursue and scatter themselves over the field; for they saw that if they could once get their enemies to break their ranks, they might be attacked and discomfited much more easily. As they had said, so they did. The Normans by little and little fled, the English following them. As the one fell back, the other pressed after; and when the Frenchmen retreated, the English thought and cried out, that the men of France fled, and would never return.

Thus they were deceived by the pretended flight, and great mischief thereby befell them; for if they had not moved from their position, it is not likely that they would have conquered at all; but like fools they broke their lines and pursued.

The Normans were to be seen following up their stratagem, retreating slowly so as to draw the English further on. As they still flee, the English pursue, they push out their lances and stretch forth their hatchets; following the Normans, as they go rejoicing in their suc-

cess of their scheme, and scattering themselves over the plain. And the English meantime jeered and insulted their foes with words. "Cowards," they cried, "you came hither in an evil hour, wanting our lands, and seeking to seize our property, fools that ye were to come! Normandy is too far off, and you will not easily reach it. It is of little use to run back; unless you can cross the sea at a leap, or can drink it dry, your sons and daughters are lost to you."

The Normans bore it all, but in fact they knew not what the English said; their language seemed like the baying of dogs, which they could not understand. At length they stopped and turned round, determined to recover their ranks; and the barons might be heard crien Dex Aie! for a halt. Then the Normans resumed their former position, turning their faces towards the enemy; and their men were to be seen facing round and rushing onwards to a fresh mêlée; the one party assaulting the other, this man striking, another pressing onwards. One hits, another misses; one flies, another pursues; one is aiming a stroke, while another discharges his blow. Norman strives with Englishman again, and aims his blows afresh. One flies, another pursues swiftly: the combatants are many, the plain wide and the mêlée fierce. On every hand they fight hard, the blows are heavy, and the struggle becomes fierce. The Normans were playing their part well, when an English knight came rushing up, having in his company a hundred men, furnished with various arms. He wielded a northern hatchet, with the blade a full foot long; and was well armed after his manner, being tall, bold and of noble carriage. In the front of the battle where the Normans thronged most, he came bounding on swifter than the stag, many Normans falling before him and his company. He rushed straight upon a Norman who was armed and riding on a war-horse, and tried with his hatchet of steel to cleave his helmet; but the blow miscarried, and the sharp blade glanced down before the saddle-bow, driving through the horse's neck down to the ground, so that both horse and master fell together to the earth. I do not know whether the Englishman struck another blow; but the Normans who saw the stroke were astonished, and about to abandon the assault when Roger de Montgomeri came galloping up, with his lance set, and heeding not the long-handled axe, which the Englishman wielded aloft, struck him down and left him stretched upon the ground. Then Roger cried out, "Frenchmen, strike! The day is ours!" And again a fierce mêlée was to be seen, with many a blow of lance and sword; the English still defending themselves, killing the horses and cleaving the shields.

There was a French soldier of noble mien, who sat his horse gallantly. He spied two Englishmen who were also carrying themselves boldly. They were both men of great worth, and had become companions in arms and fought together, the one protecting the other. They bore two long and broad bills (halberds), and did great mischief to the Normans, killing both horses and men. The French soldier looked at them and their bills, and was sore alarmed, for he was afraid of losing his good horse, the best that he had; and would willingly have turned to some other quarter, if it would not have looked like cowardice. He soon, however, recovered his courage, and spurring his horse gave him the bridle, and galloped swiftly forward. Fearing the two bills, he raised his shield, and struck one of the Englishmen with his lance on the breast, so that iron passed out at his back. At the moment that he fell, the lance broke, and the Frenchman seized the mace that hung on his right side, and struck the other Englishman a blow that completely broke his skull. . . .

And now might be heard the loud clang and cry of battle, and the clashing of lances. The English stood firm in their barricades, and shivered the lances, beating them into pieces with their bills and maces. The Normans drew their swords, and hewed down the barricades, and the English in great trouble fell back upon their standard, where they collected the maimed and the wounded.

There were many knights from Chauz, who jousted and made attacks. The English knew not how to joust, or bear arms on horseback, but fought with hatchets and bills. A man, when he wanted to strike with one of their hatchets, was obliged to hold it with both hands, and could not at the same time, as it seems to me, both cover himself and strike with any freedom.

The English fell back towards the standard which was upon rising ground, and the Normans followed them across the valley, attacking them on foot and horseback. Then Hue de Mortemer, with the sires

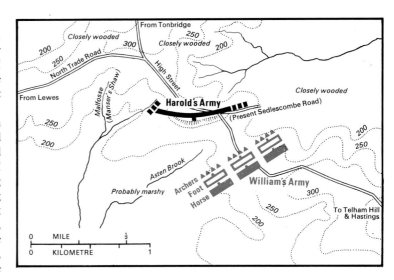

The Battle of Hastings, 1066.

D'Auviler, D'Onebac, and St Cler, rode up and charged, overthrowing many.

Robert Fitz Erneis fixed his lance, took his shield, and, galloping towards the standard, with his keen-edged sword struck an Englishman who was in front, killed him, and then drawing back his sword, attacked many others, and pushed straight for the standard, trying to beat it down, but the English surrounded it, and killed him with their bills. He was found on the spot, when they afterwards sought him, dead, and lying at the standard's foot.

Duke William pressed close upon the English with his lance; striving hard to reach the standard with the great troop he led; and seeking earnestly for Harold, on whose account the whole war was. The Normans follow their lord, and press around him; they ply their blows upon the English; and these defend themselves stoutly, striving hard with their enemies, returning blow for blow. . . .

And now the Normans pressed on so far, that at last they reached the standard. There Harold had remained, defending himself to the utmost, but he was sorely wounded in his eye by the arrow, and suffered grievous pain from the blow. An armed man came in the throng of the battle, and struck him on the ventaille of his helmet, and beat him to the ground; and as he sought to recover himself, a knight beat him down again, striking him on the thick of his thigh, down to the bone. . . .

The standard was beaten down, the golden standard was taken, and Harold and the best of his friends were slain; but there was so much eagerness, and throng of so many around, seeking to kill him, that I know not who it was that slew him.

The English were in great trouble at having lost their King, and at the duke's having conquered and beat down the standard; but they still fought on, and defended themselves long, and in fact till the day drew to a close. Then it clearly appeared to all that the standard was lost, and the news spread throughout the army that Harold for certain was dead; and all saw that there was no longer any hope so they left the field, and those fled who could. . . .'

William had conquered: Harold and his two brothers were slain. Both Normans and English had excelled themselves in valor, but the Normans, experienced warriors on horseback, were militarily the superior force. Two feudal professional armies had met and thus settled the future fate of the island. That the English Army was a professional force is beyond doubt. A military organization based on the old Germanic local levy, the *fyrd*, would hardly have given William seventeen days in which he established his base entirely undisturbed. William left the initiative to Harold while he completed his armaments. With the Anglo-Saxon army vanquished he proceeded to subject the country to his rule and on Christmas Day 1066 was crowned King. Realizing the importance of historical consciousness, legitimacy and continuity he had himself elected king by his

Right. *1600 hours: Harold is killed and the battle is virtually over. Tradition says he is the man on the left, his eye pierced by a Norman's arrow. Modern historians challenge this and using contemporary sources, such as the William of Poitiers ms, believe it more likely that he is the man on the right hacked to death by a Norman sword.*

Below. *Battle scene: the conical helmets with their protective nasals worn by these Norman soldiers were designed for maximum deflection of blows to the head.*

vassals, claiming to be the rightful successor of Edward the Confessor. By accepting the past, he secured the formality of election by the witan and was consecrated by an Anglo-Saxon bishop.

William had been elected by his vassals and followers, much in the same way as Henry of Saxony had been elected by his dukes as King of Germany more than a century before. But there was one vital difference. Henry's dukes were his equals, each commanding his own territorial base of power. In 1066 William conquered England as the leader of a comparatively small group of alien adventurers whose power other than that given to them by William was negligible. One of William's first actions was to lay claim to the whole of the land of the realm. It was his conquest, and therefore his property. During his reign

on basically still hostile soil, it lay in the interest of William's vassals to cooperate, they only stood to gain by it. And following the practice already established during the later Anglo-Saxon Kings, he avoided handing land to his vassals in large compacts that would have allowed them to develop the power of their own house and thus become potential rivals. Of course any monarchy is as strong as the man who heads it. England was lucky enough to have a succession of strong Kings for more than half a century after the conquest. After that time the negative features of the feudal system became operative, but never as strongly and with such consequences as, for instance, in Germany.

William parceled out the land to his tenants-in-chief in return for military service; they in turn divided it up into knight's fees, each fee to be used to raise, equip and support a knight. William himself was not greatly concerned about how the knights were found, as long as they were found, properly trained and equipped. However, by the end of the eleventh century it was still common for barons to hold knights in their household. Those to abandon this custom first were abbeys and monasteries, to whom the presence of men-at-arms at their establishment was bound to be a nuisance. In place of the knights they were supposed to supply, they paid scutage, the money equivalent needed for raising them. But the process of dividing up baronial estates into knights' fees was only completed towards the end of the reign (1100–35) of Henry I when the first signs became evident that the custom was being abused. Royal vassals enfeoffed more knights than they were actually required to do. The Bishop of Lincoln in place of the 60 knights he was charged to provide, had enfeoffed 102. Henry took immediate steps to have the number reduced, as he was setting out for a prolonged visit to France and wanted to be sure of the loyalty of his Anglo-Norman knighthood.

The size of a knight's fee varied, ranging between four and eight-and-a-half hides of land. But extremes at either end of the scale were not unknown. In total the feudal army thus raised in England varied between 5000 and 7000 knights, added to which must come those knights recruited on a mercenary basis, which took place in England from the twelfth century onwards. But knighthood, the distinguishing military institution of the feudal age, was now also firmly established on English soil.

On the European mainland, much more so than in the British Isles, the instrument of the territorial organization of the vassal was his land from which he derived his power. His most profitable domains were equipped with castles and fortifications, which in turn became the centers of their military, economic and judicial organization. As we can see from the castles still in existence in Europe they were of large construction surrounded by high walls, with ample room for stores and accommodation for a garrison of mounted men. The supply of castle and garrison was the responsibility of the peasants of the region for whose protection the castles, at least in part, had been built. The power of the continental territorial landholder was considerably stronger than that of the King. Kingship was elective, a dukedom inheritable within the family. In England each successor to a deceased tenant-in-chief had to render an act of hommage to the King, the sole owner of the land, whereupon he was enfeoffed with the territory of his predecessor; the proprietary right to the land was still the King's. No King in France or Germany could lay such a claim.

Originally, according to ancient Germanic custom, all free men could and should bear arms. But there were freemen and freemen, those who lived from the property they actually possessed and those, the original vassals, who lived from the land with which they were enfeoffed, land which was not inheritable except when a son was available who would be ready to take up the duties of his father. In case of the extinction of the male line the land reverted to the feudal lord, or at a higher level, to the King. However, by the tenth century in both Germany and France, the inheritability of a territorial fief had become customary. Service in arms meant a privileged position *vis-à-vis* those who tilled the soil. Military service became concentrated

The cavalry sets off at a gallop covered in front by a body of archers (The Bayeaux Tapestry). The Norman army eventually won at Hastings owing to the superiority of their cavalry and bowmen.

in those families who had always provided the knights in the first place, and from that originated military nobility of birth. The vassals of a King or prince who may have advised him on matters other than warfare, who may in fact have been precursors of higher civil servants, the ministeriales, also held their territorial fiefs, and began to provide knights for the King. In that way the military and the administrative nobility fused on the basis of the possession of land, and during the course of the thirteenth century possession of fiefs was restricted only to the nobility. The nobility was the army; the knight paid no taxation to his lord because his service for holding the land was his military service, a principle which in varying degrees and variations existed in European society until the French Revolution, the principle of the exemption from taxation of the nobility. Hence the fiscal burdens and other non-military services hit the peasant and the towns hardest particularly after the towns began to recover economically.

Yet it would be mistaken to imagine the life of a medieval knight as having been particularly comfortable. Their fiefs secured them only a modest living. Their equipment could hardly be called a luxury. They were frequently at war, if not in the host of the King, then much more often in that of their immediate lord, be he baron, graf, or duke to settle one of the many differences or feuds between feudal lords. Indeed it has been argued that one of the main motivations behind calling for the Crusades was the attempt by the Church to channel off the energies dissipated in the civil wars of feudal Europe into one major effort beneficial to Christendom as a whole and to the individual souls of the knights in particular.

Even knightly tournaments were not as peaceful as one might imagine. One chronicler of the twelfth century records that ten brothers of his father were killed in one tournament, giving rise to a serious feud which, before Church and prince could settle the matter, claimed many more victims. Intellectually the knight could lay no claims to distinction, nor did he desire it otherwise. Literacy and the arts were taught only at the abodes of the highest of the nobility. Nor can it be said that all the virtues associated with the age of chivalry were present in the medieval knight at the end of the eleventh century. That was an age which was yet to come.

*While the king lies asleep in his tent his soldiers mount guard outside.
(Histoire du Graal by Robert de Borron, thirteenth century).*

THE SOCIAL AND MILITARY ASPECTS OF KNIGHTHOOD

The ceremony of dubbing or the accolade which formally elevated a warrior to a knight originated in old Germanic custom which used this method or a formal proclamation to announce that a young man was able to bear arms and considered suitable. Among the Goths, the Visigoths and the Franks, but probably also among most of the other tribes, the ceremony was performed at the age of twelve or fourteen. However, with the growing use of heavy horses and the increasing weight of the armor, the age moved upward to about twenty. Sometimes, of course, the accolade would be given to an auxiliary warrior of non-noble descent in reward for a particular distinction in the field of battle. The aspiring knight first had to undergo a lengthy period in which he was trained, and in which he also grew strong enough to carry heavy armor, fight in it and control his horse. From the twelfth century to the end of the Middle Ages, knighthood represented its own estate; throughout Christian Europe it was a kind of closed corporation, socially cutting across the frontiers of national descent, a characteristic shown by the European aristocracy as a whole.

The outward trappings of a knight were his knight belt and golden spurs. The belt as a symbol of the warrior class is of Germanic origin. In the early phase of knighthood, it was the privilege of every knight to elevate to knighthood by accolade any man he thought fit; accessibility to the corporation was still relatively easy. But in the twelfth century this changed; only one who was of knightly parentage could become a knight. Louis VI of France is said to have ordered that any knight not of such parentage should have his spurs hewn off on the dung heap. Frederick Barbarossa expressly prohibited the sons of priests(!) and of peasants from taking the sword-belt. The knighthood of Italy, in so far as it was Italian born, was the object of contempt and derision for centuries because the Italian cities made knights of the sons of artisans. The Order of the Templars refused the white mantle to anyone not of knightly birth—rather in contrast to the Order of the Teutonic knights later. The material consequence of being deprived of one's knighthood was the deprivation of the fief held, in other words, the destruction of his economic security.

No knight could take service and a fief from his equal, since that would have made him dependent upon a person who, by being a knight, was subject to the same services. The right to enfeoff was firstly that of the Emperor or King, secondly that of the ecclesiastical princes, thirdly that of the lay princes, fourthly that of the counts, and, according to region and country, that of

Below. *Ceremony of knighthood.*

Above. *For safety and comfort while fighting on foot, knights wore doublets sewn with patches of mail beneath their armor.*

several other bodies of knightly nobility. The accolade as such would have been little more than a favor or a distinction had it not been tied to the condition to give proof of one's noble descent. In that way the accolade became an instrument of social integration and social exclusiveness, the affirmation that those who had received it belonged to the ruling class.

In England the knights were under much greater control from the monarchy than either in France or in Germany. A significant indication of that is the very term knight, derived from the German *Knecht*, connoting menial or bondman, while the German *Ritter* and the French *chevalier* literally state that they are mounted men. The knight had his shield bearer, the *knappe* or *escuyer*, the esquire who in many if not most cases was himself of knightly descent, serving his apprenticeship for knighthood in this role. In addition he had his groom, plus a lightly armed warrior for scouting purposes, and one or two foot soldiers.

This indicates that the knights were not the only warriors, but rather the upper class of the feudal army. But physical prowess, bravery and other warlike virtues can never be the exclusive property of one class, or the lack of these virtues that of another. The friction arising out of that dilemma was never fully resolved. Sons of knights who proved to be physically as well as psychically unsuited to the profession of knightly service were moved on into the priesthood or into monasteries, while the esquires supplied the fresh blood for the knighthood. Also on occasions the exclusiveness of knightly origin was broken by Emperors or Kings awarding the accolade for particularly distinguished service. There is ample evidence that such a breach of the existing rules caused protest in many quarters especially in the thirteenth century, one noble ridiculed such knights as 'scarecrows turned into knights.' On the other hand, when Frederick Barbarossa wanted to give the accolade to a particularly deserving warrior outside Tortona in 1155, the man concerned refused on the grounds that he was of low estate and should prefer to remain part of it.

Knighthood, then, is a product of many sources, some going

Above. *European sword or long dagger (fourteenth century).*

back to the tribal traditions of the Germanic tribes, but its development into a specific class has its source in the technological transformation of war. During the reign of Charlemagne, helmet, mail shirt and shield were still relatively light. But throughout the Middle Ages armor increased in weight. Whereas at first the shield was the main protection, armor increased in complexity. The helmet acquired a visor, and to the mail shirt, which originally had left the neck unprotected, armor plate was added until trunk, arms and legs were covered by armor, and finally the horse as well. Range was increased by longer and heavier lances, and the horses had to be strong, steady and sturdy to sustain the weight. The cost of all this must have been immense. Thus the economic basis, the fief, had to be sufficiently large to pay for it.

The Romans had won their campaigns employing coherent, disciplined bodies of men, tactically trained and exercised. The medieval battle was decided by the personal bravery and ability of the individual knights. They represented the main body of the army, but the heavy armor carried its own inherent limitations. When forced to fight on foot the knight could do so only in a very limited manner. Armor prevented him from charging forth afoot. Nor could he use the bow. Like modern tanks which are transported by rail or road to as near the battle zone as possible to keep down the wear and tear, so the knight's battle horse was saved for the final encounter to avoid tiring it, and it was not uncommon for a knight to have several horses in his train. Knights were incapable of carrying out the tasks of light warfare. For that purpose both foot troops and light cavalry were needed. Hence we find lightly armored cavalry forces equipped with sword and bow, and on foot, archers and men with the crossbow and swords. They were the auxiliary forces, the deployment of which was handled masterfully by William the Conqueror at Hastings. In most parts of France and Germany they re-emerged only in the course of the twelfth century as mounted bowmen, mainly as a result of the Crusades. But the soldiers on foot are in no way comparable to the

infantry of antiquity. They did not operate independently but solely fulfilled an auxiliary function. Until Courtrai the actual decision of battle lay with the knights, never with the *Fussvolk*. The knights were the army; the rest is subsidiary to it. They were a professional as well as social caste. The importance of this is born out time and again. For example, Emperor Frederick II called upon his son to send him knights, because in the knights resided the fame of the Empire and the strength of his power, or again one vassal was called upon to provide 15 esquires, 'good people, born to the shield.' The knight alone was *the warrior*. Emperors and Kings were knights; women apart, their entire court consisted of knights. The chief vassals—princes, dukes and counts—were knights, and bishops and abbots surrounded themselves with them. The only other estate represented in that society is the clergy. We do not find a single example of a knight laying down his sword belt to retire and

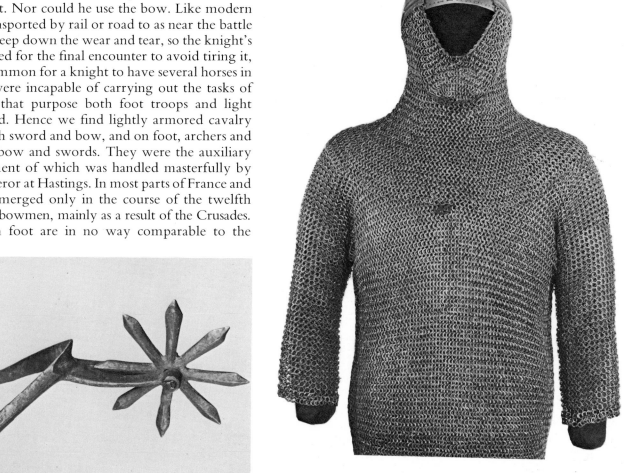

Above. *Mail shirt and aventail, 1340.*

Left. *Rowelspur, 1370.*

Left. *Servants gird medieval knights with swords.*

Right. *Two horsemen tilting with lances in a public exercise of their prowess (*Histoire du Graal*).*

Far right. *Battle scene (*Histoire du Graal*).*

Below right. *Mounted-man-at-arms, a scene from a North French manuscript illustrating the Apocalypse (thirteenth century).*

attend to the cultivation of the soil. However, there are many examples of knights retiring into monasteries.

At the beginning of the Carolingian period many knights were still known to reside in urban communities, in the towns that sprung up around burghs or castles, such as those founded as frontier defense posts by King Henry I of Germany. The *Burggraf* actually headed the town. In the early fourteenth century, in the Flemish cities, the lower knightly nobility were the allies of the burghers and artisans who, in an uprising equivalent almost to the Sicilian Vespers, tried to rid their towns of the Francophile upper bourgeoisie and French overlordship in general. Many former servants of knights settled in towns and cities to pursue trade and commerce, or a particular craft. But it seems that over the centuries the vast majority of the knights remained

on the land, on their fief, the basis of their economic and social power.

The Middle Ages knew hardly any example of the common military training of European knighthood. What thorough training they received was imparted individually, and a special profession developed: those who did nothing other than to train the sons of knights for their future task and position. First this training took place within the family, and then on active service with a knight, as his esquire for example.

Tournaments were the public exercises in which the up-and-coming future knights could display their ability. Over the years these became encounters which on occasion could be extremely fierce when it became customary to use sharp instead of blunted weapons. The tournament reflected in some aspects

real battle conditions. As in battle the horses did not charge at full speed; considering the weight they carried this would have been impossible. The knights rode together but not in a tactical formation, the prerequisite of which would have been joint tactical training, something the mounted knights of the Middle Ages never knew.

Nor did the knight know the discipline of a drilled formation. The feudal state knew order and subordination; it knew obedience, but *not* what was understood as military discipline in the Roman armies and in the armies of the European territorial states from the seventeenth century onward. Discipline is based upon command and carries with it, if the command is not obeyed, the power to punish. It implies the full command of the commander in chief over his army, its officers and generals. The medieval prince, by comparison, was rather weak in power. He could exert pressure on his vassal. He could deprive him of territory previously granted by him, as was the case when Frederick Barbarossa deprived Henry the Lion of his Bavarian possession because Henry refused to support the Emperor on his crusade. What Frederick Barbarossa could not do was to deprive him of his Dukedom of Saxony. Henry the Lion stayed at home, considering it more important to pursue the colonization of his eastern marches than to waste his resources on a far-off

Left. *Composite armor from Schloss Churburg, Germany.*

Right. *Mounted man-at-arms and horse in full armor. The horse has a protective 'chauffron' over its head.*

tary realities of the Middle Ages. Nor were there any articles of war governing the behavior of the knights during a campaign. During the First Crusade keeping the host of knights together was a greater problem than meeting the enemy in combat. The sack of Constantinople had nothing to do with the aims of the crusade and little to do with trying to vanquish heresy among Christendom, but much more to do with the desire for loot among the unruly knighthood.

Once their spoils declined, the moment they felt the economic pinch, declining agricultural production through bad harvests, or depopulation through disease, many a chivalrous knight of the Middle Ages saw it by no means dishonorable to waylay the merchant trains, or hold towns to ransom, to use the slightest pretext to feud with the object of hopefully making booty.

The right to call a feud lay with every freeman of country or town. It was possible, and did in fact happen, that bakers, cooks and kitchen-boys announced a feud with their regional nobility, who usually had a sense of humor and ignored it. Some general laws about the feud did exist; for example it had to be proclaimed three days before actually beginning. A feud announced applied not only to the person who had given cause for it; it applied to his kith and kin, to his servants, free and unfree, as well as to the entire community which might want to assist and protect him. If the object of the feud was a town, then it applied to all its inhabitants. In the fourteenth century it was common usage that prisoners taken in a feud could be killed, if keeping them alive would endanger one's own life, and the vanquished in a feud lost his property. At a higher level, the prisoners of an Emperor, King or prince became his servants.

The property of the loser was that of the victor, including people that were unarmed. Accounts are frequent of entire harvests having been ravaged, villages burned down, livestock driven away, the peasants either killed or carried away as serfs. Only Christian women were not allowed to be touched. They were left their clothes and other parts of their wardrobe. In the conquest of castles an even greater degree of chivalry is alleged to have prevailed. The ladies, apart from their wardrobe, were also allowed to keep their jewelry. Whether this rule was always observed is a little doubtful. The wars of medieval Europe were mostly caused by family feuds among and between related dynasties. The wars of the Plantagenets in France, the Hundred Years' War, the wars between Germany and France, the Bohemians and the Hungarians all started as family feuds. Large armies banded together, but scarcely fought more than one major battle, after which they drifted home again, both because of the lack of money to keep the army in the field, and because the vassals were anxious to get back at the earliest possible time. In the history of the Holy Roman Empire of the German Nation there is not one Emperor who succeeded in persuading all his vassals to support him on a campaign. Strongly fortified towns were difficult to conquer. In 1447 the city of Nuremberg conducted a feud with the majority of the German princes. The city then comprised 20,000 inhabitants; the struggle lasted for three years, Nuremberg surviving because the princes never thought of laying siege to it. Sometimes when a town captured its feuding opponent it dealt with him leniently because to do so was to its own advantage. In 1373 the knight Hennele von Streif proclaimed his feud against Worms, because the city had captured two waylaying robber knights whom it promptly hanged. Hennele found support among the knights of the castles in the vicinity and began to despoil the countryside around Worms. For the burghers of Worms this was rather too costly. They cut their losses by taking Hennele into their service at a price of 200 guilders annually, and Hennele subsequently

adventure. Even the Italian communes swore an oath to Frederick Barbarossa, after he had restored his position there, in which they promised to carry out every order of the Emperor which he gave *in the exercise of his rights*. In other words, they were not prepared to obey *any* order. The fief could be withdrawn by the lord, a process which was more easily done further down the feudal pyramid than near the top where the vassals were princes of territories which their ancestors had owned long before a kingdom of France or Germany existed. The Norman dynasty in England had the advantage of being able by what one might call—grossly oversimplified, of course—one vast act of expropriation to assume all land and thus make themselves into the sole source of power.

When family quarrels tore the dynasty apart, as under the successors of Charlemagne or under the Saxon Kings, both under Otto the Great and in the eleventh century under Henry IV, the weakness at the apex of the feudal pyramid was felt down to its very bottom. The centrifugal forces inherent in the feudal system began to be felt disastrously, and could only be curbed but never retarded by another strong dynasty or monarch. Exceptions to this pattern were the knightly orders, such as the Templars and later the Teutonic Knights, orders which had firm rules which had to be obeyed to the letter, rules derived from the Order of the Cistercians of St Bernhard of Clairvaux, the initiator of the Cluniac monastic reform movement.

Military discipline therefore was an artificial product, inapplicable to and contradicted by the political, social and mili-

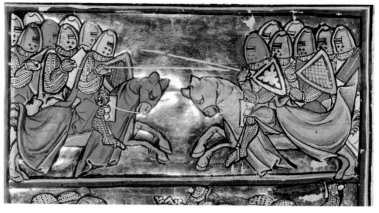

Above. *Horseback battle scene* (Histoire du Graal).

Left. *Four mail-clad men-at-arms slaughter Thomas à Becket. Their attire is a good example of the armor of the period.*

proved to be a very loyal and efficient servant of the interests of the city of Worms.

While the cities took recourse to a feud only as a last resort—commercially in the long run they stood to lose more—for princes and nobility it was a source of income, and needless to say even more for the lower rungs among the knighthood. Many of the medieval feuders became infamous. Only very few remained alive in popular folklore, like Apel of Gailingen, a knight renowned for the frequency with which he sought feuds with financially rewarding victims, as well as for his waylaying activities. His major enemy was the city of Nuremberg, into which he rode one day, halting before a smithy to have his horse shoed. As the smith completed the work Apel asked him to whom the pair of boots hanging at the gate of the city wall belonged. He got the reply that these were Apel of Gailingen's boots. Apel pulled them down, thrashed the guard at the gate with them and told him to tell the magistrate that Apel had come back to fetch his boots. Freebooting stood at one of the extremes of the development of medieval knighthood.

If one looks at the military aspect of medieval knighthood one finds that the warriors of Charlemagne and Otto the Great had much in common. They bore much the same weapons and were not excessively heavily armed. They were prepared, and capable if need be, to fight on foot. This also holds true of the Normans of William the Conqueror. Foot soldiers as such, and men equipped with bows were the exception rather than the rule. From the late eleventh century however, a greater degree of differentiation can be noted between heavy cavalry, light cavalry, bowmen on foot and sword fighters on foot. Theoretically two possibilities of their deployment were possible. To group each arm, if we can call it that, separately, or simply to group them around the main body of the army, the armed knights. Hastings seems to have been an illustration of a partial application of the first possibility, but generally the application of the second dominated. Not one of the auxiliary branches would have been able to engage the mounted knights. The light cavalry, almost unarmed, was no match in combat for the heavily armed knights unless they fought with bow and arrow, which they did not. The one with the greatest chance of engaging the knight at a distance was the bowman on foot. That would have required very strong nerves, because he had to let the knight come quite close for the arrow to be lethal (the kind of nerve required in the Second World War to let a Russian T-34 tank come into a range of 40 feet and then launch the *Panzerfaust*). The greater the safe distance between knight and bowman the

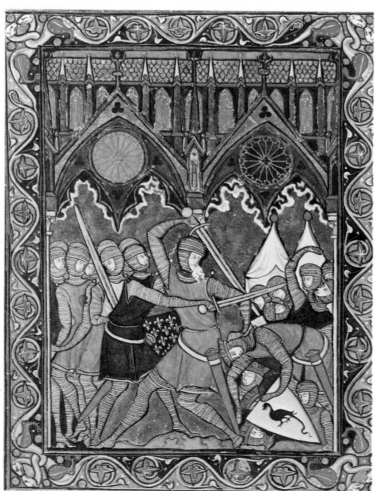

Left. *Foot soldiers in armor* (Psautier de St Louis, *1270*).

surer was his own survival. Therefore a body of bowmen without being covered and protected by the heavy knights, or by protection afforded by geography as in Wales and Ireland, faced no alternative other than its own destruction.

Another opportunity among those on foot lay with the warrior with a blank hand weapon. What havoc they could cause with their axes or halberds we have seen in the Norman chronicler's account of the Battle of Hastings. With strong nerve, good luck, and circumspection they could get at the horseman from the side by killing the horse and dismounting him. Should the knight not have been killed as a result of being trapped by the horse, he would still have been at a position advantageous to the footman, because of his lack of physical maneuverability constrained as he was by his armor. Also troops of foot soldiers forming up as groups with the use of spears and pikes could ward off the heavy cavalry, but once a gap was cut the infantry was lost.

In fact prior to the Hussites and the Swiss the only offensive actions by infantry against mounted hosts of knights seem to have been the Battle of Courtrai in 1302 when the Flemish cities won over the French and the Battle of Bannockburn in 1314 when the Scots defeated the forces of King Edward II. For the rest, the function of the foot soldiery was always subsidiary and auxiliary in function. Therefore they were deployed to support to the best of their ability the action of the main arm, which was the only arm expected to bring about a decision. They operated partly on the flanks and partly mixed within the main con-

Below. *European armor in the Middle Ages.* Above. *Foot soldiers prepare for battle.*

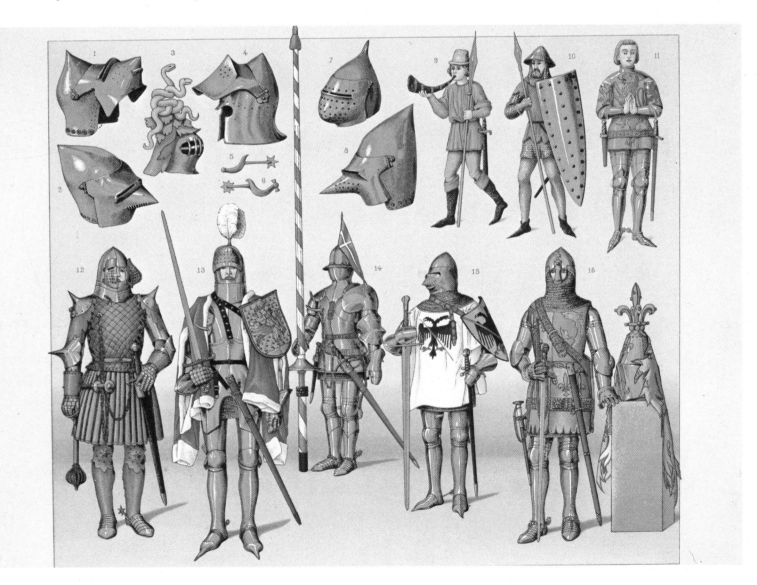

tingent. In this manner foot formations appeared in the battles of the Middle Ages.

It has been suggested that these auxiliary arms were of three-fold origin. Among them we find those of the old warrior class who did not become part of the knighthood; secondly, the burghers of the cities anxious to obtain training and experience in the profession of arms entered the medieval host as pikemen and bowmen; thirdly, of course, they were recruited from every knight's immediate entourage in the field, his esquire and other servants who until the twelfth century had remained non-combatants. For a knight, heavy and clumsy on his horse, it must have been an asset to have by his side a rather more flexible individual.

The nature of the mixed forces and their respective tasks are illustrated in a speech which Charles of Anjou is claimed to have made to his soldiers before the Battle of Benevent in 1226. He advised his men that it was more important to hit the horses than the men; deprived of their horse the enemy, almost immovable in his armor, could be easily felled by the foot fighters. Therefore every horsemen should be accompanied by one or two of his entourage, and if there were no others they should hire a mercenary, because experienced in war they would understandably kill horses as well as their toppled masters.

As the cavalry with its slow pace caused by the heavy armor rode on, it was not difficult for a footman to keep pace. The chronicler of Henry II's conquest of Ireland, Giraldus Cambrensis, renders a good account of the different systems. Although the Normans had understood perfectly how to transfer their military system to England it was quite different from that encountered in Wales and in Ireland. While the Normans sought the open plain, the Welsh and the Irish preferred mountainous territory, or simply as difficult a physical terrain as possible. The Normans preferred the field; their opponents preferred the woods. The Normans armed themselves heavily which was quite suitable for open combat, but along narrow, mountainous paths, in swamp-infested woodland, he who travels light travels easiest. The warrior on foot had the advantage over the warrior on horse. This was even more true if he were armored, for it would be difficult to dismount on a forest path, let alone fight.

A knight and his immediate entourage in combat were generally called a lance. Precisely how many there were to a lance is impossible to say, perhaps up to ten men. However, medieval chroniclers, or for that matter the commanders of the feudal host, counted the number of their army not by the total number of combatants present but solely by the number of knights, an important illustration of the military and social importance of the role of the knight.

In battle the bowmen advanced ahead of the knights and did as much damage to the enemy as possible, but still proceeded close enough to the cavalry to be able to withdraw quickly into the folds of its protection, as demonstrated in 1066 at Hastings. Pikemen, or foot soldiers with sword, adopted the role of advance guard if they had to clear away obstacles designed to delay or hold off the cavalry. At Hastings they were clearly not warriors with pikes but only with swords. Knights fought on foot only under rather exceptional circumstances, as in many engagements in Crusades when the supply of horses had become scarce.

The knights did not range themselves in any particular tactical order. They just advanced on their mounts with little attention being paid to a straight linear approach. Only the Order of the Templars had issued a rule saying that no brother was to attack on his own initiative or to ride outside the formation. They did not attack like modern cavalry, aiming at achieving maximum impact and maintaining, insofar as this was possible, the impetus of the attack. Instead they rode on slowly to engage the enemy riding equally as slowly towards them in combat. The medieval battle compared with those of later periods must almost have been a slow-motion study of individual combat, of knights encased in their armor slowly raising their heavy weapons and bringing them down on their opponents. It must have been a far cry from the speed, cut and thrust operations of the cavalry engagements of the eighteenth century.

Left. Rustic vassals conscripted into the army as foot soldiers formed an invaluable part of any fighting force. (Latin ms 1390, eleventh century).

Below. Armor-clad knights armed with lances and hafted arms ride slowly to engage in individual combat with their opponents. Compared with the speed of eighteenth-century cavalry engagements, these medieval operations must have seemed like studies in slow motion.

Boatloads of troops assault the strongpoints of the ancient city of Tyre
(History of Alexander the Great, *fifteenth century*).

SIEGE
AND SIEGECRAFT
FORTIFICATIONS

Fortifications are as old as is the history of warfare. Protective fortifications of an army camp protected it against surprise attack; the city walls insured the safety of its citizens. In the successor states of the Roman Empire, defense became the primary consideration in the reconstruction of the cities razed by the Barbarians. This was also the origin of the medieval castle, the defensive center against the attacks from the Saracens, Norsemen and Magyars, especially in the course of the ninth century. Henri Pirenne provides a description of them which applies, a few minor details apart, to them all:

'They were walled enclosures of somewhat restricted perimeter, customarily circular in form and surrounded by a moat. In the center was to be found a strong-tower and a keep, the last redoubt of defense in case of attack. A permanent garrison of knights (*milites castrenses*) was stationed there. This was placed under the orders of a castellan (*castellanus*). The prince had a home (*domus*) in each of the burgs of his territory where he stayed with his retinue in the course of the continual changes of residence which war or administerial duties forced upon him. Very often a chapel, or a church flanked by the buildings necessary to house the clergy, raised its belfry above the battlements of the ramparts. Sometimes there were also to be found by the side of it quarters intended for the judicial assemblies whose members came, at fixed periods, from outside to assemble in the burg. Finally what was never lacking were a granary and cellars where was kept, to supply the necessities of a siege should the case arise and to furnish subsistence to the prince during his stays, the produce of the neighboring demesnes which he held. Prestations in kind levied on the peasants of the district assured the subsistence of the garrison. The up-keep of the walls devolved upon these same peasants who were compelled to do the work by statute labor.

Although from country to country the picture, which has just been drawn, naturally differed in details, the same essential traits were to be found everywhere. The similarity between the *bourgs* of Flanders and the *boroughs* of Anglo-Saxon England is a striking one. And this similarity unquestionably proves that the same needs brought in their train similar results everywhere.

As can be easily seen, the burgs were above all, military establishments. But to this original function was soon added that of being administrative centers. The castellan ceased to be solely the commandant of the knights of the castral garrison. The prince delegated to him financial and judicial authority over a more or less extensive district around about the walls of the burg and which took, by the tenth century, the name castellany. The castellany (or *burgschaft*) was related to the burg as the bishopric was related to the town. In case of war, its inhabitants found a refuge there; in time of peace, there they repaired to take part in assemblies of justice or to pay off prestations to which they were subject. Nevertheless the burg did not show the slightest urban character. Its population comprised, aside from the knights and the clerics who made up its essential part, only men employed in their service and whose number was certainly of little importance. It was a fortress population; it was not a city population. Neither commerce not industry was possible or even conceivable in such an environment. It produced nothing itself; lived by revenues from the surrounding country, and had no other economic role than that of a simple consumer. . . .

The towns and burgs were merely fortified places and headquarters of administration. Their inhabitants enjoyed neither special laws or institutions of their own, and their manner of living did not distinguish them in any way from the rest of society. . . . The towns and burgs played, however, an essential role in the history of cities. They were, so to speak, the stepping-stones thereto. . . .'

In case of war the castle or the fortified city represented a strategic objective which had to be isolated or, if need be, taken. As Sir Charles Oman rightly observed, there is a greater continuity in the history of siegecraft and siege-machines through the whole of the Middle Ages down to the invention of gunpowder than in any other area of the military art. Two weapons in particular can be encountered throughout the Middle Ages,

the ram and the bore. The ram aimed at battering a particular section of the castle or city wall to pieces. The bore, a very strong, pointed metal pole, aimed at breaking loose particular stones of the wall until by this systematic method a hole and finally a breach had been made. These siege instruments are found in the sixth century during the Gothic siege of Rome, during the First Crusade in the eleventh century when Godfrey of Boullion besieged and captured Jerusalem, and throughout the Middle Ages and beyond, during the peasants' risings in the sixteenth century, and even as late as 1705, when Bavarian peasants tried to take Munich in a vain bid to expel the Austrians from Bavarian territory during the Wars of the Spanish Succession. Of course their effectiveness depended on the ability to overcome the defensive devices of the fortress attacked. Vittigis failed because he did not manage to overcome the moat surrounding the Eternal City. Godfrey, before Jerusalem, had the moat filled in at the position where the battering ram was to be erected, and to protect its crew from the arrows and other missiles of the defenders he covered it with a strong roof. Both ram and pole were 'slung by ropes or chains from two solid perpendicular beams, drawn back by the workers as far as the chains allowed and then released to dash itself against the wall.' In spite of protective roofing, and finally protective sides, so that the ram was covered virtually by a house, it was not safe from all means of defense. Raw hides, tiles and the like would resist Greek fire, pitch or other liquid combustibles only for a limited

Storming of a town in 1529: soldiers break through with a battering ram.

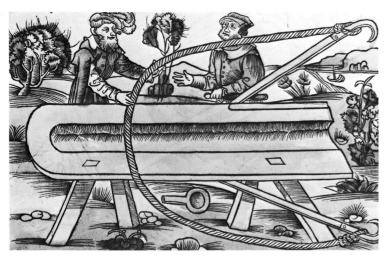

Above. *Early ballistic siege weapon.*

Below. *Tending the wounded outside the city walls during the Battle of Jacob on Bir (Swiss ms, fifteenth century).*

period. Therefore the protective house had to be put on wheels for the crew to be able to withdraw and repair the damage before the next attempt was made. Even the ram itself was exposed and could be caught by the defenders with sharp beams which held it fast, or one could cushion its impact by letting down protective matting sacks, or hides at the point of impact.

Sappers also were an early branch of the military services. Their task was to approach the fortification at its most vulnerable point, and since such an approach could rarely be made on the plain ground surrounding a wall, a network of trenches was excavated leading to the wall. Once the wall was reached a hole was dug under the wall and filled with brushwood and straw, which was set on fire. Until the invention of gunpowder this method had only a limited effect and was characteristic of the early Middle Ages when many walls and other fortifications consisted of wood or were constructed with mortar of a kind that had a very low degree of resilience to heat, became brittle and crumbled away with the stones it held.

But, of course, there were other offensive siege weapons of

which perhaps the siege ladder is the simplest and probably also the oldest. After all, the most direct approach to climbing a wall is to use the ladder. To check the defensive forces on the wall it was necessary for some of the siege forces to fight at the same level or higher than the defenders. This was the origin of the siege tower, constructed of wood with a platform from which the bowmen would discharge their arrows. When it first appeared is unknown. The Goths used it before Rome in 537 and it recurred only during the course of the eleventh century. It was a very prominent instrument during the siege of Jerusalem. Being made of wood it was of course, as vulnerable as the protective house of the ram or pole, but its effort to cover the crew of a ram made it unnecessary to get as close to the defenders as the ram. It

was another matter, however, when it was used as an offensive instrument. As such it contained a drawing bridge, which meant the siege tower had to be moved close to the wall before the bridge could be let down and members of the siege forces could sally out onto the wall as well as seek refuge in the tower again if necessary. But its weight was considerable, and even on wheels it was immensely difficult to move. For forces advancing towards the walls large shields, almost segments of walls themselves were made, and they were carried right under the wall. They had the advantage of being lighter and much quicker to make.

Primitive forms of artillery were known from earliest times, the bow being probably their forerunner, since the tension of a crossbow, operated by tension rather than torsion. Procopius wrote:

'These machines have the general shape of a bow; but in the middle there is a hollow piece of horn loosely fixed to the bow, and lying over a straight iron stock. When wishing to let fly at the enemy, you pull back the short strong cord which joins the arms of the bow, and place in the horn a bolt, four times as thick as an ordinary arrow, but only half its length. The bolt is not feathered like an arrow, but furnished with wooden projections exactly reproducing the shape of feathers. Men standing on each side of the ballista draw back the the cord with little devices; when they let it go, the horn rushes forward and discharges the bolt, which strikes with a force equal to at least two arrows, for it breaks stones and pierces trees.'

The ballista could also fire javelins, and was more accurate in its aim than the magnon, but in contrast to the magnon it was more of an anti-personnel weapon than one to breach fortress walls. Furthermore it was a weapon that could be used by attackers and defenders alike, as the Norsemen experienced when they besieged Paris. It was also the ancestor of the crossbow in full use in Europe since the eleventh century. One chronicler reported:

'That weapon is not a bow held in the left hand and bent by the right, but can only be spanned by the bearer stopping and placing both feet against it, while he strains at the cord with the full force of both arms. In the middle it has a semi-circular groove of the length of a long arrow, which reaches down to the middle of its stock; the missiles, which are of many and various kinds, are placed in the groove, and propelled through it by the released cord. They pierce wood and metal easily, and sometimes wholly imbed themselves in a wall, or any such obstacle when they have struck it.'

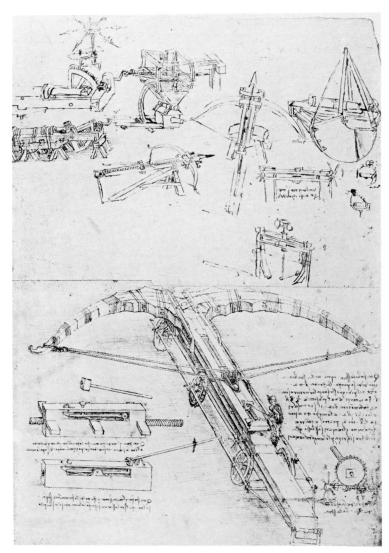

Above. *Studies of a crossbow by Leonardo da Vinci (1452–1519) who was employed as a siege engineer at the court of Francis I of France.*

Left. *Assault of a fortified city like that of Calais in 1347 using a mobile siege tower and trebuchet (see foreground right hand side).*

Right. *Diagram of an attack tank on wheels (Vigevano's military treatise, fourteenth century).*

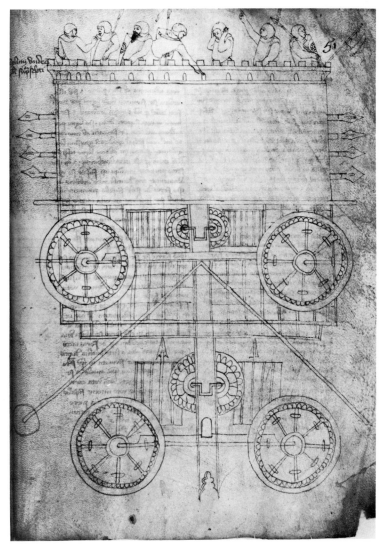

stretched chord released the bow and provided its propelling power. But it was torsion which provided the power for the siege machinery throwing heavy missiles against the wall, its defenders or, for that matter, into the fortress itself. A beam with a shallow hole at one end, into which the missile was put, was placed between two sets of horizontally stretched ropes. These were then twisted to a maximum by several men. The beam, when released had accumulated considerable power, and hurled its missile against its target. Naturally the target had to be large because with that type of machinery precision in aiming was almost impossible. Within these machines one can in fact distinguish between light and heavy artillery. The size of the missile was not the decisive criterion, but rather the range obtained. The beam when very long, between 25 and 30 feet, could be placed on a tower, its 'loading end' on the ground while the ropes would tighten at the top. When released this vast beam would jerk upwards with tremendous force sending its stone or ball far into the interior of the fortress. The name for both the short- and long-range machines was the magnon. The major impediment to the efficiency of magnons was the weather, for rain would slacken the ropes to the point where they were useless, about as effective as wet gunpowder later on.

The large-scale successor of the bow was the magnified

Above. *The mining of Riolle Castle: sappers digging a gallery under the castle wall* (Chroniques d'Angleterre *by Jean de Wawrin, fifteenth century*).

Below. *Medieval siege of a stronghold in Africa showing tented encampment, crossbowmen and artillery* (Chroniques de Froissart, *fourteenth century*).

These weapons were known in the early Middle Ages, and most of them were known and available to the Norsemen when they besieged Paris in the ninth century. They must have acquired familiarity with them from their enemies but did not know how to use them effectively, for the entire siege of Paris displays an almost complete absence of any strategic concept of siege warfare by the Norsemen.

Medieval castles, as we know them now, were the immediate consequence of the Barbarian invasions of the ninth and tenth centuries. Indeed, it would not be incorrect to say that this period was marked by a renaissance of military architecture, as well as by the restoration of old fortifications originally built by the Romans but then left neglected to crumble away. Old fortifications, such as those of London, Chester and York, were restored and brought up to date. The earliest of the new castles were made of wood, because of regional scarcity of stone. William the Conqueror brought his own wooden prefabricated castles from Normandy. King Henry I of Germany's first castles in the Harz region were built of wood, probably because of the abundance of timber in the region and surrounded by wooden palisades. Once the principal structures of the castle had been built, they were rebuilt stage by stage, with stone, first the walls and then the interior buildings. With materials other than wood it would have been impossible to erect as many castles as Henry did in such a short span of time. Their primary function was that of defense and control of the immediate surrounding area. They were not a place of residence of the magnates at first. They became so only in the course of time. During the course of eastward expansion in the thirteenth century in northeastern Europe, the first castles of the Teutonic Order at Kulm, Löbau and Thorun were first constructed of wood and later replaced

Above. *Turtle device for defending attackers during the siege of a moated castle.*

Left. *The taking of Rouen 1418–19 by Henry V, in which significant use was made of cannon warfare (Vigiles de Charles VII, fifteenth century).*

Below. *Siege instrument (Renatus, 1529).*

by stone buildings. Only Marienburg at the River Nogat, ultimately the Order's center in the east, was constructed from stone from the very outset, but only at a time when the Order's position in the region had, on the whole, been secured.

The early castles of the Normans in England served that purpose, and because control of the region had to be established quickly, so were the castles. Therefore they too were initially wooden structures. The castle of York was built by 500 men in the summer of 1068, too short a time to erect a castle of stone, at a time when William was ferociously subduing the rebellious north of England. At the same time the beginnings of castles built from stone took place, such as the Tower of London, constructed with such solidity that it has endured into our own day. The keeps of Colchester and Richmond castles also date from the same period. But it was not before the twelfth century that the great age of castle-building began in England, Dover and Norwich being two of the first.

Naturally the castle architect was the prisoner of geography. An ideal site was on a location high above the surrounding countryside, such as the site of the Hohenzollern Castle near Hechingen in southwestern Germany. The present castle there, although not the original, but a reconstruction on the original site, offers a free view into the Swabian Alps in all directions. Another ideal site on which to build a castle was on a strategically important point, such as the fortress of Ehrenbreitstein, towering massively above Koblenz at the point where the River Mosel coming from the southwest joins the Rhine. But where, as in the Netherlands or parts of England, the country is flat, the architect was compelled to build an artificial mound as in the vale of York, at Ghent or Leiden or in the plains of northern Italy at Milan. On flat ground, a deep ditch or a moat proved indispensable.

As the building of castles transcended the stage in which they were mere defense posts, they became more expansive and so did the residences of the magnates of Europe's knightly nobility. As such their fortifications were extended: to the wall outer-walls were added to extend the defensive glacier as widely as possible from the actual center of the residence. Fortresses became impregnable much to the desperation of those lords

Stained glass window depicting a kneeling German knight.

low wall, another outer wall with towers at all strategically important points at a distance of 60 yards from each other. They all projected outwards, thus insuring that no attacker could utilize the wall as protective cover. Behind this wall, the wall of Constantine, ran a covered road between the inner and the outer wall, a major artery of communication within the fortress for the transfer and supply of troops. Only then came the inner wall, 30 feet high above the covered road, with a drop of 40 feet further to the city. It was also amply equipped with towers, all positioned so that the view from them was not impeded by the towers of the outer wall, and they were also twice as tall. They were of such massive construction that their roofs could carry heavy ballistic machines, while their wall contained plenty of openings for archery and crossbow fire. From land the fortress was impregnable, but it was vulnerable from the sea. Therefore a strong and efficient naval force was essential to its defense. Because the Emperors in the late twelfth century had seriously neglected their naval forces the Venetians were able to attack by sea in 1204 and caused Constantinople to fall for the first time in its history to outside attack.

Most of the castles which the Crusaders encountered on their way to the Holy Land were constructed according to similar principles. Once taken, they immediately repaired them and put them to their own use.

Inevitably Byzantine influence made itself felt in the construction of castles in Central and Western Europe thereafter. Outer walls and defense posts beyond them made their appearance, one of the most prominent examples being Château Gaillard of Richard the Lion Hearted, which covered Rouen from any attack coming from the direction of the Seine, its main works protected by four successive lines of outer defense. The concentric castle, from the point of view of military architecture, represents the final form in the development of castle-building.

Siegecraft could not keep pace with them. In the fourteenth century the balance was still heavily weighted on the side of the defender. The siege machines were roughly what they had been three centuries before. Details improved but not the underlying principles, with the exception of one which Oman calls the counterpoise, an engine depending not on tension or torsion for its propellant energy but on the sudden release of weight. The so-called trebuchet was in fact the adaptation of the long-range magnon, but it worked on a different principle. The long pole on the end of which the missile was placed, was secured to the ground while its upper end rested at the top of a wooden construction not dissimilar to a siege tower but conical in shape. The shorter end of the pole rested on top of the structure, and fastened to it by chains was a large box containing a heavy weight of metal or stone. Upon its sudden release the pole jerked upwards with great vehemence, catapulting its missile to the target area. Needless to say, it was as inaccurate as the magnon. Several versions of the trebuchet came into use but they did not differ in principle and effectiveness—or lack of it—from the original.

One siegecraft which appears to have experienced further development in siege warfare was the craft of mining, its prime being in the thirteenth century. But mining no longer meant making a hole in the palisades, filling it with inflammable material, and setting fire to it in the hope that the palisades would burn down. The mortar would grow brittle under the heat, so it was a hopeless undertaking against a moat surrounding the castle, or against a castle built of solid stone. What mining meant in the thirteenth century was virtually burrowing a route of access into the castle underneath the castle walls. As soon as the garrison became aware of what was going on,

who had to bring their overmighty subjects to heel. None of the existing siege equipment was capable of breaching the formidable defenses of a substantial castle. The only way was to starve it out and devastate the surrounding countryside. A well-supplied castle could hold out for months as Henry III was to experience at Kenilworth and Pevensey, or as the first Hohenzollerns were to find out when dealing with their unruly Brandenburg nobility. Sieges could last longer than the feudal host was prepared to support the King. The vassals had to attend to their own affairs as well, particularly when their own territories were threatened. Hence scutage or commutation proved a vital source for the hiring of soldiers. The advent of the mercenary soldier took place in England in the years of anarchy which followed the death of William's successor William Rufus and the disputed succession of Henry I. At least mercenaries could serve all the year round, providing the paymaster did not run out of funds.

The Crusades added further impetus to castle-building when the medieval knights were confronted for the first time in the twelfth century with the fortresses of the Byzantine Emperors and the Arabs. Constantinople was the most perfect fortress of them all. It was surrounded by a triple system of defenses, consisting of a moat of about 20 yards wide and approximately seven yards in depth, spiked with sharp poles and riddled with other obstacles. Of course its effectiveness depended on the presence of water, which, according to some chronicles, seems not always to have been the case. This was followed by a low wall over six feet high which gave excellent cover to defending archers. But the main line of resistance was 60 feet behind this they set their own sappers to work countermining to meet the attackers and slay them or smoke them out. One account of such an action exists of the siege of Carcassonne in the autumn of 1240.

'The attackers began a mine against the barbican gate of Narbonne. And forthwith, we, having heard the noise of their work underground, made a counter-mine, and constructed a great and strong wall of stones laid without mortars in the inside of the barbican, so that we thereby retained full half of the barbican. When they set fire to the hole in such wise that the wood having burned out, a portion of the barbican fell down! The outer defense line, the barbican of Carcassonne, was then still constructed of wood.

They then began to mine against another turret of the *lices*; we counter-mined, and got possession of the hole which they had excavated. They therefore began to tunnel a mine between us and a certain wall and destroyed two embrasures of the *lices*. But we set up there a good and strong palisade between us and them.

They also started a mine at the angle of the town wall, near the bishop's palace, and by dint of digging from a great way off arrived at a certain Saracen wall, by the wall of the *lices*; but at once, when we detected it, we made a good and strong palisade between us and them, higher up the *lices*, and counter-mined. Thereupon they fired their mine and flung down some ten fathoms of our embrasured front. But we made hastily another good palisade with a brattice upon it and

Capture of Constantinople by the Latins in 1204 during the Fifth Crusade. (Painting by Tintoretto now in the Ducal Palace, Venice).

loopholes; so none among them dared to come near us in that quarter.

They also began a mine against the barbican of the Rodez Gate, and kept below ground, wishing to arrive at our walls, making a marvelous great tunnel. But when we perceived it we forthwith made a palisade on one side and the other of it. We counter-mined also, and, having fallen in with them, carried the chamber of their mine.'

Mining failed to take Carcassonne as did attacks from the outside, and with relief coming from the outside, the siege was abandoned. Mining played its part in England as it did in Germany and in the Levant during the Crusades, where in fact the Egyptians under Sultan Kelaun caused the fall of Markab held by the knights of the Order of St John in 1285.

As long as siege warfare had no other weapons than those mentioned fortresses remained almost impregnable. To achieve success in any siege operation required time, more time than was available to feudal hosts of siege armies whose services could not be compelled for periods longer than three months out of twelve. Mercenaries, though available, were very costly, nor were they very particular in their behavior. German mercenary forces in the service of the French Crown, as much as French ones in the service of the English Crown, tended to treat the population of the host country not much differently from their enemies, giving cause for complaint and for pressure to be exercised by the magnates to have them withdrawn. Until the invention of gunpowder success in siege warfare generally favored the defenders.

*Close-up of horseback battle scene (*Histoire du Voyage et Conquête de Jerusalem, *1337).*

THE CRUSADES

Pope Gregory VII had seen it as his life's task to unite Christendom under papal supremacy. Canossa on the one hand, his death in exile on the other, are the hallmarks of the victory as well as defeat of his policy. It was up to his second successor, Pope Urban II, to issue the call on all knights of Christendom to take up arms against the infidel who were in possession of the Holy Land and to reconquer it. But the original idea for a Crusade goes back to Gregory, when he received an appeal by Emperor Michael VII of Constantinople for assistance against Turks and Muslims. For Gregory it must have been an ideal opportunity to attain his three major aims: firstly, to subject the heretic Eastern Church to Rome; secondly, to turn the Kings and princes of Christendom into his vassals under the banner of a Crusade; and thirdly, by the Crusade itself to retrieve the land from which Christianity had sprung forth and return it to its rightful owners. His preoccupation with Emperor Henry IV in the investiture contest dominated all other activities. Added to the Papacy's own motives for a crusade came other factors such as the rapid rise of a feudal aristocracy in Europe, which tended to pervade the surrounding regions, the growth of the cities and the rise of their prosperity with a population eager for mercantile expansion.

Christianity's counterattack against Islam had already begun. Perhaps Charles Martel can be considered its first representative. But in the eleventh century the Genoese and the Pisans had driven out the Muslims from Sardina and thus achieved supremacy of the Tyrrhenian Sea. The Normans had begun to gain a foothold in southern Italy which they were quick to expand in order to conquer Sicily from there in 1060, a task not accomplished until 1091. On the Iberian peninsula the attack was well under way as well. The Ommiad Caliphate of

Right. *Crusader. (Westminster psalter, twelfth century).*

Below. *Knights before and during battle* (Histoire du Voyage et Conquête de Jerusalem, *1337).*

Above. *Battle outside the walls of a town (Egyptian ms, twelfth century).*

Below. *Crusaders, c 1100.*

Cordova, after reaching its height and splendor in the early tenth century, had broken apart, leaving behind a number of independent emirates. This had provided the opportunity for a Christian offensive. At the eastern end of the Pyrenees Charlemagne's Spanish March had become the county of Barcelona. To the west the Basques in their mountain country had managed to defend themselves successfully against Muslim and Frankish dominance alike and in the process create their own kingdoms of Aragon and Navarre. Other Christians in the mountains of Asturias had given birth to the kingdom of Leon, extending south to the Douro River. A frontier region on the east, named for the castles built to defend it, became the kingdom of Castile. Aided by Frankish knights from the north and west these kingdoms during the course of the eleventh century managed to make considerable inroads at the expense of the territorial holdings of the Muslims in Spain. In 1085 Alphonso VI of Castile conquered Toledo, the fall of which resounded throughout the world of the Islam, while two years later an expedition made up of Pisans and Genoese captured Tunis and burned the whole Muslim fleet there.

Furthermore, throughout the ages the lands of the Orient, though strange to Occidentals, had never become fully alien. Byzantium, the islands of the Aegean, and Asia Minor had always remained important stations for trade. The Venetians, the Genoese and the Pisans brought the luxuries of the east to the west in their vessels. But more important, Christianity's most holy relics attracted masses of pilgrims every year, particularly since the Cluniac reform movement of the tenth century. Pilgrims from central and western Europe upon their arrival in Byzantium were overpowered by the splendor of its architecture, its basilicas and palaces, its vast markets and the abundance of merchandise they had to offer, which contrasted so sharply with the stark simplicity of their own homelands. Byzantium's

ويحمل النقص والجمالة والفبرى والإبالة انها لضفت علي بالة فانضاعت نفض مذهبها
فسدم مذرجها فلما دانبي وزنت بالرقعة درهما وقطعة وقلت لها ان رغبت في المشوف المعلم
وازن الى الدرهم فوجى بالسر المهم وان ابسان ان نترجي خذى القطعة واسبرجن

نالت الى استخلاض البدر النم والابلج الهم وقالت دع جدالك بناعما بدالك فاسطه
طلع الشيخ وبلده والشغر وابج بردنه فقالت ان الشيخ من اهل يروج وهو الذي وفتى

Left. *The Sultans' Guard sound a trumpet blast to inspire the Muslim troops (*Séances d'Harari, *Arab ms, thirteenth century).*

Above. *Stragglers in First Crusade being set upon by Hungarians.*

military forces were largely mercenaries from the Germanic tribes. Descendants of the Norsemen served side by side with those of Anglo-Saxons, Franks, and Normans. Greece still had lost nothing of its intellectual reputation. But the connection which tied the Occident closest to the Orient was that of the religious faith. The Holy Land was the ultimate aim of any pilgrim. Since the days of the Great Migrations, pilgrims, after they had visited the graves of the Apostles in Rome, gathered in the harbors of the Italian coastal towns to sail to Constantinople, and from there made their way into the Holy Land. It was a venture not without serious dangers from marauders who might lie in wait for pilgrims anywhere along the long route. But the Caliphs themselves never obstructed the pilgrimages. And upon their return home they spread the news of ventures and splendors encountered far and wide, in the cities as on the land.

Hence when Pope Urban II called upon Christendom to liberate the Holy Grail from the hands of the infidel the overwhelming response came from a climate of opinion that psychologically as well as practically had been well-prepared for such a vast undertaking. From the Roman Catholic Church comprising the French, English, Spanish, Danes, Germans and Italians, the call for the Crusade originated, and for the bulk who followed it, the mystical current of this call dominated all other considerations and motivations which also played their part. This mystical current is one reason for the failure of the Crusaders to develop a rational strategy. But that really is a characteristic adhering to most of medieval warfare. Although tactical and strategic concepts never completely disappeared, the product of the feudal system, the feudal knight, was too much of an individual, too independent to accept the kind of leadership capable of applying firm tactical schemes. And without tactics there can be no strategy. When in the course of the fourteenth century the beginnings of the great transformation in warfare emerged, the picture changed entirely.

In the two years from Pope Urban's original summons, hosts

of preachers had carried it into all corners of Christendom. Urban himself spared no pain or hardship to spread the message in person, traveling from palace to palace pointing out the importance of eternal salvation which could be gained in the Crusade, but also rather more the gains to be made this side of eternal life: new lands for Kings and vassals, the profits to be made by the merchants and craftsmen in equipping this crusading host, and to the unfree of both town and countryside, the status of a freeman if he enrolled under the banner of the cross.

The nobility of Europe assembled, particularly the French. However the first shortcoming, after the Crusades had assembled at Constantinople, was that no supreme commander was appointed. There was no united crusading army but a confederation of forces. Strong rivalry existed between both the forces themselves and their leaders. Prominent knights in the ranks included Robert Rufus, son of William the Conqueror; Godfrey of Bouillon, Duke of Lorraine; Hugh, Count of Vermandois, brother of Philip I of France; Robert II of Flanders and Raymond, Count of Toulouse, leader of the largest contingent of the Crusaders.

At Constantinople the first problem was encountered in the person of Emperor Alexius who respected the motives of the Crusaders from the west as much as the Czechs appreciated the forces of the Warsaw Pact powers who had come to rescue them from the dangers of imperialist aggression in 1968. Unlike the Czechs, Alexius was still in a strong position. To safeguard his own situation he demanded that each crusading leader swear an oath of allegiance to him. Only Godfrey of Bouillon sub-

mitted to this. The others ignored it. The problems which they encountered thereafter were mostly of their own making. One major problem, however, was not: their lack of geographic knowledge. An utter lack of geographical information about the countries of the Levant and Asia Minor in general existed

The First Crusade 1097: the Christians fight against the Turks at Constantinople (Engravings after medieval sculptures).

among the Crusaders. The only ones with any knowledge at all in the west were the Genoese and the Pisans, but their knowledge was primarily restricted to sea routes. The route from Europe to the Bosporus was well-known and well-traveled since the beginning of the eleventh century, but what lay beyond that on the way to the Holy Land was *terrum incognitum*, except to the Byzantines of course, and the Crusaders had to accept their guidance or ignore it. Since they were suspicious of the Byzantines they usually ignored it. In 1101 Raymond of Toulouse marched with his contingent by an incredibly circuitous route from Abcyra to Gangra and from there to Amasia. It was a choice made by Raymond himself, in place of the route recommended by Emperor Alexius. Raymond was to repeat this mistake more than once and illustrated that most of the troubles which the Crusaders encountered once they had moved into Eastern Europe on their way to Constantinople were of their own making. Presumptuousness, selfishness, improvidence and downright carelessness marked their course, so much so that it is astonishing that they achieved anything at all.

Once in Asia Minor they were incessantly harassed by Turks and other tribes. The territory was unsuitable for the battle formation's usually made by feudal knights. Often, crusading contingents, such as that of William of Poitiers, were attacked when crossing streams surrounded by rocky highlands. Too scattered to form a line of battle, hemmed in by geographic obstacles, they were surrounded by the Turks, and those who did not manage to cut their way through into the hills and mountains were slaughtered. Those on foot stood no chance at all. The Crusaders, equipped only with the tactical knowledge of the knight, the shock tactics of heavily armed cavalry, had

treated the other arms merely as auxiliaries. Compared with them Byzantine tactics were infinitely more sophisticated, an asset which they owed mainly to what they had learned from the Turks and the Arabs. As Sir Charles Oman stated:

'They were (1) always to take a steady and sufficient body of infantry into the field; (2) to maintain an elaborate screen of vedettes and pickets round the army, so as to guard against surprises; (3) to avoid fighting in broken ground where the enemy's dispositions could not be described; (4) to keep large reserves and flank-guards; (5) to fight with the rear (and if possible the wings also) covered by natural obstacles, such as rivers, marshes, or cliffs, so as to foil the usual Turkish device of circular attacks on the wings or the camp guard; (6) always to fortify the camp; (7) never to pursue rashly and allow the infantry to get separated after a first success.'

In spite of these tactics the Byzantines had suffered severe setbacks at the hands of the Turks. The Crusaders, totally ignorant of them, too arrogant to stoop to adapt anything from

Top. *Crusaders crossing the Bosphorus, 1097 (After a drawing by Weber).*

The powerful Eastern fortress of Jordan, Shaubak Castle.

Above. *Assyrians at the siege of Jerusalem, 1099* (Silos Apocalypse, *1109*).

Left. *The horsemen of the Four Seals armed with crossbows and swords like Saracens* (Silos Apocalypse, *1109*).

the 'Greek monkeys,' stumbled into their own disasters.

At first this did not seem to be the case. In 1097 they laid siege to Nicaea which surrendered after little more than a month. Then they moved on to Antioch and from there to Tripoli. Finally in January 1099 the crusading armies set out for Jerusalem. En route, Godfrey's younger brother Baldwin turned east with his forces on the pretext of protecting the flanks of the main army; in reality, however, he was looking for land which he could conquer for himself. As the armies advanced on Palestine, they traversed territory short of water supplies and almost barren in foodstuffs. But upon entry into Palestine the environment changed. The country was full of fruit and vegetables; the towns had plenty of wine, bread and cheese.

Three years after the beginning of the Crusades they reached Jerusalem, positioned high on its hills and surrounded by strong walls and towers. Its defenders had driven away all the livestock and poisoned the wells around the city. The siege was established along the traditional pattern. The Crusaders built siege towers, siege ladders, ram and pole, magnons, ballista and trebuchets.

'Before we attacked, our bishops and priests preached to us and commanded that all men should go in procession in honor of God around the ramparts of Jerusalem . . . Early on Friday we made a general attack but were unable to do anything and fell back in great fear. Then at the approach of the hour at which our Lord Jesus Christ suffered for us upon the cross, our knights in one of the wooden towers made a hot attack, with Duke Godfrey and Count Eustace among them. One of our knights, named Letold, clambered up the wall. As soon as he was there, the defenders fled along the walls and down into the city, and we followed them, slaying them and cutting them down as far as the Temple of Solomon, where there was such slaughter that our men waded in blood up to their ankles . . . The Crusaders ran about the city, seizing gold, silver, horses, mules, and pillaging the houses filled with riches. Then, happy and weeping with joy, our men went to adore the sepulcher of Our Lord, and rendered up the offering they owed. The following morning we climbed to the roof of the Temple and fell upon the Saracens who were there, men and women, beheading them with our sword.'

The chronicler who has left us this account indicates the priorities existing among the knights quite clearly: first to render unto themselves the plunder they believed to be their's and then after that accomplishment to perform their act of worship. The city had been won, but the conquest did not establish unity among the conquerors, some of whom now wished to return home. Godfrey of Bouillon was acclaimed King of Jerusalem, an honor which he enjoyed for only one year before he died of typhoid fever.

In the meantime the Crusaders consolidated their success by defeating an Egyptian army sent to reconquer Jerusalem. Generally speaking, non-Turkish Muslims proved an inferior fighting force, less ably led than the Turks, and after the Egyptian defeat at Ascalon in August 1099, the Crusaders dominated the interior of Palestine. Only Damascus, Emesa, Hama and Aleppo were still held by the Muslims. Very important was the capture of the harbor city of Jaffa, without which the Crusaders could not have been supplied. But the Muslims rallied once again and by 1144 recaptured Edessa, the fall of which reverberated throughout Europe and caused the preaching of the Second Crusade by St Bernhard of Clairvaux. Godfrey of Bouillon before his death had recognized the dangers inherent in the lack of any formal organization in the Crusading army. What was needed was a tighter reign of order and discipline. He ordered as a preliminary measure that there should be 20 canons of the Holy

Sepulcher, monks whose task it was to guard and defend the tomb of Christ. They were required to swear obedience to the prior of this order. Soon these knights became known as 'the most worthy' they carried white mantles decorated with the red cross of Jerusalem. This order was soon followed by that of St John. Up to the end of the Crusades, the military orders represented the very backbone, the elite of European knighthood, of the Crusading movement.

St Bernhard of Clairvaux was one of the men instrumental in founding the Order of the Templars which he described in 1125:

'They are not lacking in proper bearing at home or in the field, and obedience is not lacking in esteem. They go and come according to the order of the Master; they put on the clothes he gives to them and demand from no one else either clothing or food. They avoid opulence in both; only essentials are cared for. They live with one another happily and with modesty without wenches or children in order that they do not lack evangelical perfection, without property in one house, of one spirit, endeavoring to maintain the bond of peace and tranquility so that in all of them one heart and one soul appears to live. At no time are they idle or wander about with curiosity. When they rest from their struggles against the infidels, in order not to eat their bread for nothing, they improve and mend their clothes and arms. Chess and boardgames they despise, they do not cherish the chase nor the bird-hunt. They hate the vagabonds, the minstrels, all excessive singing and acting as excessive vanity and stupidity of the world. They do not go into battle stormily and without thought, but with due consideration and caution, peaceful like the true children of Israel. But once the battle has begun then they press into the enemy without fear, considering the enemy mere sheep. And if there are only a few of them they trust in the help of Jehovah. Therefore one of them has managed to drive a thousand before him, and two ten thousand. Also in a curious combination they are gentler than lambs and more ferocious than lions so that one has doubts whether to call them monks or knights. Yet they deserve both names, because they partake in the gentleness of monks and the bravery of the knights.'

*Crusaders attacking a castle using a ballistic siege weapon: see bottom left (*Histoire du Voyage et Conquête de Jerusalem, *fourteenth century).*

Siege of a fortress, 1438.

This was the ideal, and St Bernhard's description is the vision of this ideal, which was to give new impulses to the Crusades and its preachers. Their success was considerable. Emperor Conrad III of Germany and King Louis VII of France took to the cross in the spring of 1147. On their way through Asia Minor they met with various disasters which decided Conrad to take his forces by sea to the Holy Land while Louis opted for the land route. In the Holy Land they united and met up with Baldwin, the brother of Godfrey of Bouillon, who by then had become Baldwin III, King of Jerusalem. At Jerusalem Conrad,

Above. *The Saracen horsemen on the left are unencumbered by heavy suits of armor, giving them that definitive advantage over the Christians (right) which led to the Christian defeat at the Horns of Hattin.*

Right. *The siege of Antioch (*Histoire de Jerusalem *by William of Tyre, c 1250).*

Below. *Attack on Castle of Emmaus: a wooden tower is used to assault the dungeon where only women are left (*Histoire de Jerusalem *by William of Tyre, c 1250).*

Right. *Richard I (1157–99) and the Saracens making a treaty (Corpus Christi ms, c 1240).*

Below. *Fleet of the Crusaders before the coast of the Holy Land, 1386.*

Louis and Baldwin together with the grand masters of the Templars and the Knights of St John held council and decided to attack the city of Damascus. It was the largest army the Crusaders had so far put in the field, though precise numbers are impossible to obtain. For instance, the sources of the First Crusade speak of a 100,000 knights and some 900,000 others. Subsequent studies have shown that the highest number of knights engaged in any one battle in the Crusades cannot have

been more than 1200 and, as at Ascalon, 9000 foot soldiers; after that the knightly hosts seem to have ranged between 260 and 1100, with foot soldiers numbering 2000 to 3000 at the very most.

As they laid siege to Damascus the question arose as to who was to have the city once it had been conquered. As no straightforward answer could be decided, the siege was declared a mistake, and since Turkish relief forces were on their way, the

Crusading army left. Conrad returned to Germany in 1148, and Louis to France in 1149. The Crusaders were pushed back by the Muslims. Among them was a sixteen-year-old boy named Saladin. Devoutly Muslim and fanatically anti-Christian, he grew up to become one of the great characters of medieval history, a man who in spite of his fervently held convictions retained, as a politician as well as a general, a cool head throughout his life. Since Mohammed, no Muslim succeeded in uniting the peoples of the Islamic world more than he. By 1169 he had established himself firmly in Egypt and was intent upon expelling the crusaders from Palestine where they occupied parts of it, supplied by sea, which was also the protection of one flank, and on the other by a chain of mighty castles. As long as these castles could hold out and as long as the lines of communications and supplies in the eastern Mediterranean could easily be maintained, their position, if not unassailable, was from the point of view of defense, a very strong one. Although relations between the Crusaders and Constantinople were difficult at the best of times, as long as Byzantium threatened the Syrians from the north, enough Muslims were diverted from the Crusaders. This changed drastically for the worse when Emperor Manuel of Byzantium decided in his turn to take the offensive against the Muslims, but he was defeated on the 17 September 1176. Without Byzantium the Crusaders could not hold Palestine in the long term. The collapse was delayed until

Above. *Saladin's troops ravage the Holy Land (*Histoire de Jerusalem *by William of Tyre, c 1250–60).*

Left. *Crusaders process round the walls of Jerusalem.*

Below. *Siege of Antioch (*Histoire de Jerusalem *by William of Tyre, c 1250–60).*

Manuel's death in 1180 and the quarrels over the succession to the throne of Byzantium weakened it to an extent from which it never recovered.

In the meantime in 1177, Saladin had taken his forces across the Egyptian frontiers, heading for Jerusalem. But caught unaware his army was routed by the Crusaders. However, he quickly recovered and resumed campaigning the following year. The campaign proved inconclusive and since both sides were tiring over the struggle for Palestine, Baldwin and Saladin agreed to a two-year truce. It provided that Christian and Muslim merchants could cross each other's territory. The sight of so many rich caravans, full with merchandise was too strong a temptation to be resisted by Reynald of Chatillon. One day he waylaid a caravan and plundered it. As far as Saladin was concerned the truce had been broken. In September 1183 he invaded Palestine, but the knights would not do battle in the open, they stayed in their castles. Another truce was arranged, and broken again by Reynald.

Saladin was enraged and concentrated his troops on the frontier. This time the Crusaders emerged under the command of Guy à Lusignan, who after his death had succeeded Baldwin to the throne of Jerusalem. Marching towards Saladin, who was encamped near the Sea of Galilee, they had among them the Bishop of Acre, who is said to have carried the most holy of relics, the Cross on which Christ had died. They camped on some rocky heights of a pass, called by its two peaks, the horns of Hattin. Water was scarce; plagued with thirst, exhausted by the march, the soldiers looked down upon the village of Hattin and beyond at the glimmering waters of Lake Galilee.

The Muslims took the initiative. Setting fire to the dry grass leading up to the Crusaders, they followed with a massed attack of arrows. Many knights are said to have fallen from their horses, not because they had been hit by a weapon, but from sheer exhaustion. The following day Saladin reinforced his archers with horsed archers and seventy camels carrying nothing but arrows. Parts of the Crusaders were cut off from the main body of the King's army. The Saracens cut their way into the ranks of the knights and their foot soldiery and, as one Arab chronicler said: 'Terrible encounters took place on that day; never in the history of the generations that have gone have such

Saladin defeats the Christians and captures the Holy Cross, 1187.

feats been told.' All order disappeared; charge after charge mounted by Saracens scattered their enemies, many of whom, including the King, they took prisoner. Finally they also captured the Holy Cross. Saladin had Reynald of Chatillon beheaded. The Kings and the other nobles were spared. Saladin's victory, conducted as it was literally against the Cross, was a blow from which the Crusades never recovered.

The defeat gave birth to the Third Crusade, the signal being Saladin's capture of Jerusalem where in place of the Red Cross

Above. *Crusaders bombard Nicea with captives' heads (*Les Chroniques d'Outremer*).*

Left. *Frederick Barbarossa about to embark on his crusade (*Chroniques des Rois de Bourgogne, *c 1500).*

Far left. *Richard the Lionhearted and Philip II of France during the Third Crusade.*

Below. *Richard I unhorsing Saladin, Sultan of Egypt.*

against the white background the golden banner of Saladin now fluttered. This new crusade was to be led by Emperor Frederick Barbarossa, Conrad's successor, accompanied by Philip of France and by Richard the Lionhearted who as a soldier was Barbarossa's equal. Barbarossa was considered a worthy foe, a true successor of Charlemagne and Otto the Great. But Barbarossa's role in the crusade was cut short; he never reached the Holy Land. He drowned in an unexplained accident in a little river in Cilicia. The army at first tried to come to an agreement with Saladin. It had captured Acre in 1191 but then Richard and the Duke of Burgundy beheaded 2600 captives. In the September of that year the Crusaders achieved a magnificent victory at Asouf. It was mainly Richard's victory; he deployed his knights and foot soldiery more judiciously than any of his predecessors and contemporaries. Saladin withdrew and resumed his old policy of harassment. The fact that the Crusade did not achieve its objective has more to do with the self-seeking ambitions of the monarchs concerned than with anything else. Consequently in 1198 Pope Innocent proclaimed the Fourth Crusade. Its leader was the semi-blind Doge of Venice, Enrico Dandolo, at the ripe old age of eighty. His main task was to assemble the fleet to carry the Crusaders to the Holy Land. As they assembled in Venice, there was no money to pay for the vessels. This diverted them into Dalmatia and into the heart of the Byzantine Empire until they arrived at the gates of Constantinople where the Byzantine Prince Alexius Angelus, son of the dethroned Isaac II, persuaded the Crusaders to reinstate his father. On the 7 April 1203 the Crusaders stormed the city from the water side and Isaac was restored. The Crusaders now waited outside the city for payment of 200,000 marks. No money was forthcoming, and worse still another palace revolution deposed Isaac II again. Considering themselves freed from all obligations the Crusaders set about to storm the city by land and sea. The city held out a few days, but ridden by internal dissensions it no longer mustered the strength it once had. On 13 April 1204 it fell and for three days it was a scene of carnage and plunder. For the Crusaders Byzantium was a heretic empire, to a Christian worse than infidelity. But more attractive, the riches it offered outdid anything the Holy Land could offer. Byzantium, so far the bulwark in the East against the Turks and Asia, was destroyed. For more than two centuries it lingered on, but politically it ceased to play a serious factor in European politics.

Politically the Crusades had crushed such barriers which existed between the Muslim world and the West since the days of the Arab invasions. In spite of the petty squabbles, treachery,

Defeat of the Turks before Antioch (Bibliothèque Nationale ms 5594).

and deceit, they were the last grand demonstration of the Christian Universalism that was the bracket holding together the successor states of the Roman Empire. Among the French, who always considered the Crusades as a predominantly French affair—which, on occasions, it was—it kindled the spirit of nationhood, in the same way as the *reconquista* kindled that spirit among the peoples of Spain and Portugal. The Church under Innocent III reached its zenith. The Pope was the King of Kings; his spiritual control, however, required an economic basis, supplied ultimately by indulgences and clerical tithes. Opposition to that, combined with an increased knowledge gained at Byzantium and from the Arab world, led to speculation, to doubt. The cross of Hattin had not been able to hold back the conquering hordes of Saladin. Did this not reflect upon those who claimed to be its bearers and upholders? Heresy was rife; speculation, doubts all nourished man's innate spirit of inquiry. The questions asked, more so than the answers given, were the great driving force that was to change the world—or the picture which medieval man had of it.

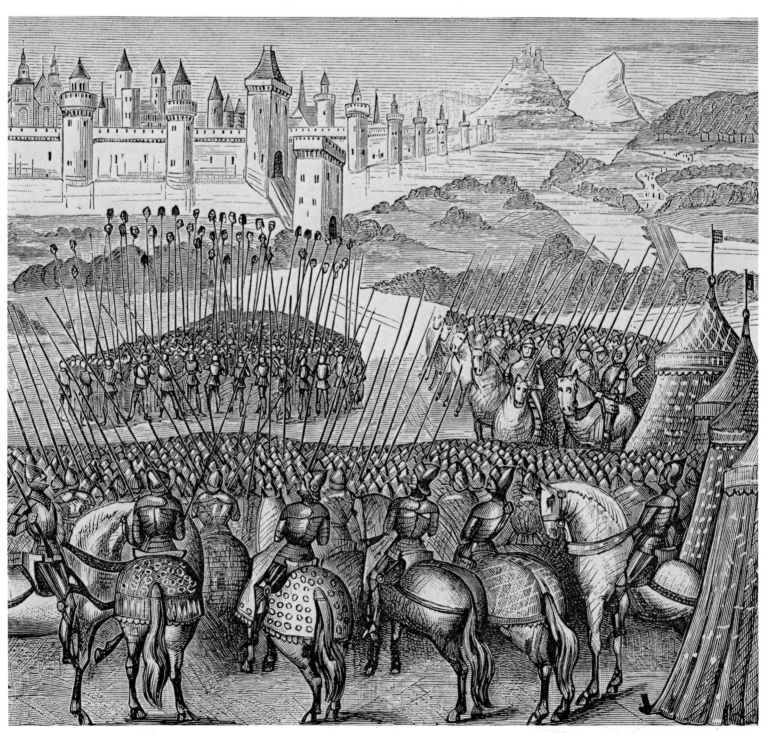

Below. *Knights of the Holy
Ghost embarking for the Crusades.
This voyage, in fact, was never
undertaken, but the knights were
told to prepare for their departure
pending a final decision concerning
their future to be taken at Rome
(After a fourteenth-century French
miniature from* The Statutes of
the Holy Ghost at Naples *now at
the Louvre, Paris).*

TEUTONIC ORDER

*Defeat of the Turks at Dorylaeum 1097 by Godfrey de Bouillon during the First Crusade. The Crusades inspired the formation of the knightly orders such as the Teutonic Knights. Initially they functioned as a medical order similar to the Knights Hospitallers of St John but they eventually developed an exclusively military role (*Saintes Chroniques d'Outremer*).*

Quite distinctive from medieval knighthood are the knightly orders which date back to St Bernhard's appeal for support to mount the First Crusade. He had issued the rules of the Templars to two knights, Hugo of Payens and Godfrey of St Omer, and called for recruits in a tract which he wrote:

'The warriors are gentler than lambs and fiercer than lions, wedding the mildness of the monk with the valor of the knight, so that it is difficult to decide which to call them: men who adorn the Temple of Solomon with weapons instead of gems, with shields instead of crowns of gold, with saddles and bridles instead of candelabra; eager for victory not for fame; for battle not for pomp; who abhor wasteful speech, unnecessary action, unmeasured laughter, gossip and chatter, as they despise all vain things: who, in spite of their being many, live in one house according to one rule, with one soul and one heart.'

St Bernhard's foundation did not put an end to the 'hero of the Age of Chivalry' and his courtly pursuits, but encountered the restless, vacillating secular knight errant, who flew from adventure to adventure, or sacrificed himself in the service of his lady-love, leading his individual life and entirely destructive to the firm fabric of the state, with a closed, rigidly disciplined corporation, dedicated to the service of Christ, the spiritual head of the knightly corporation. They were monks and lay brethren, actively serving a common purpose with the New Testament and the sword, men who subordinated themselves to a common master. In modern terminology they were activists of the sword and the word, recognizable by uniformity of dress, the mantle with the cross, and their uniformity in style of life.

Like the original idealistic impulse, often at the root of the origin of many human institutions, the first impetus could not be sustained indefinitely. By the end of the twelfth century

Above. *Among the European warrior nobles who considered it an honor to serve with the Teutonic Order was Henry Bolingbroke.*

Left. *Emperor Frederick II (1194–1250), the greatest of the Hohenstaufen emperors.*

spiritual knighthood seemed almost at the point of extinction. The institutions of Knights of the Templars, whose members were mainly French, and those of the Knights of St John, composed largely of English and Italian members, were on the wane and near the point of disintegration. Yet precisely at this point in time, in 1190, a new order made its appearance, one which was to be called the *Deutschritterorden*, the Teutonic Order. The initiative for it, however, did not emanate from the clergy, nor for that matter from German knights, but from German burghers, merchants from the Hanseatic cities of Bremen and Lübeck.

These merchants in the Holy Land showed compassion for their compatriots among the disease-ridden siege army encamped on Mount Turon outside Acre. They established a hospital, dedicated to the Virgin Mary, in which sick German knights were cared for by the merchants. Once Acre had been taken, they obtained a land grant there on which a church and hospital were built, and they then applied for official recognition as a spiritual corporation of the Brothers of the Hospital of St Mary of the German Nation. This was granted by Pope Coelestin III in 1196, and again confirmed by Pope Innocent III in 1199. The latter confirmation, however, insisted that the corporation become a knightly order which would take its rules from the Templars, while its hospital rules were to come from the Order of St John.

This new order of German knights never distinguished itself in the Holy Land; it fought no famous battles there, nor did it enjoy that abundant wealth which had been the cause of the corruption and decay of the older orders. It was, and remained, a purely Germanic movement, one of the most significant features of which, particularly in the context of its long-term development in the colonization of the German east, was its close association with the German burghers. As a founder of cities and towns, and as a protector of and participator in the trading ventures of northeastern Europe, it established its reputation. But once the interests of the cities and merchants on the one hand, and those of the Teutonic Knights on the other began to diverge, the order declined. Throughout its history the Teutonic Order consisted of three main branches. Firstly there was the German branch, concentrated primarily in southern and southwestern Germany, including Alsace, with possessions in Burgundy. Secondly there was the branch in Livland (Latvia) and thirdly, the Prussian branch with its center at Marienburg. After the residence of the Grand Master was transferred to this castle, it became the center of the Order as a whole.

The inner core of the order comprised clergy and laymen. Their way of life was governed by strict rules; personal property had to be renounced. Each house of the Order consisted of twelve brothers, in accordance with the number of Christ's disciples. Their head was a bailiff, called the *Komtur*. A brother of the Order was to have neither his own seal or coat of arms. His was the only white mantle with the black cross.

When a Master of the Order died, his deputy convened all the *Komturs* of Germany, Prussia and Livland, as well as of Apulia. Their function was to elect thirteen members who in turn would elect the new Master. Qualification for this office, as well as for membership in general, was not noble origin, but to be a freeman and to have been born in wedlock.

Throughout its duration the Teutonic Order was never an

Marienburg Castle, the principal fortress of the Teutonic Order.

aristocratic body, nor was it a corporation which accepted only people of knightly origin, or those who in fact had had knighthood bestowed upon them by the Grand Master. The first masters of the Order were burghers of the city of Bremen. But that Grand Master, Hermann von Salza, whose personality determined to a large extent the early fortunes of the Order, had probably risen to his high rank from that of a *ministeriale* at the court of Emperor Henry VI and his son Frederick II. Only in 1216 did Pope Honorius III insist that the Grand Master of the Order should be of knightly or of honest birth to ensure that he could be made a knight. This was to prevent illigitimate sons of princes, or those of the Grand Master himself, from turning the office into a hereditary commodity.

Nevertheless knightly ethics determined the institutions, attitudes and behavior of the Order. Its highest officer was the Grand Master. Although obliged in all important matters to take control from experienced brothers and to take into consideration the decision of the Chapter of the Order, he was, during the heyday of the Order an extremely powerful man. Only during the final stages of the Order's disintegration did the Grand Master's government degenerate into a government in which the other officers of the Order shared.

Below the Grand Master were the offices of the central administration: the *Grosskomtur*, the *Ordensmarschall* or *Grossmarschall*, the *Spittler* (hospitaller), the *Tressler* (treasurer) and the *Trapier* (quartermaster). Following the occupation of Prussia, the office of the *Grosschaeffer* gained in significance, since it acted as Ministry of Trade, administering and guiding the continually expanding commercial relations of the Teutonic Order. The territory of the Order was divided into *Komtureis*, each headed by a *Komtur*; smaller territorial subdivisions were headed by *Vogts* or caretakers. In spite of the fact that the Order

was a specifically German institution, it did accept foreigners into its ranks, particularly Poles, as well as other Slavs.

The Order's rise was closely linked with the rule of Emperor Frederick II. He was quick to recognize the potential of this relatively new and unknown Order. Unlike the other orders, this one, free from both feudal ties and the influence of temporal and spiritual lords, was still capable of being turned into an elite body for the Emperor's purposes; Frederick's greatest confidant was the first Grand Master of stature, Hermann von Salza. For over two decades Hermann was his counselor and friend on account of his personal qualities which combined unflinching loyalty with stable judgment and political good sense. These qualities enabled him to act time and again as a mediator between Frederick and the Papacy, without losing the respect and high esteem of either.

The Order's most prominent period began when Konrad of Masovia, Duke of Poland, found himself unable to repel the heathen Prussians. And so he turned to the Teutonic Knights, the *Deutschritterorden* for help, and provisionally gave a verbal undertaking that, in return for their services, he would reward them with the territories of Kulm along the River Vistula.

Hermann von Salza immediately received backing from Frederick and then from the Papacy which issued the Golden

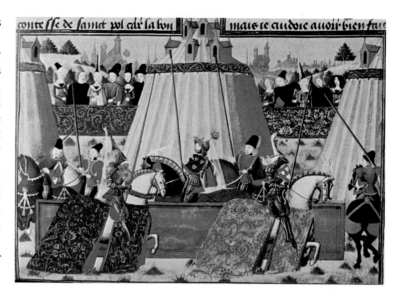

Bull of Rimini of 1226. This laid down the future task of the Teutonic Order, as well as setting out in minute detail the constitution of a future state in northeastern Europe. The privileges accorded to the order included that 'all gifts and conquests are to be the free property of the Order, which is to exercise full

Above. *Medieval tournaments provided a public arena in which knights could display their military prowess* (Chroniques de Froissart, *fourteenth century*).

Left. *A German tournament of the fifteenth century: the object of the tournament was to unhorse one's opponent and break a lance against his armor.*

Below. *Jousts were perfect occasions on which to vaunt heraldic Coats of Arms.*

Above. *In this assault on a medieval city, the lancers engage in battle in the foreground while soldiers scale the walls armed with handguns (Ghent ms, fifteenth century).*

Left. *German knight pierces the neckpiece of his opponent.*

Below. *Saladin and his Saracen horsemen* (Histoire du Voyage et Conquête de Jerusalem, *fourteenth century*).

territorial rights and be responsible to none. The Grand Master is to enjoy all the privileges that pertain to a Prince of the Empire, including all royal privileges, and in Prussia the Order shall be free from all Imperial taxes, burdens and services.' The future territory of the Teutonic Order was to be 'an integral part of the monarchy of Empire.'

Obviously the importance which the undertaking was to acquire could not have been foreseen in 1226, but the position of the Order and its future was assured by the charter. Beside the Teutonic Knights, another order was and had been active in the conversion of the heathens in the northeast, namely the Cistercian monks. These Hermann von Salza also managed to win over so that they became his allies, and the two orders together represented the main pillars of the missionary activity in the northeast.

The heathens, occupying the coastal plains of the Baltic Sea from the Vistula to the River Memel, had already been subjected to unsuccessful attempts at conversion earlier. The rivers flowing into the Baltic gave access to the interior, and on land the territory was traversed by traders making their way to Poland and as far as Novgorod. The territory around Kulm and Löbau had become Polish but, like the entire region between Vistula and Memel, was not exclusively inhabited by Prussians but by numerous other tribes as well. Even before the arrival of

the Teutonic Knights, German colonists brought in by the bishops of Kulm posed a threat to them from the west and south; furthermore Germans had settled along the Baltic coast under the protection of the Bishop of Livland. They traded mainly with the interior, protected by a knightly Order foun-

MACHINES of WAR &c. used in the ATTACK & DEFENCE of FORTIFIED PLACES.

Dadley sculp.

1 Section of the Wall of the Ballium.	5 Crenelles & Oilets.
2 Section of a Machicolation.	6 The Sow.
3 A Plan of ditto.	7 The Cattus.
4 A Perspective view of ditto.	8 A Dart called a Quarrel.
9 A Moveable Tower of 3 stages.	13 Darts for the Balista.
10 A Battering Ram.	14 Herse or Portcullis.
11 A Bridge to let down for storming.	15 The Balista.
12 Onager or Scorpio.	16 A Catapulta for discharg.ᵍ Darts

Above. *Heralds proclaim a tournament.*

Left. *An eighteenth-century engraving depicting medieval siege instruments.*

ded by the Bishop of Riga, which ultimately fused with the Teutonic Order. They were instrumental in spreading German rule, language and occidental culture across Courland, Latvia, and Estonia.

In fact the Teutonic Knights arrived rather late at the scene. Indeed, in the context of the thirteenth century, they can be considered almost an anachronism at a time which saw the beginning of the decline of medieval knighthood. Time and again nobles refused to support their lords. Poetry, inspired by the cult of courtly chivalry, was on the decline; no further epics were forthcoming: no *Chanson de Roland*, no *Nibelungenlied*. Louis IX of France represented the swan song of European knighthood; a new order was on the threshold of power, whether represented in France by Philip the Fair and his *Realpolitik*, or by England in the form of the House of Commons.

During that epoch the Teutonic Knights set about creating a new state of their own, thus forging the last link of the colonization that had begun with Charlemagne's subjection of the Saxons and which in the course of the next two centuries had moved across the Elbe to the Vistula. Without being aware of it, the Teutonic Knights lived on borrowed time. They set about their task speedily, the land around Kulm and Löbau was converted, and by 1230 Konrad of Masovia handed it formally over to the Order. But the creation of a German state was bound to be felt as a potential threat by the Polish nobility. The common interest of the religious cause stopped at the point where practical political conflicts of interest began to emerge.

Yet during its early years, around 1230, the Teutonic Order showed little inclination to carry out its missionary activity by force of arms, since their initial number were rather small. Also its economic base was rather weak. Only after 1230 did growth set in, through additional land grants made to the Order elsewhere, and through the increasing land taken under cultivation in Prussia. In one report, the membership of the Order in Prussia in the days of Hermann von Salza was listed as approximately 600, while in the late 1270s the membership had increased to over 2000. It was not the brothers of the Teutonic Order who alone conquered and settled the land, but the crusading folk, recruited by the brothers throughout the German Empire and beyond. Whoever participated in the crusade in Prussia would be relieved of penance for past wrong doings. In 1231 the Master Hermann Balke, sent by Hermann von Salza together with seven other brothers, headed a crusading army and crossed the Vistula. German vessals sailed up the Vistula with supplies and building materials, and the first castles of the Teutonic Order began to raise their powerful and arrogant silhouettes against the eastern skyline: Thorun, Kulm and Marienwerder, bases from which further expansion could be undertaken, and the centers upon which the attacks of the natives were concentrated.

But the Prussians and other tribes in the region were at first totally unaware of the threat facing them; they did not even obstruct the building of the castles. Doubtless in a majority *vis-à-vis* the invading Germans, politically they were too divided among themselves to rally together for effective action to eliminate the new threat. When they did take the first steps in this direction, they had to give way to a German minority far more effectively organized in military terms. Then the Germans drove them relentlessly into the wilderness, secured the Vistula by building a fortress at Elbing, destroying the heathen shrines, subduing and converting the natives at the point of the sword. In 1239, when Hermann von Salza died, the Order controlled more than a hundred miles of the Baltic coast; less than two decades later in 1255 Ottokar, the King of Bohemia, joined the crusade in Prussia, and there in Samland, in his honor, a new fortress was built by the name of Königsberg.

It would, however, be a serious error to equate the crusades in the Holy Land with those in northeastern Europe. In the former the territories conquered were exploited; the majority of the Crusaders returned home after a year or more service in the Holy Land. It was essentially a knightly venture. In Prussia the ties between knights and burghers were inseparable, and the newly founded settlements were established with a view to permanency. The settlers came from all parts of Germany as well as from the Netherlands. Once again this Flemish song enjoyed popularity:

> *Naer Oostland wille wij rijden,*
> *Daer isser en betere stee.*
> (To the East we will ride,
> There is a better home.)

The initially low number of the brothers of the Order and crusading folk determined, of course, the kind of warfare, as well as the relationship between the Order and the natives. With few in number it was hardly advisable to provoke a surrounding majority into active hostility. But with the increasing number of crusaders, together with the increasing number of castles and their steady eastward advance, ultimate intentions could no longer be hidden. In addition there emerged the inner contradiction arising from the religious motivation of the crusade and the political realities. The Germans subjecting the Prussians were in the minority but were determined to maintain their dominance. Consequently they considered it politically unwise to convert the Prussians in excessive numbers, for that would have given them rights almost equal to the Germans, and consequently would have threatened the political position of the Prussians. Until 1241, however, the progress of the Teutonic Order remained relatively unimpeded, but then, for eleven years, unco-ordinated uprisings against the foreign invader took place. The Germans maintained the upper hand and by 1260 it seemed that the Order's hold on Prussia had been secured.

Yet the picture was deceptive. Hardly any of the Order, lay or clergy, troubled to acquire any knowledge of the language of the natives. The priests arrogantly destroyed ancient shrines, imposing the symbols of the new religion by force rather than persuasion. A people of peasants and shepherds was forced to bear the heavy burdens placed on them by the Order, to build castles and carry out other services. Mutual suspicion was rife, so much so that no Prussian might offer a German a mug of mead unless he had himself taken the first sip.

Moreover, what happened in Germany almost at the beginning of our time scale when Arminius the Cheruskan, educated and trained in Rome, vanquished the Roman legions, was very nearly repeated in 1261, when Prussian noblemen, educated in German monasteries, were ready to beat their masters with their own weapons. The imminent danger was recognized by one German knight who invited them to his castle and then burned it down over their heads. But the flames of the Castle of Lenzenberg became a signal for a general uprising against the Germans, lasting ten dreadful years in which German rule in Prussia was almost at the point of disappearing. Only under the Land Marshal Konrad von Thierberg did the tide turn again in favor of the Teutonic Knights in 1271. But another decade had to pass before German rule was once again established and firmly consolidated.

The uprising marked a turning point in the attitude of the Teutonic Knights toward the natives. Whereas so far, in spite of their arrogance and occasional excesses, they had been prepared to deal with the individual tribes, conclude treaties and end feuds by elaborate peace agreements, they now demanded complete and utter submission. Large numbers of the Prussian nobility were reduced to serfs, while potentially dangerous communities were deported from their native villages and re-settled in regions where they might be less harmful. Feudal obligations were imposed on them in their full severity. The system of centralized administration, introduced in Europe first by Emperor Frederick II, was adapted by the Teutonic Knights and put into operation throughout Prussia. To the natives only possessory rights were granted but not those of a proprietor. These were reserved for the influx of colonists.

In the long run this policy led to complications with Prussia's most powerful neighbor Poland, especially after the Order had established its dominance over Danzig. The first Grand Master to reside in the Marienburg at Elbing, Siegfried von Feuchtwangen decided in 1309 to place great emphasis upon the further consolidation of the territories of the Order: in his view the limits of expansion had been reached. But the threat of Prussia to the Poles was too serious to be ignored. They attacked the knights in typical medieval battle style and were defeated. After that the Order resumed the policy of aggressive expansion. During this period, between 1329 and 1382, a period in which the order reached the zenith of its secular power, it was a particular point of pride to serve as a knight in Prussia not only for Germans but for many members of Europe's warrior nobility, such as Henry Bolingbroke or Jean Bousicaut.

Warlike activities and the spread of the Gospel were not the Order's only business. Rising corn prices made the region's crop highly attractive, thus providing a powerful incentive for increased cultivation of the land and further territorial expansion. This is the time when the office of the *Tressler* and *Grosschaeffer* gained great influence. The Order introduced a principle hitherto unknown in the financial practice of the European states, namely the separation of the budget of the state from that of the Order. The *Ordensstaat* prospered at a time when the knights of Imperial Germany took to making the land routes of commerce unsafe. With the growing importance of the cash nexus the Order was quite prepared to have feudal services commuted into money payments.

The intellectual development of the Order during the fourteenth century is hardly worth discussing. There were Grand Masters who could neither read nor write. A law school at Marienburg soon withered away into obscurity. The suggestion of founding a university at Kulm was never acted upon. Indeed,

Crow and battering ram.

CROW.

monks belonging to orders of intellectual distinction such as the Benedictines were not tolerated on the territory of the Order at all. The Cistercian monks were tolerated only on account of the part they had played in the past. On the whole the Order preferred monks from the mendicant orders. The single lasting impression of the arts was the Order's architecture, which included its castles, and in particular the Marienburg, completed under one of the Grand Masters, Winrich von Kniprode. This vast Gothic brick structure is symbolic of the entire architecture of the Order. Its stylistic severity exudes the spirit of a military state, Gothic architecture devoid of the more sophisticated refinements which this style achieved in France and England. If

Above. *Two combatant knights* (Tristan et Yseult *by Maître Lucès, fifteenth century*).

Left. *Tournament armor for man and horse.*

Below. *Helmets and visors for tournaments (*Traité de la Forme et Devis comme on fait les Tournois *by René d'Anjou, fifteenth century*).*

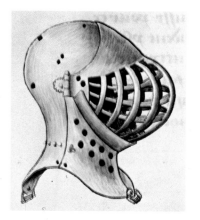

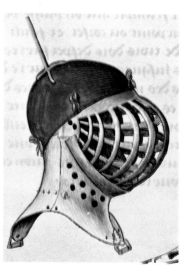

Knights engaged in a tilting match.

anything characterized it then, it was the spirit of the functional. If constrasts in attitude are expressed in architectural styles, then one need only look at the Hermannsburg on the west bank of the Narva and opposite it, the Ivangorod, at Novgorod on the east bank: the one challenging, aggressive and symbolic of the advance of Occidental Christian culture; the other of low structure, essentially defensive in appearance, nestling into the countryside rather than dominating it.

The Teutonic Order had conquered, but it also began to rest upon its laurels. It no longer cultivated the interests that had once existed between the Order and the immigrants who had settled and cultivated the country. The Order consisting of celibate monks had institutional but not personal roots in the land. Its members became estranged from their own people, in particular those living in the cities. Even members of the landed gentry who were not members of the Order believed themselves to be living under a hard, strictly centralized regime. Peasants saw their way of economic development blocked by what were taken to be the Order's restrictive policies. Gradually they began to turn for support to those who had formerly threatened them, the Poles and the Lithuanians. Pomerania too, fearing the dominance of the Order, looked toward Poland. The territory of the Order was about to be cut off from its hinterland, and thus with its lines of communication with the Reich.

Not that the Reich was much concerned with the problems facing the Order. Prussia was far away; there were problems enough without it. But after Poles and Lithuanians had concluded an alliance, the Grand Master, Ulrich von Jungingen, staked all on one card. With an army of almost 50,000 men, one-third of which was on horseback, supported by artillery which in the final analysis rendered the basic function of knighthood obsolete, he confronted the Poles and Lithuanians on the 15 July 1410. The Grand Master left the initiative to the enemy, deciding to fight a defensive-offensive battle. Once the Teutonic Knights had formed their order of battle within sight of the Poles, they stayed put and waited. The Germans were strong in cross-bows and in their artillery which was positioned in front of the cavalry. When the Poles attacked, the German infantry armed with crossbow and archers immediately achieved success against

the left wing of the Lithuanians who quickly retreated. But at the very center where the main force met, the Germans fared disastrously. A sudden and prolonged rain shower reduced the effect of the artillery pieces to insignificance as the gunpowder failed to ignite. In addition the Teutonic Knights adhered to traditional obsolete tactics, while the Poles concentrated their attack at one point of the German front, broke through and then with their numerical superiority of 3:1 engulfed the army of the Teutonic Order and defeated it. Among the dead was the Grand Master.

Tannenberg was not the end of the Prussian state of the Teutonic Order, but its beginning. Several more engagements followed, until the combined pressure exerted by military defeat, internal dissension within the Order and the German settlers of Prussia in town and country compelled the Order to submit. By the Peace of Thorun in 1466, Prussia became a vassal state of Poland.

Military disaster had its parallel in the economic field. The agrarian crisis which in Germany occurred during the middle of the fourteenth century and lasted for more than a hundred years, caused a serious decline in the price of wheat, while at the same time wages and prices of manufactured goods increased. Most seriously affected by this crisis were the lower ranks of the nobility, insofar as this group derived its income from the rents of tenant farmers. A strong inflationary tendency made it, on the one hand, easy for the peasants to pay their dues, and on the other hand more difficult for the nobility to live on fixed rents. The Teutonic Order as a whole was seriously affected by this, and in Prussia, whose economic base lay on the export of wheat, impoverishment set in. For the same reason the other branches of the Order were unable to inject financial aid into their Prussian branch.

Eastward expansion of German and European knighthood had come to an end. They were the last of the truly medieval knights. A century later, during the Reformation when the last Grand Master decided to secularize the land of the Order, the *Deutschritterorden* in Prussia also came to an end. What remained was the state of Prussia.

HERALDRY

True heraldry involves the hereditary use of an arrangement of charges or devices centered on a shield. The concept originated in the feudal society of the High Middle Ages in western Europe.

Many forceful arguments and categorical statements defining the exact nature of the origin of heraldry have been offered and yet the exact purpose for which it was intended remains obscure. Much favored is the argument that heraldry owes its existence to the need for identification in battle and this is likely to have been a contributory factor. However, it must not be forgotten that the flag in various forms existed long before the advent of *true* heraldry in the twelfth century. Flags flying high above the battlefield were and continued to be far more effective for identification purposes and rallying points than any device worn on a shield and borne close to the ground. Furthermore, civilians for centuries used heraldic symbols on personal property, particularly on seals, and this influence must not be overlooked. To suggest that the only purpose of heraldry was military would anticipate its decline and ultimate extinction

Above. *Armorial Bearings of Thomson; the use of vert or green was seldom found in the Middle Ages. Its failure to contrast with the countryside was doubtless responsible for this lack of favor (Property of Mr J C Thomson).*

Left. *The French Dauphin, later King Louis XI, painted c 1450; he incorporates the dolphin in his Arms and Crest as a punning allusion to his style or title. The use of puns has always been favored in heraldry (The Hyghalmen Roll, College of Arms ms).*

Corona granducale

Above. *Armorial Bearings of the Devonshire family of St Leger exemplify the use of quarterings and supporters. The 'sinister' supporter is a male gryphon, a monster peculiar to English heraldry (College of Arms ms).*

Left. *Armorial Bearings of the Italian family of Medici: the mantling is lined with vair, a fur made from the back and belly skins of a species of European squirrel. These skins are shown alternately blue-black and white. The confusion between vair and the French word* verre *gave rise to the celebrated error of Cinderella's glass slippers (Taken from* Pompeo Litta*).*

with the disappearance of medieval warfare. This did not happen; the Battle of Bosworth in 1485 and the start of the Tudor period ushered in perhaps the richest and most creative periods of English heraldry. Thus factors other that its practical use in medieval warfare must be sought.

In 1127 King Henry I of England invested his son-in-law, Geoffrey Plantagenet, with a blue shield charged with little gold lions. This shield was used by Geoffrey's grandson, William Earl of Salisbury, which indicates that its hereditary nature was well-established. The investing of Geoffrey Plantagenet is generally regarded as the first known instance of *recorded* heraldry in Europe. The significance of the event is that it coincides with the sudden explosive advances made by European civilization and known as the Twelfth Century Renaissance. The sheer exuberance of spirit and self-confidence inspired by this movement was manifested in a delight in visual decoration which found an obvious outlet on the personal shields of individual knights. It is perhaps with this spirit rather than with military tactics that the real origin of heraldry should be sought.

In the half century between the First and Second Crusades, instances of heraldry occur almost simultaneously in several countries of Western Europe. Undoubtedly the Crusader played an important part in the later development of heraldry, but it was the Tournament which provided the background for the initial meetings, and the resultant interchange of ideas. Tournaments were occasions admirably suited for that self-confidence and pageantry so characteristic of the Twelfth Century Renaissance and thus served to encourage the beginning and growth of heraldry.

The first Shields of Arms were essentially simple. Many

Sir Thomas de Montacute, Earl of Salisbury, knight of the Garter, who died in 1428, and his wife Eleanor Holand. Sir Thomas greatly distinguished himself in the Anglo-French wars of the early fifteenth century (Wrythe Garter Book, Buccleugh ms).

knights adopted unadorned stripes or crosses, which may well have owed their origin to bands of metal or boiled leather which served to strengthen the wooden shield and so offered an obvious surface for paint. Others were not content with the abstract, and so, for reasons which can only be guessed, chose a specific object such as a lion. Thus King Richard I, the first English monarch known to have made use of heraldry, is believed to have placed on his shield two rampant lions facing each other. These lions appeared again on his first Great Seal which he lost during his captivity in Germany. In about 1195 Richard replaced the two lions with three golden lions on a red field, which ever since have remained the Royal Arms of England.

With the proliferation of Arms among the knightly classes of western Europe, groups of families connected by blood or feudal tenure began to incorporate the same charge or device in their Arms. These charges were tinctured differently, arranged in a new fashion or combined with other charges to ensure that the Arms of each family in the group was distinctive in its own right. One well-known example of this is the golden wheat-sheaf or garb of the family of Meschines of Cheshire, which also features in the Arms of many other Cheshire families.

During the second half of the thirteenth century individual knights began to acquire more than one Shield of Arms. The additional Arms were nearly always obtained through a favorable marriage to an heiress. The importance attached to the wife's Arms seems unlikely to rest with the wife herself but rather with the lands she conveyed to her husband. Heraldry had therefore obtained a *territorial* significance.

This new development gave rise to several experiments as attempts were made to combine several Arms. The grouping together of the devices on separate shields was adequate and aesthetically pleasing for example, with seals. Nonetheless it failed to satisfy the desire to incorporate all the Arms on a single *shield*. This difficulty was overcome by taking selected elements from two separate Arms to create a new Arms to be placed on, for example, one shield. This process was known as compounding. In this way the Arms of de Bohun Earls of Hereford, came to consist of the bends, attributed to earlier Earls of Hereford, set between six lions attributed to the earlier lions of Geoffrey

Plantagenet. Such a process worked well for bringing together the Arms of two families but clearly the amalgamation of a greater number presented problems of design. Furthermore, some recognizable hereditary elements stood a good chance of being lost altogether. The answer lay with quartering.

Quartering was devised at the end of the thirteenth century and gradually all other experiments were abandoned in its favor. In quartering all the Arms are placed on a single shield which is divided in four quarters. If the Arms of two families are involved, the most important, usually the paternal Arms, is placed in the first *or* fourth quarters and the lesser Arms in the second and third. With the Arms of three or four families, the paternal Arms are placed in the first and fourth quarters with the other two in the second and third in order of their acquisition. If more 'quarterings' are subsequently required, the shield can be divided again to accommodate any number of Arms.

As might be expected, the early years of heraldry witnessed something of a free-for-all. Knights adopted devices as their fancy moved them; some degree of regulation became necessary. Moreover the adoption of Arms was considered a manifestation of gentility and it was necessary to have some form of supervision to prevent the assumption of Arms by commoners. Another problem was that as the simple geometrical and other more obvious devices were adopted one by one, more complex designs were appearing. It was desirable that some rules be set down to govern design generally and to facilitate the deciphering of Arms by the onlooker.

Heraldry took its name from the herald. Like heraldry itself, the origin of the herald is obscure. Early references in the twelfth

century nearly always connect heralds with the Tournament, proclaiming this event, announcing the name of the combatants on entry to the lists and acting as masters of ceremonies. These activities necessitated a special knowledge of the Arms of the participants. It is therefore likely that it was the heralds who devised the rules and regulations which developed in the thirteenth century. The earliest known treatises on heraldry date from the fourteenth century and many authors of these treatises are known to be heralds. From the fourteenth century also come the earliest references to cases heard in the Court of Chivalry arising from unconnected persons bearing identical Arms. This court remains in existence today.

Early examples of specific grants of Arms by an English king date from the reign of King Richard II. By the end of the fourteenth century self-assumption of heraldic Arms had come to evoke disfavor. In 1417 King Henry V proclaimed that no persons should bear Arms unless by inheritance or by the grant of some person having the requisite authority. Such authority was vested in the senior heralds or Kings of Arms.

As the feudal system died away and the Middle Ages came to an end, heraldry experienced an upsurge in the number of grants due to the increasing number of new Tudor gentry. At the same time it captured the spirit of the new Renaissance in a flamboyance of design unknown in previous centuries. This trend was suddenly broken in the later Tudor period when a return to simplicity was effected only to be reversed again some 150 years afterwards with the complexities of Hanoverian heraldry. Heraldic designs of the Victorians often reached a level considered by many today as little more than ill-composed clutter. Twentieth century heraldry has once more placed the emphasis on simplicity and many new grants are surprisingly medieval in appearance.

Left. *Early Tudor Armorial Bearings; the complex designs contrast with the simplicity of those of the early Middle Ages (College of Arms ms).*

Left. *Ladies watching tournament. The tournament was a popular form of medieval entertainment and was often put on to celebrate special occasions (Traité de la Forme et Devis comme ou fait les Tournois by René d'Anjou, fifteenth century).*

Above. *The recording of medieval Armorial Bearings was made in Rolls of Arms. Originals of these manuscripts are rare; more frequent are copies made in the sixteenth and seventeenth centuries. (Fenwick's Roll of Arms Temp HV and HVI, College of Arms ms).*

To provide a full account of the technicalities of heraldry with its rules and vocabulary is beyond the scope of space available here but the basic features can be covered quite briefly and will serve to explain the examples depicted here.

Armorial Bearings consist of several component parts – the principal factor is the arrangement of charges or devices set on the shield and known as the Arms. In the thirteenth century it became fashionable to place the Arms on a surcoat, hence the term *Coat of Arms* which has colloquially been extended to embrace the Armorial Bearings as a whole.

During the fourteenth century the practice of placing an object modeled in wood or boiled leather on the helm (helmet) developed; this is known as the crest. The buckles or straps attaching the crest to the helm were hidden from view by either a coronet or a wreath of twisted silk encircling the helm. From

the latter there also flowed the mantle a cloth originally intended as protection from the heat of the sun. Supporters or figures standing on either side of the shield appeared in the fifteenth century. Because of their comparatively late arrival on the heraldic scene they have been largely confined to a two dimensional medium and seldom modeled in the round or animated in the form of human beings dressed or disguised appropriately. The use of supporters was always limited; today they are restricted to Peers of the Realm, Knights Grand Cross and important corporate bodies. Mottoes, evolved from battle cries, and badges, additional devices borne by retainers or followers, are further aspects of heraldry.

The most frequent geometric charges found in heraldry are sometimes termed the Ordinaries. Although there has always been disagreement as to which devices qualify for this term, most writers would not dispute the inclusion of the *chief* (a broad horizontal band) running across the center of the shield, the *pale* (a vertical band running down the center of the shield), the *bend* (a diagonal band running through the center of the shield), the *chevron* (similar to a sergeant's stripe), the *cross*, and the *saltire* (a St Andrew's cross).

The tinctures used in heraldry comprise the colors: *gules* (red), *azure* (blue), *sable* (black), *vert* (green), with the three additional varieties of *purpure* (purple), *tenne* (orange) and *murrey* (reddish-purple), and the metals *or* (synonymous with gold) and *argent* (normally represented by white). It is one of the fundamental principles of heraldry that a metal is never placed upon a metal nor a color upon a color. Various forms of fur and other exotica are also found.

The variety of charges or devices which can be used is un-limited. The Middle Ages drew heavily on the animal world largely ignoring flora with a few exceptions such as the rose, fleur-de-lis and cinquefoil. Later on, it made use of charges which were suggested by the knightly environment of Tournament or battlefield such as swords, arrows, horseshoes, spurs and the maunch or lady's sleeve.

Once the above terms are grasped, an understanding of blazon or the description of any Armorial Bearings can begin. A few technical terms must not be allowed to confuse; it is always the intention of any good blazon to describe as clearly and succinctly as possible the ingredients of the Armorial Bearings under observation.

Above. *A tournament (Cotton Nero ms).*

Below. *Quartering of Arms of France and England.*

TRANSFORMATION OF WARFARE

The Battle of Crécy, 1346: flying their banners aloft, the French and English engage in battle (Chroniques de Froissart, fourteenth century).

Largely because of the Crusades profound military changes were taking place. They precipitated a boom in castle building in central and western Europe, until in the fourteenth century the feudal castle dominated every region. They had also fully opened up the Mediterranean again and restored the flow of commerce. This was reflected in the growing wealth of the towns, which helped them to gain greater political consciousness. In part, their loans had financed the Crusades and they began to recruit their own militias. How effectively they could be used against the feudal host the Battle of the Golden Spurs amply demonstrated. Yet the increasing wealth of both town and country, through the revival of commerce and the price rises during the fourteenth century, had rather adverse effects upon the feudal system, based as it was economically on static feudal duties and services in money or kind. The rising need for hard cash by the nobility caused them to commute many of the duties and services into money payment. But even commutation was a static feudal fee which with increasing prosperity the peasant found easier to pay while King, vassals and knights found it increasingly difficult to make ends meet with a static income in a world of rising prices. Hence the monarchies of Europe had two alternatives open to them. First, the extra sums needed for their expenditure could be raised from additional taxation and from loans raised from cities and merchant corporations or from private bankers. Such loans had their price, not only in money but in political terms. The lenders could and did put forward their own demands. In that way the German Hanseatic League in England obtained considerable privileges from Edward III who needed all the cash he could raise for the conquest of France. But even more important it weighted power more in favor of the House of Commons than it had done in the fourteenth century. In France it brought greater power to the parliaments until the advent of Francis I. Second, the monarchs could raise increased revenue by greater

Above. *Edward III (1312–77). From his effigy in Westminster Abbey, London.*
Left. *Edward III met at Amiens by Philip VI the other contender to the French throne (Cotton Nero ms).*

centralization in all spheres of government. In Germany it was not so much the *Reichstag* which gained by this process but those territorial princes who within their principalities could through various reforms adjust to the changed environment by a greater degree of administrative and economic centralization. The Teutonic Knights had given a splendid example of this. But while the first alternative largely took away powers from the crown with little sign that this erosion of royal power would cease, the second alternative implied the rise of the modern state, the product of the conflict of the princes with two primary forces.

The princes had to acquire unrestricted access to financial resources. In the final analysis they could not afford to rely on the resources in the possession of private financial monopoly. Those monopoly holders, families like the Fuggers and the Welsers in whose hands economic power was concentrated by the end of the fifteenth and early sixteenth centuries, could bridge the endemic gap between the declining feudal revenues of the prince and his actual requirements if it lay in their interest. Jakob Fugger had no qualms in writing blandly to Emperor Charles V: 'Without my aid Your Imperial Majesty would hardly have obtained the Roman Crown.' In the long run the majority of Europe's princes were not prepared to commit themselves into that state of dependence, either on monopoly holders or representative assemblies and instead entered the path towards centralization which led to the princely absolutist state.

The second force which they had to confront and over which they needed to obtain control was the power of the traditional estates of the realm, the political and social structure of the Middle Ages: the nobility, the church and the towns. In many cases the estates had succeeded in twisting medieval feudal tradition into something akin to democracy, insisting that public power resided in the hands of those strata of society which in fact formed the primary components of the state. What the prince had to achieve was the transfer of all power into his own

Below. *England and the English Possessions in France, 1154.*
Right. *Battle of Sluys, 1340: Edward III won a brilliant naval victory.*

hands, by turning public power into personal private property, property which had previously been run more or less together, or against one another by the estates of the realm, the holders of financial monopoly and the princes.

This successful transfer of power required changes in several directions, only one of which affects the discussion here, the change in the field of warfare, meaning the 'nationalization' of armies. However, this was a process stretching over several centuries, but at each point it marked a further decline of the feudal system. The need for mercenaries was one of the early signs, mercenaries hired not simply because one wanted to increase the feudal host, but simply because the traditional feudal host no longer met the necessities of prolonged warfare;

Incident from the Battle of Crécy, 1346 (Cotton Nero ms).

Above. *The Black Prince
(1330–76) being invested with the
Duchy of Aquitane, 1363 (Cotton
Nero ms).*

Right. *The Tree of Battles: the
Hundred Years' War.*

Far right. *The coronation of Henry
IV, 1399.*

Below. *The funeral of Richard II,
1400, son of the Black Prince who
was deposed by Henry IV
(1367–1413).*

for example, the Hundred Years' War between France and England.

In France the Capetian line had become extinct. King Edward III as the nephew of the last King put forward his claims to the French Crown against Philip of Valois. It was foreseeable that the campaign would be a formidable venture requiring capital resources not obtainable within the realm of England. He concluded numerous treaties with German princes including the Emperor, Ludwig the Bavarian. In addition to the sums obtained from Parliament and the loan from the Hanse, he granted export licenses to many of the German Rhenish princes to ship wool to England in lieu of payment. The abbeys were compelled to make their contributions. Yet the army with

Below. *The siege of Calais, 1347.*
Right. *Guy de Greville taken prisoner at* Château d'Evreux.

Above. *Funeral attire of the Black Prince (d 1376) in Canterbury Cathedral.*

which he invaded France in 1339 was not a very impressive one, and that year brought no decision. The Anglo-German army quickly broke up and Edward was compelled to return to England. To muster again an almost exclusively feudal army no longer seemed possible. Apart from his own native feudal nucleus he had to turn to the recruitment of mercenary troops, who in the absence of ready cash were given the right to plunder in conquered territory. Bands of veteran mercenaries were

recruited serving on 'indentures,' under professional officers, English and foreign. Among the mercenaries could also be found specialists for whom there was no place within the feudal hosts such as sappers, miners and those who constructed and worked the siege engines. The mercenaries equipped themselves, an important factor in the fourteenth century which saw the full development of armor plate, an enormously costly item. And mercenaries could remain indefinitely in the field, as compared to the forty days, extended on many occasions to three months, of the feudal host.

When in 1340 Edward achieved a naval victory over the French fleet giving him naval supremacy, he could land wherever he desired. He chose Normandy in 1346. Meanwhile the French had turned towards Edward's possessions in France such as Gascony. Almost without hindrance he could capture Norman towns and plunder them. When the French forces turned towards him, Edward decided to move towards Flanders which was allied with him. He crossed the Seine with a degree of urgency, because the captains of the naval vessels had decided to return home, which cut Edward off from his English base and made it therefore all the more necessary to reach Flanders and with it the support of his ally. At Crécy he met the French army under Philip IV.

Again, figures of the size of the English army are a matter of dispute, estimates ranging between 14,000 and 20,000. What is certain is that the French army, coming in rapid marches from Gascony, was numerically inferior. Rather more important as far as the outcome of the battle is concerned is that a very large contingent of Edward's forces were longbow foot soldiers.

The history of the longbow is shrouded in obscurity. The

Right. *John of Gaunt (1340–99), fourth son of Edward III, returning from one of his numerous missions to France, 1373.*

Below. *Pikeman's helmet.*

Left. *Battle scene during the Hundred Years' War: horsemen versus foot soldiers (Vigiles de Charles VII, fifteenth century).*

Below. *After a short period of peace following the siege of Calais, war broke out again in 1355; and at the Battle of Poitiers, 1356, the Black Prince won his second great victory over the French. (Chroniques de Froissart, fourteenth century).*

Bottom. *Scene from the Battle of Agincourt, 25 October 1415 in which King Henry V of England resoundingly defeated the French. (Vigiles de Charles VII, fifteenth century).*

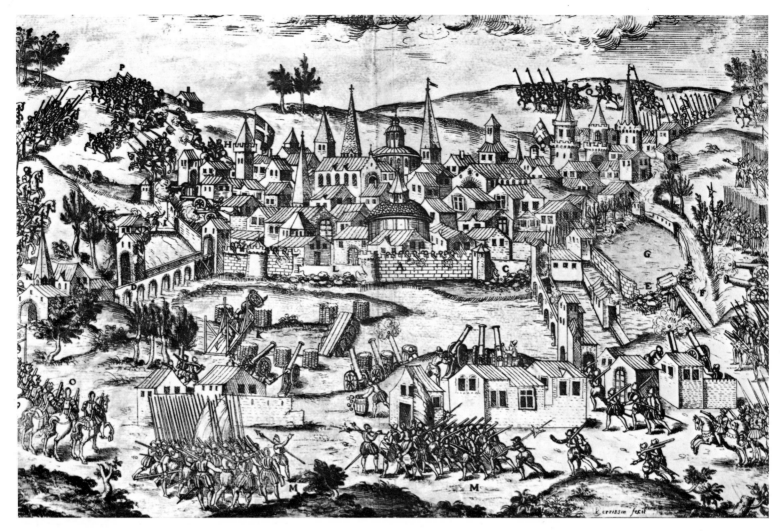

Above. *Pike transformed into halberd – typical of the period. The knightly host on the left and the artillery on the left.*

Left. *Expedition of the Duke of Bourbon (*Chroniques de Froissart, *fourteenth century).*

Right. *Fourteenth-century armor.*

bow as such has been in use for centuries. As a weapon we have met it on many occasions before. But that it was not held in very high esteem in England is shown by the fact that it is not listed in the Assize of Arms of 1181. Perhaps it was not the weapon of a 'gentleman.' The crossbow derived directly from the short-bow was a weapon which Richard the Lionhearted very much admired and he went to considerable expense to hire mercenaries skilled in its use. This seems to suggest that he possessed no previous familiarity with it. The longbow appears to have been used first by the Welsh; the difference between the short and longbow is that the former is drawn to the breast and the latter is drawn to the ear and has both a greater range and a higher velocity. The crossbow was more difficult to load and therefore required more time; that problem did not exist with the longbow. During the Welsh wars of Edward I the long-bow established itself firmly in the English army.

At Crécy there was no reason why the traditional knight's battle should not have been fought, except that Edward III decided to deploy his weapons in a way which the Middle Ages had not seen before. Previously infantry soldiers armed with bows, pikes and swords had fulfilled a purpose subordinate and auxiliary to that of the feudal host. Edward decided upon a change. To insure that his firing line of longbowmen remained in combat continuously right to the last moment, he ordered his knights to dismount and to take their place between the long-bowmen, the pikemen and the other infantry. He wanted to give his infantry the kind of moral backbone which the medieval infantry had so far been lacking, and that backbone was best supplied if the knight himself would fight on foot, important when one bears in mind the eternal grudge of the infantry, that they were butchered while the lords on horse could ride away.

Philip unwittingly aided Edward's scheme by having his

Left. *Henry V (1387–1422) of England.*

Below. *Battle of Crécy, 1346.*

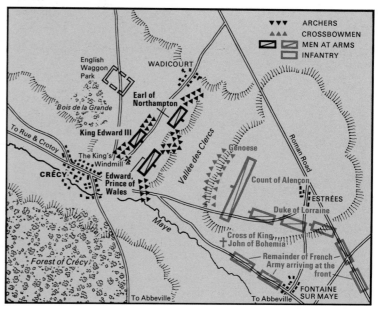

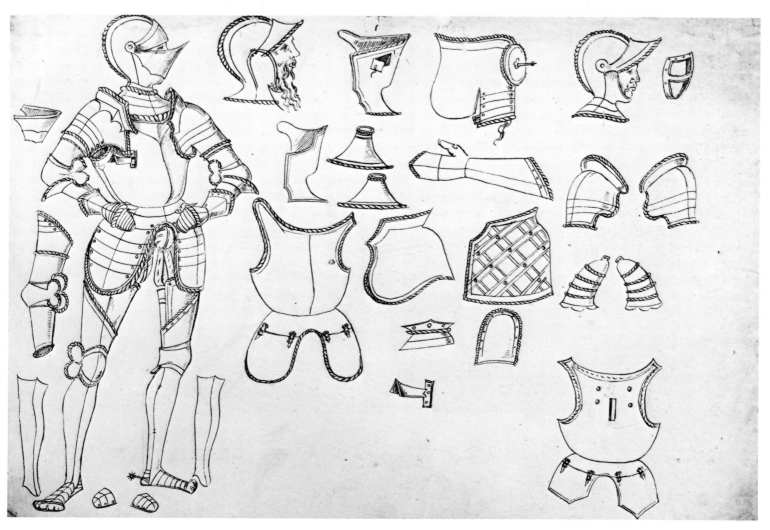

Above and left.
*The siege of Orleans,
1428 (*Vigiles de Charles VII,
fifteenth century).

*Right. Battle of Agincourt, 1415: with archers to the fore and the cavalry massed behind (*Chroniques d'Enguerrand de Monstrelet, *early fifteenth century).*

*Below. Joan of Arc (c 1412–1431) directing the attack on Compiègne, 1430 during which she was taken prisoner. She was subsequently burned on charges of witchcraft (*Vigiles de Charles VII, *fifteenth century).*

Below right. The Hundred Years' War: Battle of Patay, 1429 *(*Chroniques de Charles VII, *fifteenth century).*

knights attack in individual contingents and not *en masse.* Edward's forces, positioned on a minor height, could see them come while the short uphill stretch slowed down the attacking French. Many of them were killed or unhorsed by the long-bow before reaching the actual battle-line and those who did were quickly dealt with by the knights on foot and the pikes. A crisis occurred only once on the English right wing, commanded by Edward's son, the Black Prince, then sixteen years of age. Reinforcements dispatched by his father from the center restored the situation. When Philip had his own horse shot from under him, he realized that he could not conquer and left the battlefield. Among those killed were numerous famous noblemen and over 1200 knights.

It was one of the very rare instances when a victory had been achieved purely from a defensive position. It was not the long-bow which had brought victory but the manner in which Edward III had decided to fight the battle, to dismount his feudal host against all canons of tradition and conduct the battle as a combined operation. The French did not lack bravery, but they lacked what was new in battle, the discipline of a closely organized and centrally directed body.

Almost seventy years later Crécy was to be repeated, but with a difference. Henry V had landed in Normandy in 1415 and was making his way towards Flanders. But unlike Edward III he could not cross the Somme. The French prevented this by marching for five days parallel to the English army, then overtaking it and positioning themselves across his path, compelling Henry to attack. In other words, in comparison with Crécy, the position was reversed. Tactically the environment favored the English in a space of about 500 yards near Agincourt. Both sides of the battlefield were heavily wooded. Originally it had not been Henry's plan to attack; the objective was Calais, which by then had become his property. It was the French who forced him into an offensive battle. Approximately 9000 Englishmen faced the French, estimated to have numbered between 4000 and 6000. The French dismounted some of their knights and,

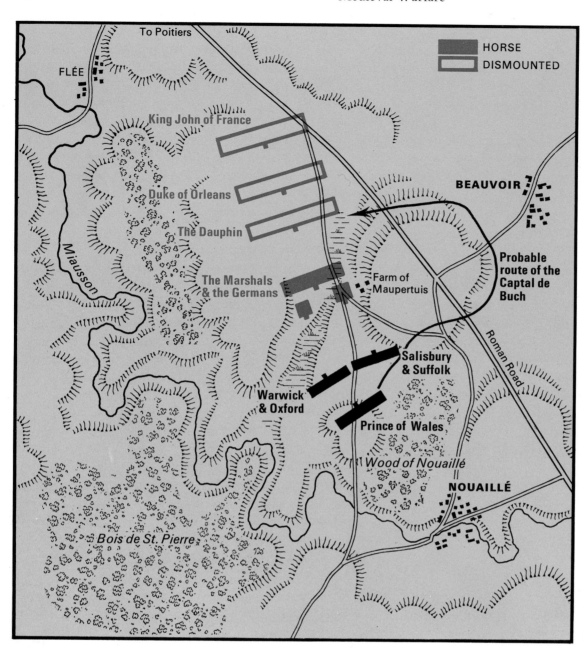

like the English at Crécy, put them with the infantry and crossbowmen. Two contingents of knights remained mounted on each wing.

The largest portion of Henry's army consisted of longbowmen to whom he added his knights, dismounted as at Crécy, but deploying them for the offensive. The French were sadly deficient in bowmen and their crossbows could never match the speed with which the English longbowmen discharged their missiles. Keeping knights and infantry in a tight body Henry's army advanced to a point at which the longbowmen rammed spiked poles into the ground before them, surprising in view of the fact that the French cavalry could have attacked at any moment, and that the poles could have become a hindrance to the English themselves in their advance. Be that as it may, the French left the time unused and the poles can be assumed to have been placed not across the entire front but at the wings, precisely the points opposite which the French mounted knights were positioned. Once that was done the English advanced on foot, using a hail of arrows to provoke the French cavalry into attacking them. The attackers were bloodily repulsed, or run up against the obstacles erected, behind which the longbowmen dispatched them with careful aim. Then English infantry and knights, swords ready, attacked and overwhelmed them. Hindered by their heavy armor the French knights on foot were no match for the lightly armored English on foot.

At Agincourt the principle first deployed by Edward III at Crécy had been applied to the offensive. It would, however, be a gross exaggeration to see in this the transformation of warfare in the fourteenth and fifteenth centuries. Important though they were, they were nevertheless merely stages of a transformation taking place at the end of the sixteenth century. They were the birth-pangs of modern infantry as was the Battle of Courtrai. The old order did not give way all that quickly. There were battles in which knights refused to dismount to do combat and

*Siege scene depicting incendiary
missiles (Detail from the
Firework Book, c 1450).*

Right. *The Knight and the Devil (Painting by Albrecht Dürer 1471–1528.)*

Below. *Helmet, sword, shield and saddle of Henry V. The helmet on the right is Henry VII's.*

had to be forced to do so under penalty of death. English knighthood during the Hundred Years' War proved superior to its opponents because it was more disciplined in the military sense of the term. Though considering itself still a feudal army, it had to break with principles held sacrosanct by medieval knighthood to achieve what it did achieve. The precedent, once established, was on its way to becoming the rule. It even became fashionable for a knight to display his chivalry; to dismount and fight on foot and lead his men—a fashion which perhaps can be considered the root of the modern officer corps.

At a time when the Holy Roman Empire was showing all the signs of rapid decline, matched only in speed by that of the Papacy, out of the Hundred Years' War emerged the national consciousness of two European states, symbolized in France by Joan of Arc and the siege of Orleans and in England by Crécy and Agincourt, which signaled to Europe England's arrival as a military nation. The battles against the Welsh and Scots had taken place on Europe's periphery, and little notice was taken in Europe. But what happened in France could not be overlooked. And for England, at long last, Anglo-Saxon and Norman had fused.

Transformation of warfare had, at its roots, many influences and causes. Cities soon developed to the point where they required their own defenses both in terms of architecture and personnel. Mercenaries came to dominate the entire European military scene until the seventeenth century. In Italy the mercenaries formed close corporations who elected their own leaders or *condottieri*. In other parts they formed marauding bands for hire to the highest bidder. Eventually soldiery became more highly organized and professional (as exemplified by the *Landsknechte* in Germany) but this was not for many years to come.

Piece by piece the old feudal order was breaking apart, and in its place stepped new forms of military organization which corresponded more closely to the political and economic en-

Above. *With lances couched at the ready, the Baron of Normandy and his troops attack.* (Vigiles de Charles VII, *fifteenth century*).

Right. *Hundred Years' War: Henry V storms the walled city of Rouen with cannons during the siege of 1419* (Vigiles de Charles VII, *fifteenth century*).

vironment of the time. The German Empire tried to adjust to this development by recruiting forces consisting of urban mercenaries. But they lacked the cement which had held the Swiss together; they lacked the Swiss fighting morale. Furthermore, they lacked experience as well as the ability to make independent tactical decisions within the context of large armed formation. Towards the end of the fifteenth century greater emphasis was placed on copying the Swiss model rather than adapting what had already become obsolete.

The military system of the feudal age had become obsolete, a fact which was underlined by a bang which came from the first piece of artillery fired with gunpowder. No one knows who invented gunpowder nor precisely when. Whoever the inventor, whatever the date, it was a long time before the first gun made its appearance. The first document dates from February 1326 and authorized the Priors, Gonfalonier and twelve others to appoint persons to superintend the manufacture of a brass cannon and iron balls for the defense of the city of Florence. But cannons were known or had been heard of in England in 1327, and a chronicler of the siege of Metz in 1324 records that cannons were used. But once known, like the printing press, the cannon made rapid progress. Even the Scots used it at the siege of Stirling in 1339. The Germans were using it in 1331 at the siege of Cividale in Friaul, and in 1342 King Alfonso of Castile made use of artillery at the siege of Algeciras. Guns are known to have been used by Edward III in the Hundred Years' War, but precise information about their use is lacking. They were

Above. Scaling the walls of a city during an attack (Chroniques de Charles VII, *fifteenth century*).
Below. Besieging a fortress with longbows and cavalry.

not evident at Crécy nor seventy years later at Agincourt. Although guns could have fulfilled many functions at this time, they seem to have been predominantly used for sieges, not very effectively at first as at Rouen and Meaux. The one successful siege of the Hundred Years' War in which artillery was used was that of Harfleur by Henry V. But it is only from the middle of the fifteenth century that the new weapon began its triumphal march.

CITIES
IN WARFARE

Battle scene (Chroniques de Froissart, *fourteenth century*).

The cities of the successor states of the Roman Empire during the Early Middle Ages were only a shadow of their former selves. The decline of commerce, partly the result of the Islamic invasions, partly due to the lack of commercial institutions among the Germanic tribes, caused many cities to decay, even to disappear. After the Romans had withdrawn from England, society regressed dreadfully. The same can be said of Gaul and Rome's former possessions along the Rhine and south of the river Main. The imperial city of Trier, cut off from its Roman lifeline, became a ghost town as did most of the cities in Gaul. Whatever urban culture had existed, declined, and the economic base of European society was until the end of the eleventh century purely agrarian, its aim subsistence and not the production of surplus. What trade existed was mainly in the form of barter, because no domain could live exclusively on its own produce. Wine was imported from the south, corn exported from the north. In addition there were the weekly markets, at which goods were exchanged, at which artisans sold their boots, weavers their cloth, in return for victuals. Where a craft was particularly highly developed, such as weaving in the coastal regions of Flanders, demand went further afield, across the sea to England, and up the rivers into the interior of the European mainland.

The only exception to this general economic condition of Europe occurred in southern Italy and Venice. The harbors of the Campagna, Apulia, Calabria and Sicily still maintained regular connections with Constantinople. In exchange for wine and corn, the Italian vessels returned with the manufactures from the east. But soon Venice overtook them all. The city, at first a settlement of Longobards, built upon a collection of islands, originally based its trade on the two immediately available commodities, fish and salt, both derived from the sea. The cities nearest Venice had their own subsistence economies and had little use for the surplus produce of Venice. The major market was Constantinople and Venice's trade with it quickly overtook that of its southern Italian competitors. Without actually breaking with Constantinople, Venice became a free city, free from Byzantine suzerainty. Under its *Doge* or Duke it became a commercial republic. Since the tenth century its politics had been determined solely by its trading interests. It

Below. *Aerial view of the fortified medieval city of Naarden.*

achieved naval supremacy in the Adriatic, by clearing it of pirates off the Dalmatian coast, and once the Normans had conquered southern Italy and Sicily it prevented their further expansion into and settlement along the Greek coast. In 1082 the city received the privileges of buying whatever goods it needed throughout the Byzantine Empire and of selling all its produce there. The factors favoring this development came from outside Europe, but it was a development paralleled on a rather smaller scale along the coasts of the North Sea and the Baltic, especially among the Scandinavian countries which traded furs and corn, and developed a commercial route straight through Russia to the Black Sea and from there with Constantinople. What at first were armed raids became trains of merchants protected by armed men. Cities on their route such as Kiev prospered. Venice operated its overland trade routes across the Brenner Pass into southern Germany and from there on two main arteries, one leading to northwestern Europe, the other directly west, across the heights of the Black Forest into the plain of the Rhine and into France. It was a development stretching over three centuries in which those cities that lay along the trading routes revived while others were left behind.

Above. *A tenth-century interpretation of the story of David and Goliath showing Byzantine warriors armed like Roman legionaries.*

That in fact many cities did survive and that in addition new ones were created is in no small measure also due to an old church ruling which determined that bishoprics could be erected only in cities. Wherever the cathedral spires of a bishopric rose to the sky, the surrounding environment was populous and its abodes were numerous. All had to be protected from the dangers lurking outside the city walls. Bishoprics and abbeys, the great sponsors and developers of medieval culture, attracted to their residences the skilled work of the free, for whoever resided in a city lost, at least within the area of the control of the city, the burdens of serfdom. The relics of a saint made the church in which they were deposited. The city therefore became a focus of attraction. Pilgrims came from near and far, spent what they could spend, and provided further impetus to the economic life of the city. City markets were frequented and finally dominated by the merchants, who found the best protection within the confines of a city.

The same occurred where a King or one of his major vassals

Below. *Armored horsemen* (Histoire du Graal, *thirteenth century*).

Above. *Twelfth-century ms illustrating the life of St Guthlac showing warriors clad in hauberks of mail and helmets with nasals.*

Below. *Eleventh-century Catalan ms depicting contemporary warriors fighting like Saracens.*

Below right. *Thirteenth-century battle.*

had established his residence, such as Aix-la-Chapelle, Nancy, Goslar or Ingenheim. Goslar, for instance, originally a protectorate burg on Germany's eastern marches, through the Saxon and Salian Kings and Emperors, became an imperial residence endowed with all the splendors of late Romanesque and early Gothic architecture of the Middle Ages. The walling-in of cities was an immediate response to the invasions by the Norsemen and the Magyars. Even outlying buildings and establishments, like abbeys, were surrounded by protective walls. But the city containing a bishopric or the residence of a powerful magnate in the early twelfth century bore little resemblance to what a city of a later age was eventually to be like. The area within the walls still contained agricultural land and large gardens. Most of the population were still peasants. At this stage most of them were still unfree, owing service to the bishop, abbot, Kings or lesser members of the higher nobility. To them came the free, mainly merchants, artisans, landowners, and the entourage of the magnate. But whether free or unfree, they all enjoyed the protection of a powerful lord who ruled their community. Common interest and daily contact soon blurred the distinctions between the free and the unfree.

A traveler journeying in Germany from Cologne to Hamburg bothered little about the fact that one city was a thousand years older than the other, that one had been fully exposed to the history and the influence of the Roman Empire. What the traveler would notice is a difference in appearance and wealth that distinguished the older cities of the Empire from the younger ones, once commercial life regained its momentum.

In the eastern as well as the western provinces of the former Roman Empire towards the end of the tenth and throughout the eleventh century a process of inner colonization took place, accompanied by a substantial demographic movement in the course of which many of the people of the land moved into the cities which in turn grew bigger. Walls were widened; settlements directly outside the old walls were protected by new outer walls; the core of the old city acquired its suburbs. In this process the landowner within the city had the greatest advantage. He could sell his agricultural land to the prospective builder or simply lease the ground. An able worker could obtain more for his effort in the towns than in the countryside, and if he was unfree, was in a position to earn enough to buy himself freedom. If defense had been one of the reasons to build houses closer together, the growing scarcity of building land was another—one aspect that has many parallels in our present-day society. Soon the extent of cities outgrew their physical ability to protect their inhabitants effectively from attack. The citizens themselves raised their levies, and became, after a fashion, soldiers in times of need. This inevitably implied a bourgeois

Attack towers carried by elephants (Bible of Rhodes, Catalan, tenth or eleventh century).

countervailing force to the lord's feudal levy, the practical results of which became noticeable once lord and citizens clashed. When, during the investiture contest of the eleventh century, Emperor Henry IV was banned and excommunicated by Pope Gregory VII, his sons and the majority of his vassals used the occasion to further their own interests at the expense of those of the Empire. The one opposing force which they had left out of their calculations was the political, economic and military power which the cities had acquired by then. Most of the cities rose in revolt against their lords and sided with the Emperor. In the course of time the burdens of service still resting on the shoulders of the burghers were reduced. The unfree within the cities acquired both the privilege and the right to bestow their property upon their children, and they prevented the lord whose serf had escaped to the city from demanding his return. *Stadtluft macht frei*, the city air makes one free, was the saying.

Of course the cities did not always have it their own way, nor were the interests of their inhabitants always undivided. Flanders was the scene of much urban unrest in the Middle Ages, an unrest closely linked with the politics of the French crown and its vassals. For centuries it had been one of the principal objectives of the French Crown to annex the northern territories bordering on the North Sea to the French crown lands and

Left. Two foot soldiers in armor (Grandes Chroniques de France, fifteenth century).
Below. Battle incident (Tristan et Yseult by Maître Lucès, fifteenth century).

Right. Medieval tournaments with their colorful pageantry were put on as much for the entertainment of the spectators as they were for the training of knights for the battlefield (Chroniques de Froissart, fourteenth century).

Left. *Knights leaving their castle en route for military training (Bodleian ms 264).*

Below. *Mêlée in the lists.*

lance luy auoit faille et pala z chabenet
le suuirent / z Oustra Trist contre les
ditz pala et chabenet / et tous deux
les abati luy emprez lautre

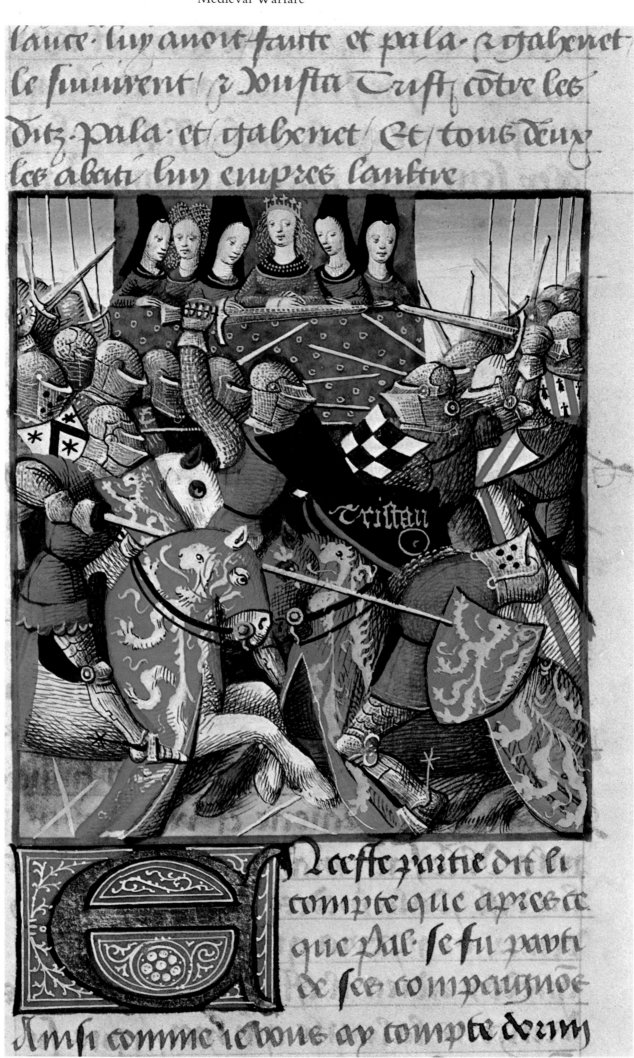

Cn ceste partie dit li
compte que apres ce
que pal se fu parti
de ses compaignoe

Ainsi comme ie bous ay compte derini

Far left. *Tristan engages in a cut-and-thrust with his opponent.*

Left. *A lady onlooker parts the two combatants, Tristan and Sir Galahad (*Tristan et Yseult *by Maître Lucès, fifteenth century).*

Below left. *Mounted knight enveloped in a gambeson richly decorated with heraldic devices.*

acquire a further and strategically well-placed base for the French operations against England. Philip of Alsace was the Count of Flanders who confronted King Philip Augustus of France. At the beginning it was a contest between these two men. But by the twelfth century the Flemish cities had acquired such power and their commercial interests had become so far-flung, that whether they liked it or not their interests were closely tied to those of their prince. But the French Crown exercised its attractions as well, especially to the urban upper class consisting of the merchants, often French-born, who had not been assimilated into their Flemish environment. On the other hand, the artisans and workers of the cities of Flanders feared that the establishment of French dominance would curb, if not eliminate, the liberties they enjoyed. The reign of Countess Margaret in Flanders from 1244 onwards was marked by the favors she showed to the artisans, particularly to the wool workers, while the patrician rulers of the towns, fearing the reduction of their own powers, looked for support from the French Crown. The patrician council of Ghent, which ruled that city until its powers were broken by the Countess, appealed against this to the parliament of Paris. When the Countess died in 1278 and was succeeded by Guy of Dampierre, the ruling oligarchy concluded a formal alliance with the French King, a step very much resented by Guy who now leaned on the lower orders of the town for support. Guy, however, was a vassal of both the French King Philip the Fair as well as the German Emperor. The lawyers of Philip the Fair argued that the alliance was a fully legal instrument on the basis of which France could now appoint its own royal agent in Flanders, an action no sooner suggested than it was implemented. In France Philip had almost completely suppressed the privileges of the communes. In Flanders he pretended to be their supporters—at least until

the moment when he had defeated Guy. The lower orders, or
the commons of the Flemish towns, felt utterly frustrated since
they had been almost within reach of obtaining their ultimate
aim, the removal of oligarchic government. Philip the Fair's
interference re-established their supremacy and caused the commons to take up their cause against the oligarchy to which the
French Crown was added with a vengeance. The supporters
of France, the enemies of the liberties of the people, were label-
led the *Leliaerts*, the men of the lilies, the sword lily being
the symbol of the French monarchy. The struggle between the
privileged and the less privileged, between the rich and the
poor, soon acquired a national perspective in the sense that it
rapidly furthered the growth of a Flemish national consciousness, much in the same way as the Hundred Years' War was to
further national consciousness in both France and England. Or
an even more important analogy is Bohemia, where the Hussite
Wars became the basis of Czech nationalism.

For the commoners, the Lion of Flanders, the symbol of the
banner of the count, became their rallying point. When war did
break out in 1300 between Guy and Philip, Guy was defeated
and imprisoned. Flanders was united with France and a French
governor, Chatillon, was dispatched. Upon his arrival he had
nothing more urgent to do than immediately levy taxation on
the towns to defray the expenses incurred by Philip in his
campaign against Guy. The outcry of the Flemish people was
great. Their champion having been defeated was bad enough,
but to be made to pay for their own suppression caused the
simmering pot to boil over. The commoners rushed to arms,
embittered, emboldened and audacious. French soldiers failed

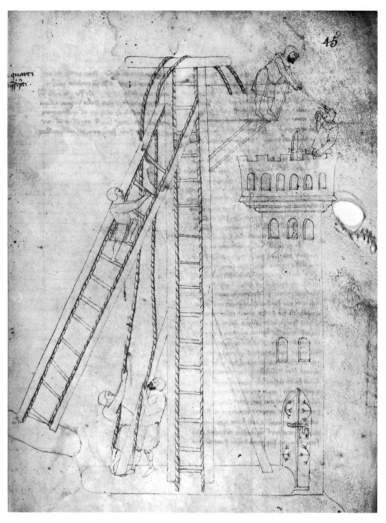

Right. *Mobile tower constructed with rope and ladders.*
Below. *Attack on a walled city (early fourteenth century).*

to restore order. At Bruges, Peter de Coninc, a hitherto unknown weaver, put himself at the head of a conspiracy which struck suddenly and for the French quite unexpectedly during the night of the 17 May 1302. *Schild en vriendt*, shield and friend, was the parole, and everyone unable to pronounce it with a pure Flemish accent was butchered, including the patricians. Throughout Flanders patrician government was overthrown and revolutionary governments were set up.

Having seized power, their problem was to maintain it against an army which Philip dispatched under the command of Robert of Artois. The sons of Guy of Dampierre, John and Guy of Namur, as well as his grandson, William of Jülich, rushed to Flanders, realizing that supporting the urban forces of Flanders represented the only opportunity of regaining their inheritance. Though they spoke only French, their arrival caused great rejoicing and with them at their head the men of Flanders marched into battle against Robert who was aided by the lords from Hainault, Brabant and Luxemburg. The size of the army cannot have included the 7500 horses and 40,000 foot soldiers claimed, but irrespective of that it was a sizable feudal army in which the cavalry dominated, supported by Genoese mercenaries as cross-bowmen. By comparison the army of Flanders was hopelessly destitute of cavalry; Guy of Namur and William of Jülich led infantry levies of burghers. Knights who were few and far between acted as sub-commanders. The nobility of Flanders, believing that they had more to lose than the burghers, was either lukewarm and preferred to sit it out or joined the French.

Robert of Artois crossed the frontier on 2 July and met the Flemings at Courtrai. The Flemings, well-protected by marsh and streams, positioned themselves behind the Groening-hebeke, a small stream running to the river Lys. The Lys and a

Fortified city enclosed by walls to protect it from marauding troops.

Franciscan convent protected their left flank; swampland and ditches the right flank. It was a good position, but only if the Flemings would hold fast to it, because behind them was Courtrai, still in French hands. Their retreat was virtually cut off. Their tactical position was that of a phalanx with a reserve held at the back of the center. A small number were equipped with crossbows, the bulk were armed with iron helmets and breast plates and carried pikes and swords. The pike was more in the nature of a club with a spike at the end and could be used for striking as well as thrusting.

Robert of Artois, deciding that a hundred men on horse are worth a thousand on foot, decided to attack. His crossbowmen advanced against those of the Flemings, who were forced to retire, in the process uncovering the front of their phalanx

Left. *City attacked by warriors using crossbows, catapults and an early example of a cannon (Bodleian ms 264, fourteenth century).*

Below. *Pigeon post was a swift and convenient postal system favored during times of war. Here the sender prepares to release the bird. (Fifteenth-century woodcut reproduced in* Der Soldat in der deutschen Bergangheit, *1899).*

necessitating its withdrawal some distance to get out of range of
the missiles of the Genoese. Robert interpreted this as a general
withdrawal and ordered his feudal host to attack. In so doing,
confusion ensued and when Robert's cavalry arrived at
Groeninghebeke it was rather disorganized. Moreover, the
stream itself was deeper and muddier than had been anticipated,
and the other bank was firm enough to support men on foot but
not firm enough for heavy cavalry. Many were trapped in
bogs, but when finally some semblance of order had been
restored the French found the Flemish phalanx with its weapons
leveled advancing towards them. The knights were now on the
defensive, the impetus of their attack had been broken by the
difficult terrain. The battle was joined and the French were
beaten back to the stream. Robert of Artois now led the main
body which he commanded forward, and the previous spectacle
was repeated. The French knights were slain mercilessly by the
Flemish infantry. Robert himself, dismounted and on his knees,
asked for quarter. None was given. 'We don't understand

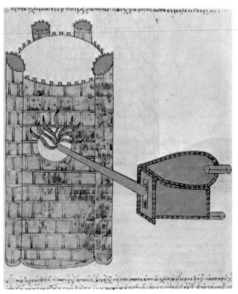

Above. *The burghers of
Calais giving up the keys
of the city* (Chroniques
de Froissart, *fourteenth
century*).

Left. *Eleventh-century
Byzantine machine for
attacking fortress with
hot oil.*

Right. *Warriors scale the
walls of a besieged city
(Bodleian ms, fourteenth
century).*

Far right. *Standard
bearer (Painting by
Albrecht Dürer).*

French,' the Flemings are alleged to have replied to such requests. The confused and struggling masses of the French knights were pushed into the stream. The reserve which Robert held back did not even bother to renew the attack. Sixty-three French counts, barons and baronets had been slaughtered, excluding a great number of other knights. The Flemings stripped the victims of their golden spurs, 700 pairs of which were hung up as a thanksgiving in the church of Courtrai. The Battle of the Golden Spurs was a shock to the knighthood of Europe; for the first time an army almost exclusively on foot had unhorsed and beaten the mounted feudal host. From a military point of view the battle is almost a copy of that of Bannockburn when Edward II was beaten by Robert the Bruce, but Bannockburn lacks the social aspect which characterizes the Battle of the Golden Spurs. Here the levies of the Flemish towns had not merely brought about the decision; it had kept in its hand the political as well as the military initiative. Their rising was their own. They did not play a role subsidiary to any other interests. In other words, the medieval city had flexed its muscles and shown that there was an abundance of strength. It had exercised its political will and was not found wanting in a spirit of decision. The French were not slow in finding their own explanations for their defeat. They contained every factor save that of the bravery of the Flemings, and of their strategic and tactical good sense. But the fundamental lesson—that under the right circumstances with the right tactics, infantry could beat cavalry—was ignored.

In Flanders the house of Dampierre was restored and a form of government established acceptable to all the citizens of the towns. Though the French tried on several more occasions, each time they were beaten by the burgher armies, until in 1320 the peace put an end—for the time being—to the French quest for

Flanders. All the French had gained was a small portion of the French-speaking part of Flanders.

Bishoprics and castles had been the origin of the medieval city, a community with a different social stratification to that of the land, and ultimately also a different political consciousness. A structure had developed in them which remained in existence, if not always intact, until the French Revolution. The bourgeoisie had come into being as a politically relevant social class next to the clergy and the aristocracy, although that political relevance was often not recognized and was downright ignored until this very relevancy enforced its recognition.

In Italy as well as in Germany development of new cities in the Middle Ages differed from that of former Roman establishments. The older Roman cities from the tenth century onwards received new life either through the gradual revival of trade or because they lent themselves to the establishment of a bishopric or a fortification. The newer cities rested on the knights within them, a class to which, in the course of time, were added the merchants. As they grew in prosperity the social dividing lines between them became blurred and extinct. But wealth alone says nothing about the ability of its owner to serve militarily. Consequently many merchants suitable to serve under arms were made knights. They became *Konstaflers* (a word from which the modern 'constable' is derived) in its original connotation meaning a member of the squad. The growing military efficiency of the burghers made itself felt against marauding knights from the outside, or even against the territorial lord, if his demands on a city were considered excessive. When a bond of common interest united several cities, as the example of Flanders has already demonstrated, they gathered in common action, in some instances institutionally forming a League for the pursuit, expansion and defense of their interests.

Bardiche (fourteenth century).

Right. *Phalanx formation favored by the Flemish from a fifteenth-century miniature illustrating Cyrus and his troops on the march.*

Below. *Staff (fourteenth century).*

The most famous of these Leagues which the Middle Ages brought forth was the Hanseatic League, comprising the cities of Lübeck, Wismar, Rostock, Stalsund, Hamburg, Lüneburg, Danzig and Riga. Its interest was trade and its ships dominated both the North Sea and the Baltic; its sphere of influence spread over the entire north of Europe. During the last four centuries of the Middle Ages no other foreign power exerted an influence so strong, widespread and continuous in the economic life of northern Europe, particularly England. As Miss Carus Wilson informs us, early in the twelfth century the wharves on the Thames were said to be packed with the goods of merchants from all countries especially from Germany. The ships of the Hanse enjoyed particular popularity because, unlike the vessels of other nations which brought into the country luxury goods for those able to buy them, the Hanse brought utility goods for all, especially grain. After the Teutonic Knights had opened up the interior of Prussia and under their guidance had converted it into the corn chamber of Europe, Prussia's grain, shipped by the vessels of the Hanse from Danzig to London and other English harbors, helped to stave off many a famine in England. In London as in other countries, it established its own settlement, the *Stahlhof*; its members were responsible for guarding London's Bishop Gate. For neglecting to do so and to keep it in proper condition they were once fined. They promptly paid and duly had such repair work carried out as was necessary. This medieval 'Anglo-German' relationship was only disturbed from the fourteenth century onwards, when English vessels began to compete with the vessels of the Hanse fishing around Iceland and when England became a cloth exporting rather than importing country. The English merchant adventurers successfully challenged the privileges which the English Crown had granted them over the course of previous centuries. This overseas trade did not go unchallenged, especially in the thirteenth century when the *Vitalienbrüder*, a band of German and Scandinavian pirates systematically seized the ships of the Hanse. The Hanse, forced to change to naval warfare, was aided by vessels of the King of Denmark and some of the Teutonic Order which put an end to piracy in the Baltic and the North Sea.

Inside Germany the city Leagues were more temporary and designed to meet a particular threat, and once it was eliminated they dissolved. The armies which they raised were always well-equipped and often well-led. Princes and vassals found them a force which it was advisable to evade rather than provoke. When knighthood declined to the level of highway robbery the German cities alone accounted for the destruction of over a hundred castles of the robber barons. Throughout the Middle Ages they had never been a bellicose force. To call the burghers to arms and to set out with them to do battle was bound to cost money and interrupt trade. They acted for reasons of self-defense, nothing else.

In Italy during the reign of the Hohenstaufen Emperors, the Italian cities were frequently engaged in war against them. But none of them produced the kind of bourgeoisie which was as effective behind the counter as behind the shield. They preferred to rely on hiring mercenaries, which had the disadvantage that when after a campaign their financial demands were not met, the mercenaries did not hesitate to sack their employer. Insofar as citizens of Italian towns organized themselves militarily they did so only as auxiliaries to the knights, mercenaries or otherwise. However, these mercenaries could be found in Germany as well, but on a more formalized basis. In 1263 the city of Cologne concluded a treaty with Count Adolf von Berg to protect the city. By that treaty the Count formally became a

burgher of the city and he pledged himself to aid the city with nine knights and fifteen esquires, all on armored horses. In return the Count received five marks of Cologne pennies per day. Cologne itself pledged to supply a further 25 men of patrician origin, fully armed and equipped who also had 25 armored horses. The treaty must have met the needs and requirements of the partners fully, because a hundred years later it was renewed, almost word for word. This treaty is only one example of many; along the Rhine the practice seems to have been fairly widespread. Localism is a feature which describes the attitude of many burghers to warfare. If they had to they went forth, but preferably not very far away. In one resolution accepted by Rhenish and Swabian cities from 1388, a specific *passus* stated that the burghers wished to return home at sundown.

Above. *Twelfth-century siege showing warriors bearing early kite-shaped shields.*

Below. *Detail from a fifteenth-century illustration of Caesar's* The Gallic Wars *depicting soldiers dressed in contemporary armor* (Commentaries of Caesar, *Lille 1473*).

ES nouuelles dalbion
Il vous en plaist escouter
mon frere z mon compaigno
Sachiez qua mon retoürner
Ly este deca la mer

E ceu a Joyeuse chiere

CASTLE BUILDING TECHNIQUES

Left. *Tower of London. Work on the Tower was begun in 1067. In 1078 Bishop Gundulf initiated the building of the White Tower for William I. The Bell Tower was erected in 1190 and in 1354 the Wakefield Tower was added which now houses the Crown Jewels (Roy ms).*

Below. *Motte and bailey castle. This simple type of fortified building was widely practiced by the Normans and it quickly spread throughout Europe. Constructed of wood upon an earthen mound it was highly susceptible to attack by fire. (The Bayeux Tapestry).*

In the early part of the Middle Ages, fortification was a dead art in Europe; such walls and defenses which existed were almost entirely relics of the Roman occupations and so little store was set upon them that Charlemagne gave his bishops permission to pull down the walls of their towns in order to obtain material for building their cathedrals and churches. It was not until the ninth century, when the depredations of raiding Normans became a serious menace, that Charles the Bald ordered the construction of castles at strategic points. In addition to the work begun by this edict, numerous barons began building private castles and several town walls were repaired and made serviceable.

What these early castles may have resembled we cannot know, since no reliable record remains but by the middle of the eleventh century a pattern had emerged. Undoubtedly a variety of ideas had, by then, been tried and modified, rejected or adopted; in the end the *motte and bailey* castle became the standard Norman structure spreading across Europe as its utility became known to become the embryo of castle design in several countries.

Above. *An ingenious method for scaling castle walls as designed by Conrad Kyeser in his military treatise* Bellifortis, *1405.*

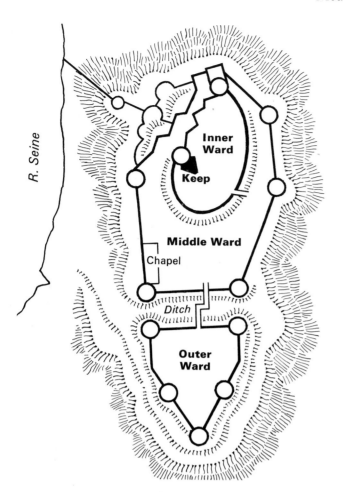

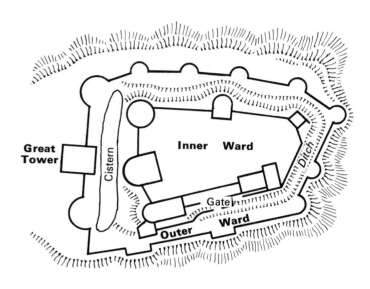

Below. *Brass rubbing of a knight in armor, c 1480.*

The motte and bailey castle consisted of an earth mound, the *motte*, which was conical and flat-topped, surrounded by a ditch, and formed from the material excavated from this ditch. Around the top of the mound ran a palisade of tree-trunks, frequently strengthened by thorn bushes and hurdles, and within the compound thus formed a wooden tower was built. The *bailey* was a second enclosure at the foot of the motte and on the outer side of the motte's ditch, generally crescent-shaped and of sufficient size to hold the domestic offices such as the stables, cowsheds, smithy, dairy, storehouses and so forth. This area was again surrounded by a ditch, the excavated material being thrown inwards to form a bank or rampart which carried another wooden palisade on its top. A light bridge connected the motte with the bailey, and a second bridge led from the bailey across the outer ditch to the country beyond.

This became the defensive complex. For minor attacks the palisade surrounding the bailey would be manned by archers drawn from the lord's retinue. Should the attack be pressed home and succeed, then the defenders could withdraw to the motte, destroying the bridge across the ditch as they went, and take up positions on the upper palisade. Should this be breached, then the wooden tower became the scene of the final stand of the garrison. This form of defense was probably more effective than it sounds; the steepness of the rampart and particularly of the motte made attack physically difficult, the wooden palisades were not easily scaled, and damage to these wooden defenses could easily and quickly be rectified.

The principal danger was, of course, fire, and in course of time, to end this danger, to reduce the amount of maintenance demanded by wooden structures, and, in all probability, to provide a castle commensurate with the owner's opinion of himself, wooden walls gave way to masonry, though the configuration remained the same. Indeed, excavation has frequently shown traces of earlier wooden structures beneath the masonry walls in a number of early castle sites.

Above left. *Ground plan of Château Gaillard, 1196.*

Above right. *Ground plan of Krak des Chevaliers, 1205.*

Building in stone upon an artificial mound was, however, a hazardous proceeding; where a natural mound or hillock existed in a suitable strategic position this was often adopted as a site for a stone tower or keep, the ditch and bailey then being constructed to suit. With an artificial mound it was necessary to sink the foundations for masonry until they reached a safe depth, either on virgin ground or at a depth where the earth had, over the years, become sufficiently compacted to take the weight of the new structure. It was probably in this way that the shell keep originated, a stone wall surrounding the mound in such a way that it enclosed a large portion of the mound's summit. The sides of the mound would be cut away to allow the wall to be built with a backing of earth, and the level of ground within the wall was considerably higher than the level on the outside. The defensive advantages of this arrangement were several: no attack by ram or mine would avail, since breaching the wall would merely lead into solid earth; the entrance, on ground level within, would be much higher than ground level outside and would only be reached by steps or ladders, easily defended against attack; and the slope of the mound from the outside of the wall would prevent any large gathering of assaulting parties close to the wall.

Left. *Rochester Castle, the eleventh century keep built by William of Corbeuil is still standing. The stone keep was the logical development of the motte and bailey castle and was virtually impregnable except to attack by mining.*

Above. *Siege of a city: castles and towns during the Middle Ages were built on naturally fortified sites such as this hill which gave an excellent prospect of the surrounding countryside. Such an elevated position gave them an added advantage over would-be attackers.*

Inside, the shell keep was simply a stout wall with buildings on its inner face, which surrounded a central courtyard. Some of the smaller keeps were completely roofed, but an open shell keep was the most common form. They were not, however, the only pattern. Tower keeps, where the structure of the mound was capable of supporting a massive structure, were the preferred form since they were more compact, more easily defended and, probably, more comfortable to inhabit.

With the masonry keep erected, the enclosure of the bailey followed, a stone curtain wall replacing the wooden palisade on the rampart. This curtain wall was continued to cross the ditch and up the side of the mound to join with the keep, or, if the terrain was suitable, ran around the motte and acted as a second line of defense around the keep, forming an inner bailey.

With this basic structure in place, subsequent improvements, as in most aspects of weapon technology, arose from the need to deal with some specific threat; in this case, some specific technique of attack.

In the first place the curtain wall had to be defended, and this required archers to be on its top; they, in turn, had to be protected, and thus arose the battlement, that most characteristic feature of the medieval castle in which the parapet on top of the wall is cut away so as to give the bowmen a firing aperture and yet allow them to retire behind the *merlons*, the solid part of the parapet, for cover from the enemy's fire.

But simply placing men on top of the wall was not sufficient, since they could only protect the foot of the wall by exposing themselves to fire in the act of leaning out so as to take aim directly downward. In order to obtain a safe vantage point the tower came into use as a regular protrusion from the curtain wall, so that men within and on top could fire directly along the wall's face and so discourage mining and similar activities. There was the added bonus that periodic towers gave greater strength to the wall, supporting the lengths of curtain.

Left. *Archers defending a castle from the battlements: the protruding towers and crenelated parapets are designed for extra defense* (Chroniques d'Angleterre, *late fifteenth century*).

Below. *Ruins of Charles VII's castle at Méhun-sur-Yèvres.*

In order to bring yet more defensive power to bear on
the wall's face, the next move was to build outward from the
parapet. Originally this involved removing stones from the
upper courses of the wall and inserting stout balks of timber
projecting out over the face of the wall. These were then used to
support a walk-way of planks and an outer wooden screen so
that the defenders could move, protected, on the walkway and,
by removing planks here and there, shoot down arrows, drop
stones or fire or boiling water (oil was too expensive), garbage
or any other handy missiles onto the attackers below. This
structure was known as a *hoarding* or *brattice*. Its principal defect
was its vulnerability to fire, and as a result this sort of structure
was gradually superseded by *machicolation*, the building-out of
the upper layers of masonry so as to form an overhang with
holes beneath through which missiles could be discharged.

Since mining posed one of the greatest threats, the walls and
towers were next rendered mine-proof by deepening the foundations and widening the wall's base. These measures made the
miner's task more difficult by virtue of the depth they had to
excavate and also, by making the wall more massive, made the
structure more coherent so that a much greater area had to be
dug away beneath the masonry before the miners could be sure
of success. Towers were strengthened by making them circular,
since the angles of a square tower were the weakest point, and
by widening the base to give a more massive structure.

With the walls secured, the focus of attack now shifted to the
gateway; since this obviously had to open in normal times, it
was likely to be the weakest part of the curtain, so the defense of
the gate became of prime importance and a system of defense in
depth gradually took shape. The first obstacle was the ditch, and

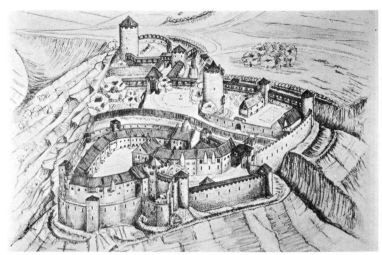

since this was normally bridged at the gateway, the bridge had
to be removed in order to give the attackers their first check.
From this requirement came the drawbridge, a bridge which
could be rapidly removed and replaced at will and under the
control of the defenders. Early bridges appear to have been
simply thrust across the ditch and drawn back into the gateway,
but these were soon replaced by the hinged form. A system
favored in England was to pivot the bridge close to the center of
its length, one section stretching over the ditch and resting on
the far side, and the shorter inner section forming a floor across a
large and deep pit. The inner end was counterweighted and the
main outer leaf could be quickly raised by chains and pulleys
until it stood vertically in the entrance way, presenting its iron-
sheathed underface to the enemy. The inner section fell into the
pit so that if the outer section was somehow forced, then the
attackers would be halted by the exposed pit immediately inside
the threshold. A variation of this was to pivot the bridge so that
the outer leaf fell downwards into the ditch while the inner leaf
rose to close the entrance, being locked and braced there by
heavy beams placed behind it and secured into slots in the
surrounding masonry.

To protect such bridges and their operating machinery the
simple gateway was enlarged into a more complex gatehouse,
towers being added on each side of the gate to contain a guard
party. To give more defensive capability the gatehouse was then
extended back into the bailey, becoming a rectangular structure
with more towers on the inner end. The entrance way was then
vaulted to form rooms in which the bridge and other machinery
could be fitted; assuming the bridge and pit to have been
surmounted, the next obstacle to confront the attacker would
be a *portcullis*, a heavy grid of oak, plated and shod with iron,
which could be hauled up and down by a windlass in a chamber

Below. *Harlech Castle, one of the*
series of Welsh Castles built by
Edward I, was begun in 1183. Note
the extra flanking towers to protect
the line of the walls from marauders
using ballistae, battering rams and
other siege weapons.

Above. *The Castle of Neuenburg*
in the twelfth and thirteenth
century, one of the many fortresses
built by the German knights and
part of an imposing castle building
program which included the Castles
of Marienburg and Hermannsburg.

above. Let down with a run it was a dangerous implement by virtue of its iron-shod feet and great weight, and any attacker beneath its fall would rapidly lose interest in the battle. The portcullis protected the main gate, stout and iron-sheathed, and the space between the two was covered by arrow-loops in the walls, possibly by traps or pits in the floor, and certainly by murder holes in the ceiling, through which the usual assortment of missiles could be discharged onto the unfortunates trapped between the closed gate and the dropped portcullis. These holes also had a useful function in directing water onto the gate area should any attempt be made to destroy the gate by fire.

Should a bold attacker manage to overcome all this and force the gate, all was far from lost. Some castles duplicated the portcullis and gate formation; other angled the entrance way and guided it between confining walls, liberally provided with arrow loops and machicolation, so that the attacker could be channeled under intense fire and forced to run the gauntlet. And if he survived that and fought clear of the gatehouse and its hazards, then he was likely, in a well-furnished castle, to have to go through it all again and force a second ditch and gatehouse in order to gain entrance to the inner bailey and the keep. As if this were not enough, in the thirteenth century the idea of the

Barbican appeared, an additional structure on the outer side of the ditch which formed an exterior gateway before the bridge could be reached, and in this, all the defensive features of the gatehouse could be repeated.

One result of all the complexities of the gatehouse was that it gradually superseded the keep as the primary strongpoint of the castle. A well-constructed gatehouse was a major work and, by its nature, more capable of being well-defended than a simple tower, and so the general form of the castle now took a gradual turn away from the motte and bailey to the *concentric* type, probably best seen today in the Welsh castles of Edward I but also common in France. Here two curtain walls exist, the outer completely surrounding the inner, and the inner much higher than the outer so that both walls could be in action at the same time. The gatehouse of the inner ward became the principal strongpoint, since here the lord had the whole machinery of defense – portcullis, drawbridge, gates and garrison – immediately under his control.

This *keep-gatehouse* was the culminating point of the medieval castle-builder's art. As the feudal struggles of the local barons subsided and concepts of nationalism arose, as the expense of construction increased in proportion to the increase in complexity of design, and as knightly warfare began to give way to the professional soldier and gunpowder arrived on the battlefield, so the castles began to move away from the essentially military character and become ornate dwelling houses with defensive adjuncts. The castle was not dead, nor was the science of fortification, but there was now to be a breathing space while the military engineers assessed the new tactics and the political changes before moving ahead in a new direction.

Below left. *Bamborough Castle. Castles were erected in suitably strategic positions which could be adapted for defense purposes. Here the castle is built on a slight mound and surrounded on three sides by sea.*

Below. *Almourel Castle, Portugal. Its isolated position amidst outcrops of rock is rendered even more inaccessible by the waters of the River Tagus.*

Wagon castle: armed carts form a tight–knit defense circle (Facsimile edition of Das Mittelalteriche Hausbuch, *late fifteenth century).*

THE HUSSITES

The Hussite movement deserves some attention because in Bohemia in the fifteenth century is found the first example in modern European history in which a state did not form its people into a nation, but that a people of a specific language group, by means of a social and religious revolution, attempted to form itself into a nation against the state of which it was part.

In the early Middle Ages a state had emerged within the lands surrounded by the Sudeten mountains. The area was composed of different tribes which very early on entered into a feudal relationship with the German crown. Its nobility had been assimilated by the Germans fairly quickly. While the heartland of Bohemia had been settled predominantly by Slavs who had flowed into the areas left by the Markomani, its border territories came under the influence of German eastward expansion. This eastward movement was also responsible for the foundation of towns in the interior, ultimately resulting in German-dominated urban communities surrounded by a Slav-dominated countryside. Bohemia had a German-assimilated native nobility, an urban largely German bourgeoisie and a Slav, or more specifically Czech peasantry and urban lowerclass.

The first evidence of conflict between the language groups goes back to the early twelfth century. An impoverished Czech landed nobility increasingly feuded with the prosperous German towns. Thus to the difference in language was added the element of social conflict. One chronicler in 1310 gave great praise to one Bohemian Duke because he had cut off the noses of all Germans and chased them out of his territory. Everything indicates that the Germans in Bohemia lived unaware of the problems coming upon them. They lacked any national con-

sciousness, living as they did in a territorial state comprising two language groups. But among the Czechs the social conflict kept their national consciousness alive and with it their own language.

When Emperor Charles IV founded the University of Prague in 1348, both Czechs and Germans participated in it. But there were plenty of causes for differences. Which nationality should occupy which office of the university and the modus of representation at the university, were two of them. In addition the emerging clamor for the reform of the Roman Catholic Church was shared by both.

Differences of nationality subtly influenced attitudes held towards differences over theological issues. The crisis over the papal authority played a major part in the disintegration of medieval universalism. Each prince and King pursued his own policy towards the Holy See, and inevitably under such conditions universities could hardly remain supranational corporations for the education of a Christian elite. The tendency of expelling foreign university teachers began in 1381 when Paris expelled German faculty members from its university. In Germany, on the other hand, this development combined with the apparent success of the University of Prague resulted in territorial princes founding their own universities.

Within thirty years of the foundation of the University of Prague differences between the German and Czechs within it erupted. The Czechs were embittered by the support which the Germans gave to the papal policy of their King and Emperor. These differences culminated in the German members of the

Jan Hus the Martyr (1373–1415).

The Wars of the Roses in England were yet another example of the decline of feudalism in Europe. Above: Cavalry skirmish with long bowmen at the Battle of Tewkesbury, 1471. *Right.* Cavalry advancing with spears and lances at the Battle of Barnet, 1471.

university, staff and students, being declared foreigners. Pressed by the Czechs into a minority position most of them left Prague and founded the University of Leipzig in Saxony. The rector of the University of Prague then was John Hus.

Hus was imbued with the sincere desire for religious reform, influenced by the ideas which John Wycliffe had propagated in his tracts. He had at his hand all the arguments needed for his cause against the Roman Church as well as against the Germans, who although they were supporters of the reform cause, preferred a course of moderation and rejected any radicalism believing that it would do more harm to the Church and society than good. In other words, to the difference in language and the social conflict now came a religious conflict was now added with the Czech rural lower stratum of society led by impoverished Czech knights on one side, and the German burghers of the towns and cities of Bohemia on the other. When Hus was burned at the stake as a heretic at the Council

of Constance in 1415, the signal for revolt had been given.

Motivated by an outraged nationalism to avenge their martyred hero and prophet, the Hussite movement led by Jan Zisca set out to expel the foreigners, resist their invasions and in turn spread terror into the German provinces bordering on Bohemia. Jan (John) Zisca was a man with considerable military experience. He had been in Polish service against the Teutonic Knights. His initial problem was forming peasants mainly unaccustomed to warfare into a fighting body with some semblance of order. Deficient in tactical knowledge, with only little cavalry, it would have been madness to expose such troops to open-field battle, in which even their national and religious zeal would be of little avail against a well-trained enemy. Consequently his policy at the outset was determined by defense until the Hussite forces had matured enough to take the offensive. Lacking firm urban bases from which he could conduct his operations, he had to keep on the move, yet at the same

time be well-protected. That protection was afforded by a device which apparently has its origin in Russia during its campaigns against the Tartars. It was the *gulaigorord*, the *wagenburg*, or simply the wagon castle. The Poles used it and so did the Teutonic Knights at the Battle of Tannenberg. The wagon castle was a moving fortress. At first Zisca had only common peasant carts which were pushed together. Later special wagons were developed, heavily boarded up on the sides, to give the defenders some protection. When on the move each wagon was drawn by four strong horses and on open ground they could quickly be turned round in a square or circular form into a *laager*. Initially the wagon castle was an improvization, arising out of an immediate need and not part of a well-thought-out scheme of tactics. When on the move they proceeded in a tactical formation which would immediately form a defensive position. Topographical conditions permitting, the Hussites moved their wagons in the forms of the letters V, C, or E. When forming into a castle, the horses were unharnessed and wagon-poles were pushed above the wagons ahead or taken off altogether. The horses remained within the *laager* to be used as cavalry horses for sudden sorties from the *laager*. Each wagon was mounted by men able to swing poles, flails and other such weapons twenty to thirty times a minute. Warriors were armed with halberds or poles with long, sharp hooks with which mounted knights could be hauled from their horses before they came near enough to wield their swords. Added to them were bowmen, crossbowmen and men armed with small hand guns. According to Sir Charles Oman, Zisca was the first general in Europe who specialized in the smaller firearms as weapons for large bodies of infantry, although they had been known since the end of the thirteenth century. Behind each wagon a reserve crew stood in wait, while at the center of the *laager* a reserve was held ready to attack the enemy in the open field as soon as he showed a vulnerable point.

A contemporary of the Hussite wars has supplied a vivid picture of their fighting methods:

'They camped together with their women and children in the open field, with lots of wagons which they had fortified. When moving into battle they formed two parallel columns between which the infantry marched while on the outside horsemen protected it from a close distance. Should a battle occur, then upon a signal given by the captain one column drove around the enemy, meeting the tail of the other column. The enemy had thus been surrounded and separated from their other fellows and became victims of the infantry or the missiles discharged by men and women. The cavalry fought outside the wagon castle, but if hard-pressed, moved back into the castle and fought like from the walls of a beleaguered city. In this way they won many battles and victories. Because the neighboring peoples were unfamiliar with this type of conduct of war, and Bohemia with its wide and extensive fields offers good opportunity to deploy carts and wagons, they spread them out as well as rapidly concentrated them. . . .

As soon as the sign for battle had been given, the wagon leaders according to . . . a sign previously given arranged their wagons into a certain pattern, into lanes which for the attackers became a labyrinth and maze from which they could not find their way out. Caught in it and cut off from their fellows, the foot soldiery completed the utter defeat with swords and flails, or they became victims of those shooting their missiles from the wagons. Zisca's army is comparable to many armed monsters, which grab their victims unexpectedly and quickly, overwhelm them and swallows its pieces. Even if individuals manage to escape the labyrinth of wagons, they fell into the hands of the horsemen outside and found their death.'

The effectiveness of the Hussites is all the more surprising in the light of the inefficiency displayed very often by peasant and burgher levies which, with some exceptions, were scattered into all directions by the mounted knights. Even national and religious zeal could not make good lack of military training. Therefore in their early phase Zisca's armies did not venture forth to seek major confrontations with the German armies which Emperor Sigismund led to Bohemia to suppress the uprising in 1420.

In their first campaign against the crusading army of Sigismund, the Hussites remained essentially on the defensive. Sigismund laid siege to Prague, but was unable to conquer it because lack of agreement in the Imperial camp prevented any major effort being made and in the end Sigismund had to lift the siege. That is not to say that the Hussites did not distinguish themselves. Their defense was tough and when they managed to defeat a small German detachment attempting to take possession of an outlying earthwork half a mile east of the city, the Hussites celebrated it as a major victory.

Nevertheless Sigismund's campaign had important consequences for the Hussites. In many of the towns and cities of Bohemia the Czechs won the upper hand and even those supporting a moderate course over the religious issue now rallied to

Zisca's side. This meant that to Zisca the manufacturing facilities of the towns were now open. He had access to arms manufacturers and lost no time in equipping his forces with small hand guns and primitive artillery pieces, mounted on board, devoid of any mechanism for aiming, elevation or depressing. During that period the war was marked by a certain equilibrium between the opposing forces.

Major offensive power was not gained until 1427 when the Hussites began to invade the neighboring provinces of Germany, mainly Saxony, Thuringia, Franconia and Silesia. Actually Silesia had already experienced its first Hussite raid in 1425 and of that one chronicler reports:

'When we wrote the year 1425 after the Birth of Christ the Hussites came before the town of Wünschelburg one Saturday evening and on Sunday at vespertime they broke through the walls. The people fled into the fortified house of the *Vogt*. Before leaving men and women put fire to the town in the hope that that would save them from the Hussites. But the Bohemians waited until the fire had died down and then set about to storm the house and to undermine it. But negotiations came about and the *Vogt* was let down to them, to talk and to negotiate with the Hussites. He was more than long enough down in the town, and people began to fear, especially the priest who was the uncle of the *Vogt*. They shouted down whether the *Vogt* was still down there, he should show himself and come back to them. After a while the *Vogt* returned. When he had arrived his uncle the priest asked him how things had gone and whether he and his chaplains would go free as well. The *Vogt* said: "No uncle, they will not grant mercy to a priest." Upon that the priest and the chaplains were very sad, and he said: "How cowardly you are leaving and despising me. This the Almighty will take note of. When some time ago I had meant to leave you, you all asked me to stay, ready to share good and bad with me, to die with me or find salvation together and you said: 'How can the shepherd leave his sheep?'" Thereupon the women and the wives of the burghers cried and said to him: "Oh, dear lord, do not cry and be sad, we shall dress you in women's garment and the chaplains as well and will all get you out." The Priest, Herr Megerlein, replied: "This is not the will of God that I deny my office and my dignity, because I am a priest and not a woman. Your menfolk will become aware of how humiliatingly they have handed me over to death in order to save themselves." Little notice of this woe was taken. Two chaplains had themselves dressed as women and they took children upon their shoulders. But not the priest.

In the meantime the *Vogt* had talked with the burghers and agreed to surrender and surrender they did. They went down one after the other. And there stood the Bohemians and the Hussites and took them all prisoners. Only the women and children they let go freely. But a great part of the women, maidens and children out of fear had hidden in the cellar; and when now fire was put to the house they all suffocated and perished. All of the house had surrendered except the priest and single men, mainly artisans, who possessed nothing with which they could have bought themselves free. The priest admonished them: "Dear fellows, now defend your necks and stand fast, because if they take you they will subject you to torture and pain." This they said they wanted to do. But when they saw that all the burghers had surrendered, they became afraid and they also went down. The priest together with a village priest, however, stayed. Then the Hussites came up and fetched them down and took them to the army and the mob. They were brought before Master Ambrosius, the heretic of Grätz, who spoke to the priest in Latin: "Priest, if you now renounce what you have preached you may keep your life, if you do not you will go into the fire." Then Herr Megerlein, the priest, spoke: "This God does not want, that I should renounce the truth of our holy Christian faith only for the sake of a short pain. I have taught and preached the truth in Prague in Görlitz and at Grätz and for the sake of that truth I will rather die." Then one of them ran away to fetch straw which they tied round his body so that he could be seen no longer. Then they set fire to the straw and danced around him until he had suffocated. Then they took him for dead and threw him in a brewing vat filled with boiling water and took the old priest, the village priest

and threw him into it as well and let them boil. But one of the other two chaplains who were dressed as women came out and the child he was carrying began to cry for its mother. The chaplain tried to calm it, but by his voice was recognized. They pulled the veil from him, he let the child fall and ran with all his strength; they followed him and clubbed him to death. The other chaplain with the woman got away.'

During that respite which the Hussites gained between 1421 and 1427 Zisca re-equipped his forces, and although they did not replace the bow and arrow, handfire weapons became widespread among his forces. A metal ball or a load of pellets were far more effective than the arrow whether fired with a bow or with a crossbow. Their psychological effect upon the morale of the attackers was immense. The noise alone coming from the massed fire of the unfamiliar weapon was bound to discourage any attempt to get too close to them. At that stage,

Left. *Wars of the Roses: the Duke of Somerset is beheaded at Tewkesbury, 1471.*

Below left. *The burning of the templars (*Des cas de nobles hommes et femmes malheureux *by Jehan Boccace, Bruges, 1470–83).*

Right. *Troops loot a house to supplement their pay.*

Below. *Kneeling knight in armor (Stained glass window, Kreuzgarten Castle, fifteenth century).*

both the handfire weapons and early artillery pieces could be used for defensive purposes only. Hence Zisca, and after his death in 1424, Procopius, placed great emphasis on perfecting their tactics of counterattack. Once the enemy had been beaten off and showed signs of exhaustion, the sword- and spear-armed cavalry held inside the wagon castle, charged forth through a gap to take up the pursuit, but never too far to ensure safe return to the castle. Bohemia was ideally suited to these tactics, but once the Hussites crossed the mountains the terrain was rather different and every wagon castle on the move was now preceeded by a far-ranging reconnaissance party which scouted for the enemy as well as for a suitable position for the wagons. Attempts at improving the cavalry were also made, firstly by trying to find among the Hussites all those who had once been riding with knights and therefore possessed the necessary

cavalry experience; and secondly, by changing over to lighter horses obtained or captured in Hungary. The use of the wagon horses had shown serious shortcomings; a cart horse did not necessarily make a riding horse even of average quality. Such a horse after it had drawn the heavy wagons was hardly fit for a spirited mounted charge, and every horse lost in such a charge depleted those necessary to keep the wagons on the move.

Like their Swiss contemporaries, and for that matter the old Germanic tribes, the basic unit of the Hussite army was the community of kinship and of settlement. There were two main Hussite armies, two because religious dissent among the Hussites had reared its head even during Zisca's lifetime and became permanent after his death. Zisca's army, after his death, called themselves the orphans, because they had lost their father. The other army under Procopius, a former priest, retained the orig-

Sallet, c 1460.

reflection of how deeply the economic basis of Europe had changed in the preceding centuries. Secular and spiritual feudal lords had to supply *Gleven*. The Electors of the Empire were the highest assessed, supplying between forty and fifty *Gleven*. The Dukes of Bavaria had to supply only eight, while the free city of the Reich, Nuremberg, at that time growing rich along the main arteries of European commerce, had to raise thirty. Actually the *Gleven* system had been introduced in the cities for some time before Emperor Sigismund used the device to raise an army of the Reich. The patricians of the city as well as wealthy artisans undertook equipping them, and their leader was often a knight who had sold his services to the city. The only difference between him and the mercenary was the considerably longer contractual length of the latter's service which had to be renewed from time to time and amounted mainly to bargaining about the price. Sigismund renewed this call to service again in 1421 and in 1431, ordering the service of every 20th and 25th man respectively. In military terms the *Gleve* proved inferior to both Hussites and mercenaries. They were not inspired by fervent national and religious zeal as were the Hussites, nor was there the monetary incentive which inspired the mercenaries. By 1467 the *Gleve* system had to be abandoned, but other expedients were equally ineffective.

For the cities to raise their own mercenary troops parallel to the burgher levy, was a measure which seemed to work for some time but also carried inherent risks. For the most part these mercenary forces were composed of the dregs of society whose fighting morale was rarely very high. Coming from all directions they lacked the experience of joint operation which only a body of men that had fought in battle together possessed and were therefore unable to conduct operations independently. If differences over the pay arose, they turned on their contractual partners with greater efficiency than they had done against the enemy. And once dissolved, without employment, they became brigands in order to live. This was true in the Germany of the fourteenth century, though on a smaller scale, as it was true of the Hundred Years' War when a peace or a truce was

inal name of Taborites. Added to them must be the Prague levy, forming its own army, and levies from regions where the Hussites enjoyed particularly strong support. In total they amounted to five Hussite armies. But on no occasion did the five armies ever operate together. Only on two occasions, one in 1426 at Aussig and in 1428 at Glatz, did as many as three armies operate together. Each army is said to have numbered at a maximum 5000 to 6000 men, and frequently rather less.

The extent to which the feudal system had decayed in Germany is best shown by its response to the Hussite threat. The Emperor's call to the estates of the Reich to supply troops for a campaign against the Hussites in 1422 took into account some of the changes that had taken place. He did not appeal to his vassals and their knights. Instead he called for *Gleven* and foot soldiers. A *Gleve* consisted of a small group of men mounted and unmounted, experienced in handling arms, often servants of a heavily-armed knight. The number of each *Gleve* varied considerably. The *Gleve* did not represent a tactical formation but was simply a means by which the number of able-bodied men could more easily be ascertained. No longer was the feudal fief the basis for the raising of a military force but actual wealth, a

The massacre of the Hussites (From a woodcut in a chronicle by Bonée, 1545).

Wars of the Roses: Battle of Tewkesbury, 1471.

supplemented by pillage and massacre by mercenaries out of work.

While the cities managed to meet their own military requirements after a fashion, the Emperor did not, obviously a serious handicap with military operations to be conducted, but even more serious in the extent to which this undermined his own authority at home and abroad. Only towards the end of the fifteenth century did the Swiss model of the mercenary army find general application within the Empire, after the boom in precious metals had begun and with it the opportunity of raising the funds for their employment by higher taxation and by credit.

When in 1426 Emperor Sigismund asked the Reichstag in Nuremberg for an army of 6000 *Gleven* to fight against the Hussites, his nominal vassals simply replied that there was no chance of raising an army of that size in Germany, and even if it could be raised, it could not be fed by the resources available in Bohemia. They were prepared to raise 3000 to 4000 *Gleven* if another 1000 could be raised by the cities. But the cities objected saying that such a number exceeded their resources. Hence with an army inferior in number to that originally expected and of doubtful fighting quality, he entered Bohemia and marched towards Aussig on the River Elbe which had remained faithful to the Imperial cause and was besieged by the Hussites. To raise the siege was the Imperial army's first objective. It is significant that Sigismund's army consisted almost exclusively of Thuringians and Saxons with a few Silesians, men from the provinces who had had first-hand experience of the Hussite raids. The *Gleven* of the Reich distinguished themselves by their absence. Numbering about 8000 men they were outnumbered by the Hussites (comprising both the two main Hussite armies and the Prague levy) more than two to one.

The Saxons mounted the attack against the Hussite wagon castle; in part they even managed to penetrate the defenses, but Procopius saw his opportunity for a counterattack. The Hussite cavalry charged from the castle and beat the Saxons, who lost a minimum of 3000 men in the battle. Some estimates put the fatal casualties at 4000. With the loss of almost half of his fighting power Sigismund had no other choice but to withdraw and return to Germany. A year later an Imperial army under the leadership of the Elector Frederick I of Brandenburg mounted another campaign, but as soon as his forces set eyes upon the Hussites at the town of Mies and heard the first volleys of their fire weapons and artillery, there was no stopping them. In spite of Frederick's attempt to hold the army together, it scattered and ran for safety.

Four years later the Reichstag decided to do what in 1426 it had considered to be impossible: to raise 8200 *Gleven*. The princes must have been aware that what they proposed lay in the realm of fantasy. The Teutonic Order in Prussia as well as its other branches were to supply forces; so were Burgundy and Savoy, although it was common knowledge that the Teutonic Order was in dire economic and political straits, and that territories as remote as Burgundy and Savoy were highly unlikely to take even the slightest notice of an order to raise forces in a war which had no bearing whatever upon their own interests. In fact, even the Palatinate and Hesse failed to send any contingents. Nothing can be said about the number of the Imperial forces when they finally assembled, but when they encountered the Hussites at Tauss, they ran away as fast as they had done at Mies. Subsequent endeavors failed equally dismally.

While new Imperial forces were raised the vassals of the Empire had more important things to do than defend the eastern provinces against the devastating raids carried out with ever greater impudence by the Hussites, who could operate almost unopposed. The Electors of Mainz and Cologne announced the feud against the *landgraf* of Hesse. A tax levied to raise forces against the Hussites could not be collected. More money was spent on tax reminders than actual tax received. Attempts to copy Hussite tactics, such as the introduction of wagon castles, proved a useless exercise. The Hussites were never defeated by the Germans. The end only came through internal strife. When moderates and radicals fought one another in 1434 at Lipen, an engagement in which Procopius was killed, the moderates won and as they were prepared to accept the toleration which the German Empire now offered.

While in England the Wars of the Roses demonstrated the ultimate aberrations of the feudal system and its end, so the Hussite Wars in central Europe underlined what had already occurred—the age of medieval knighthood and the myth of medieval chivalry, had come to an end.

*Battle scene (*Chroniques de Froissart, *fourteenth century).*

THE CONDOTTIERI
AND
MERCENARY CORPS

Medieval armies had been based on feudal vassalage, on popular levies and on the growing use of mercenaries. By the end of the fifteenth century feudal vassalage as far as its military aspect was concerned had ceased to function. So had popular levies which although they did not become extinct became militarily ineffective; what remained were the hosts of mercenaries who were to dominate the military scene until the seventeenth century. The English Crown had employed them during the Hundred Years' War. As that war grew in dimension so did the number of mercenaries.

In Italy, however, they had been on the increase since the thirteenth century. The Lombard League and the Papacy had finally succeeded in defeating the Hohenstaufen Emperors who had tried to subject Italy. But once the Hohenstaufen had been vanquished and their threat eliminated the city states of Italy began to fall out among themselves. Two centuries of internal strife between Venice, Genoa and Milan followed and ended only when a foreign power reasserted its control over the Italian peninsula under Emperor Charles V and the Spanish line of the Hapsburgs. At first these Italian civil wars were conducted using the forces raised by each city from among its own population, but eventually the perpetual warfare exhausted the citizens so that the cities were forced to hire mercenaries. Cities were not only at war with each other, they were at war within themselves for with the passing of the Hohenstaufens, the supporters of the imperial cause in the cities, the Ghibelline party, found themselves at odds with their opponents, the Guelphs over control of the cities, and when the old cause dropped into the background, rivalry between prominent families stepped to the fore; particularism and family feuds ran amok. Reliance on mercenary forces took on such proportions that the mercenary groups began to emancipate themselves from the political powers which had called them in the first place. Unlike the mercenaries so far encountered north of the Alps in Italy, they began to form closed corporations, who elected their own leaders, or they followed their captain, the condottiere, and operated as an

FRANCISCVS SFORTIA VICECOMES,
DVX MEDIOLANENSIS.

Hic FRANCISCVS *erat, qui primus* SFORTIA *genti Dux ampla Insubrium Subdidit arua suæ.*

Left. *Francesco Sforza (1401–1466); who fought for or against many masters including the pope, Milan, Venice and Florence.*

Right. *English jack, 1580.*

Far right. *Detail from a religious painting showing contemporary weapons.*

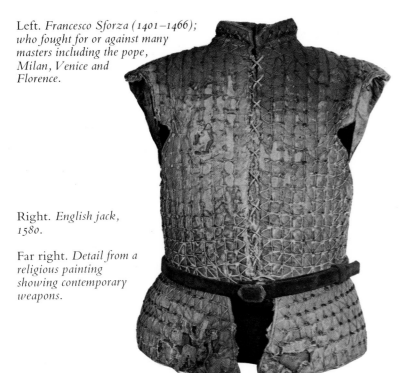

independent power. During the fourteenth century one finds many names of condottieri of famous families and some new ones who were about to establish their name: the Visconti in Milan, the Mastino della Scala at Verona, the Medici in Florence or Ludovico Gonzaga at Mantua, or foreign military adventurers like Francesco Sforza at Milan or the Swabian knight, Werner von Urslingen (who called himself a Duke because he claimed his ancestors had, under the Staufen Emperors, been Dukes of Spoleto). Werner von Urslingen had been taken into service by the city of Pisa when at war with Florence. When peace was concluded between the two cities the patricians of Pisa thought it unwise and dangerous to dismiss Werner's forces abruptly. Instead they paid them a considerable sum as compensation and instructed them to move on to the territory of the former enemy to live off his land. The mercenaries must have found some attraction in this proposal because they accepted it. They decided to remain together as an army, to organize themselves properly with constables and corporals as commanders under Werner von Urslingen's supreme command. In September 1342 they gave themselves the name *la gran Compagna*, and for six months marched from province to province, exacting money and supplies in each and if these were not forthcoming, ransacking and plundering the country. Local inhabitants were taken prisoner and subjected to torture to divulge where they had hidden their treasures. Any appeal to Werner was in vain; he called himself 'the enemy of the Lord, of compassion and of

Left. *Swiss troops besiege a castle. (Diebold Schilling Amtliche Chronik, mid-fifteenth century).*

Right. *Medal of Francesco Sforza by Vittore Pisano (c 1395–1455).*

mercy.' The booty made had to be handed in to the commander and was then distributed among the men according to fixed ratios. When this gruesome *Compagna* finally dissolved, each of its members had acquired substantial riches.

The employment of condottieri, or the reason for a member of a famous family putting himself at their head, was of course to maintain the rule of a particular family over a city. In most cases this meant upholding the dictatorship. The Viscontis and the Scalas hired whole armies of mercenaries who were reliable as long as fortune favored the family. But each city was crossed and crisscrossed with plot and counterplot, which centuries later Friedrich von Schiller dramatically sketched in his *Fiesko*: loyalty was a commodity that carried very little weight. Frequently the condottieri were among the conspirators them-

selves. Men like Sir John Hawkwood or Bartolommeo Colleone who were noted for their loyalty to their employers were very rare indeed. But, when discharged or when their contract had run out and was not renewed, they could not see any reason why they should not join their former enemies. After all, it was loyal military service over a stipulated period of time which they offered and sold, and not 'loyalty' itself.

The armies of the condottieri in Italy had one major advantage over their mercenary companions in central Europe. They remained a force-in-being; they did not disperse in all directions once a contract had ended and therefore as a military formation acquired a professionalism which other mercenary

forces did not possess. Obviously, they were also superior to the levies which the towns and cities of Italy exacted from their own population, a practice never formally abolished, but one that simply decayed. For a city state set upon territorial expansion a large army was required, larger than a city like Venice or Genoa could muster from its population by civic levy. Such numbers were simply not available and the population did not possess the proper military training. Venice and Genoa had been old enemies, rivaling each other on the trading routes of the Mediterranean, so that in its early stages the conflict had been a maritime one. The Venetians achieved maritime dominance but were not content with that and began a policy of territorial expansion reaching out into their neighbors' territory: the march of Treviso, the Patriarchate of Aquileia, and those of Padua, Verona and Milan. Experienced in naval warfare they were, but in warfare on land they were not, so Venice hired condottieri armies and achieved the improbable: the conquest and maintenance of a land empire by foreign armies commanded by foreign generals. However, many occasions did occur in which one or the other of the condottieri tried to develop his own political initiative to the detriment of his employer. But the Venetians had quick and drastic means of cutting short such attempts. Having their own spies close to the condottieri they were usually well informed and when Francesco Carmagnola, one of the greatest condottieri of his time, was suspected of treason he was lured back to Venice under some pretext and upon arrival in the city was promptly executed in 1432. The Venetians enjoyed a reputation of dealing with their own members equally as

effectively; they did not balk at cutting off the head of a *Doge*.

Venice's greatest antagonists on land were the Viscontis and the Sforzas of Milan both of whom employed and led armies of mercenaries and were as able as the Venetians themselves. They blocked Venice's bid for Lombardy. Only the invasion of Italy by Charles VIII of France in 1494 put an end to this internal strife. The Papal States having forced an alliance between Venice and Milan and supported by Ferdinand and Isabella of Spain, together fought the French intruder.

However, the condottieri had already undergone an important transformation. No longer choosing to work for an employer they began to work for themselves. The first progenitor of this new development was the renegade Templar knight, Roger de Flor, one of the captains whom Frederick of Aragon discharged after the end of his conflict with Charles II over the Crown of Sicily in 1302. Eighteen thousand Germans,

Above. *Italian condottieri: these mercenary soldiers hired themselves out to whoever required their services.*

Left. *A knight aims a lethal blow at his opponent with his sword. As revealed by skeletons exhumed from medieval graves, such a blow could split a man from shoulder to thigh. (*Histoire de Roland, *thirteenth century).*

CONDOTTIERE ITALIANO

Right. *Mounted Italian condottieri clad in fifteenth-century armor.*

French, Italian and Catalan mercenaries who were temporarily unemployed were pursuaded by Roger to stay together and embark upon an expedition into the Levant to drive the Turks from the gates of Constantinople. That was the objective which was never attained; instead the expedition degenerated into wild plundering of the Christian states of the Near East. Roger himself fell victim to an assassin and the men under his command seized the Frankish duchy of Athens and established a Duke of their own. This may well have been the example Werner von Urslingen tried to emulate with apparent success. When he returned to his Swabian home, he lived peacefully and in great prosperity until his death in 1354.

Werner' successor, *Fra Moriale* as the Italians called him (but properly Walter of Montreal), an expelled knight of the order of St John, was the archetype of the free-wheeling, freelance soldier who gave his support to whoever best suited him, broke agreements according to his own counsel and refused to be bound by any terms of contract. Building on the foundations Werner von Urslingen had laid, he developed a command and

Right. *Soldiers loading cannon. The more sophisticated firearms and cannon eventually transformed medieval warfare.*

greatest number of unemployed soldiers which Europe had yet seen were let loose. Many of them remained in compact units, dispersing to the south of France making, for instance, the region around Avignon unsafe, and from there to Spain or across the Alps to Italy. This additional surplus of soldiers enveloped Italy, but also changed her military tactics. The lessons of Crécy which these men had learned they now applied in southern Europe.

Fra Moriale's army consisted of 6000 horsemen and 2000 footmen armed with crossbows. His tactics were still those of medieval warfare in which the foot soldiers played only a subordinate role in the cavalry. This was to change within a matter of a few years. Instrumental in bringing about this change was the Englishman Sir John Hawkwood who arrived in Italy in 1361 and served in and finally commanded the 'White Company' made up largely of disbanded English mercenaries. It comprised 2500 horsemen and 2000 archers, and the proportion in favor of foot soldiery continued to change. By 1387 Hawkwood as condottiere was in the employ of the Lord of Padua, Francesco de Carrara who at that time was fighting the Veronese and the Venetians. Hawkwood had been blockading the access routes to Verona for two months, but finding himself short of food supplies as well as having his communications with Padua cut he was forced to lift the blockade. While trying to make his way to Castelbaldo where provisions were stored, he was closely followed by the Veronese and before reaching his supply base was forced to give battle near Castagnaro, not far from his objective. Fortunately he was in a tactically favorable position, his flanks protected by a canal on the one side and by marshes on the other. His battle-line consisted of dismounted knights at the center, with the archers placed along the bank of the canal. Behind the battle-line he kept a mounted reserve. Both sides possessed some primitive artillery pieces but they were not deployed, probably because the damp ground of the marshes would not carry the heavy machines. Hawkwood left the attack to the Veronese who for reasons unknown had difficulties in forming their own lines and were not ready to attack until noon. The first sally was directed against Hawkwood's flank protected by the canal and his archers. The attack was repelled; so were several others which had mounted in strength so that Hawkwood's forces had to yield some ground. By that time the full force of the Veronese was engaged

Above. *Soldiers in combat* (Histoire des Nobles Princes de Hainault, *fifteenth century*).

Right. *The rival armies of two Swiss cities met at Freienbach in 1443.*

administrative structure which for its time and in the mercenary context, was rather sophisticated. He commanded the army advised by a council (of which, of course, he was the head), ordered by secretaries and accountants, and judged by a judiciary apparatus in the form of camp judges, a provost marshal and a gallows. In 1353 he carried out a circular tour of central Italy in the course of which he extorted 50,000 florins from Rimini, 16,000 from the Sienese, 25,000 from Florence and 16,000 from Pisa. With these funds he could well afford to keep an army of 8000 men all regularly paid. A year after his 'grand tour' he hired himself out to the city league of Padua, Ferrara and Mantua against Milan. That he must have been a man of some wealth is shown by the money he lent to the Roman Senator Cola di Rienzo. En route with his forces to Lombardy he made a personal detour to Rome to collect this money and he received his due reward: Rienzo had him arrested and beheaded.

A new influx of mercenary troops invaded Italy after the Treaty of Bretigny between Edward III and John of France; the

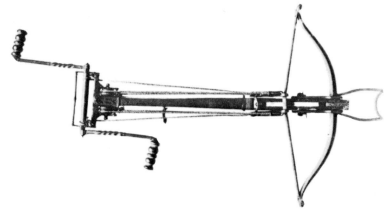

while Hawkwood still had his reserve which he now used. His horse-mounted archers crossed and recrossed the canal and attacked the Veronese on their open flank. The Veronese wavered but when Hawkwood's attack was supplemented by a frontal attack from his forces already engaged in the center, the Veronese were routed. It was a victory for Hawkwood, tactically significant because in combat all his men had dismounted.

It cannot be said that among the condottieri in Italy this change from mounted men-at-arms towards infantry was a lasting one. For infantry to be effective it must operate in large numbers. The condottieri and their troops were, however, as far as their tactics were concerned, still the product of the military tradition of the feudal age. Furthermore the condottieri themselves changed; that is to say, their country of origin changed. In the fourteenth century they were predominantly of German, or of English origin. In the fifteenth century, however, condottieri and their mercenaries were largely French. And although the lessons of Crécy and later those of Agincourt were not entirely lost, as far as the French were concerned the lessons applied to a conflict with the English and not in any other theater of war. They thought too little of their own foot soldiery to be tempted to abandon their feudal military traditions. Since the Italians themselves had no proper infantry, what, from the French point of view, was the point of dismounting? Geographical and topographical factors were ignored. Lombardy and southern Venetia, marshy and water-logged were hardly a suitable terrain for cavalry. Also, as outlined in the previous chapter, warfare became more expensive; the good condottiere had to husband his manpower carefully and avoid serious losses, as there was a limit to what the cities could pay them. The strategy pursued became one of attrition; maneuver and counter-maneuver were preferable to head-on clashes. The mercenary

Swiss infantry armed with pikes and other hafted arms attack the oncoming cavalry (Diebold Schilling Amtliche Chronik, fifteenth century).

was interested in staying in the field as long as possible, to be paid as long as possible; therefore his own pecuniary interest dictated the prolongation of a campaign as long as possible. Unlike the Swiss, he had no home to go back to and to sustain.

The campaigns of the condottieri developed into an intricate sophisticated tactical game which could only become unstuck when an unexpected novelty appeared on the field. For example, in 1439, the Bolognese put a body of hand-gun men in the field against Venetian knights and their pellets penetrated plate and mail killing a number of them. When the Venetians eventually won, they killed all the Bolognese prisoners because of their use of such a cowardly weapon. Viewed in much the same way was the use of the submarine by the 'Big Navy' advocates in the First World War. It was simply an illustration that, in Italy too, medieval warfare was coming to an end. The condottieri of the fourteenth and fifteenth centuries represented not the swansong of medieval tactics and knighthood but their death rattle.

However this does not apply to the mercenary as such. He was to occupy the battlefield for much longer. During the Hundred Years' War, France was the area most plagued with them. There they robbed, burnt and pillaged entire cities and provinces at will. After the Treaty of Bretigny serious thought was given to the problem of how France could rid itself of that cancerous growth. Pope Urban V, while still in exile in Avignon, which itself was threatened by the marauding bands of mercenaries, proposed in all seriousness to rally all the mercenaries for the purpose of another Crusade into the Holy Land to protect the faithful from the infidel. No chronicler has re-

Above left. *Fifteenth-century crossbow.*

Right. *The siege of Montagu Castle, 1487.*

Below. *Sir John Hawkwood (d 1394) an honorable man with a great sense of loyalty, he ranks as one of the greatest of the mercenary captains.*

Above. *Besieging a fortified town with cannon.*

Below. *Foot soldiers in close combat (*Chroniques de Froissart, *fourteenth century).*

corded the reaction of the mercenaries, but it it is not difficult to imagine.

Attempts were made to divert them from provinces of the
German Empire, such as Alsace and Lorraine, into Switzerland
and Spain. There were signs indicating the slow but steady
decline of these roving gangs, when the renewed conflict between England and France gave them a new temporary lease on
life and a corresponding aftermath when it had ended resulting
in some devastating raids into Germany's western provinces.

The first really practical suggestion of how to overcome this
problem came from King Charles VII who, after his successes
against the English, called an assembly of the estates in Orleans
in 1439 and proposed the creation of a standing army. The
assembly granted him the funds for a standing army of fifteen
companies, each numbering about 600 men and 9000 mounted
men. A close confidant of the king, the wealthy and patriotic
Jacques Coeur, advanced the first sums. At the same time the
assembly decided to prohibit feudal lords from keeping their
own troops. All that was allowed was a small garrison for their
castles. Only the king was allowed to have troops, appoint
officers and levy taxes for their maintenance. The captains of the

Right. *Mid-sixteenth century ms illustrating a stylized encounter between the Christians and the Tartars (Yates–Thomson ms 5).*

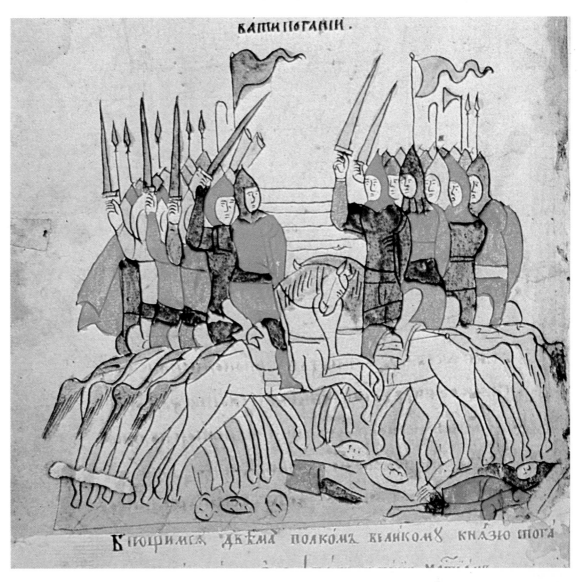

Below right. *Zurich soldiers embark on an engagement (Diebold Schilling Amtliche Chronik, mid-fifteenth century).*

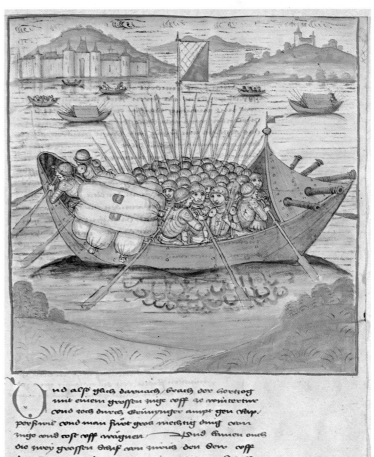

forces were made fully responsible for the conduct of their men. Armed men or gangs should be pursued, caught and handed over to the courts.

These decisions met with immediate opposition from the feudal lords, who feared the erosion of their own positions as power became concentrated in the hands of the king. The provincial estates, however, after the impact of the Orleans decisions had taken the initiative and recruited the most reliable mercenary troops, to expel the other mercenaries and force the feudal lords to abandon their opposition. Some of the mercenaries were not ready to give up very easily. Charles VII found it necessary to mount a special campaign against them. In this he was successful; several mercenary captains were executed while their men were granted amnesty on the condition that they would return to their place of origin and pursue a civilian occupation.

The first ordinance concerning this standing army dates back to 1445, six years after the assembly at Orleans. It introduces provisions for the first permanent system of taxation, a distinctive novelty since permanent taxation was unknown during the Middle Ages. Taxation was limited to the attainment of specific aims or requirements; once achieved the particular tax levied for them ended.

Of course all medieval kings had tried to circumvent these limitations by means of scutage and commutation and thus raise forces of their own, but these resources were rather more limited than the income derived from a regular tax revenue. The formation of the French 'Ordinance' companies resting on the firm foundations of enacted tax legislation was a major progressive step in the history of military forces. It ensured regular pay and more important for the future, it supplied a basis that allowed further development.

The nucleus of an administrative apparatus existed in the days of Louis IX in the thirteenth century. To administer his mercenary troops he had appointed as his deputy responsible for affairs of war, a connetable, under whom there were marshals, a grand master for the footmen, and a paymaster-general. In the organization of his army, Charles VII adapted the structure of the mercenary armies. The feudal military host had been divided up into banners; contained under the banner of each lord and his men were all the arms then in use. Their size varied according to the interest and ability of the lord to finance his banner. Once the mercenary armies appeared, the lord of the banner gave way to the captain of the mercenaries. The mercenaries of Edward I, grouped in hundreds, had their hundred leaders. And when in place of a unit of hundred, the unit of a thousand men developed, its leader in the thirteenth century was called the Millenarius.

The shape and structure of the companies of Charles VII developed slowly. One stipulation of the early phase is significant: it was desirable that the captain of each company be a man of some financial substance. Firstly, of course, he was responsible for the conduct of his men and if he possessed means of his own a heavy fine was considered a punishment of greater impact than a reprimand. Secondly, in the long term, this unintentionally ensured that captaincies and later all commissions in an officer corps (as yet undeveloped) would go to the higher social strata. No reliable figures exist about the actual size of each company. As elsewhere, it is likely to have depended on the circumstances. More important than the size was the existence of a standing military force, directly subordinated to its captain and through him to the king, a permanent force which would train and go to war together and ultimately represent an aggregate of military experience not only of the individual but of the unit and thus of the army as a whole.

However, one would be mistaken to assume that with this innovation all problems were solved. The army was far too small to meet the needs of the French Crown who therefore still had to rely on its vassals to supply men. But in that case they were divided into companies and received regular pay as did the king's professionals. However, further alterations were to follow. Already King Charles V, in the fourteenth century, had tried to order that the entire male population of his kingdom should train itself with the bow or the crossbow. But his nobility, leaving an armed and trained peasantry, successfully, insisted that he rescind the order. Charles VII in his turn decreed that every fiftieth household should train an able-bodied man with the bow. The men thus trained were to meet on every feast day in common exercise and to swear an oath to obey the call of the King when they were needed. Like the King's forces they were divided into companies. In times of war they were regularly paid and for their exercises in peace times they received certain tax exemptions.

In principle it was a sound measure, in practice it proved a failure, because however useful training with the bow might have been it did not give the men the experience and stamina required in battle. Charles VII's son, Louis XI, therefore had these companies dissolved. It was reputed that the only things they could kill were chickens. What remained were the new companies supplemented by the feudal levy but this levy too was adapted to the new structure. However, popular levies or civic levies in France proved as unreliable, unpunctual and deficient in real military training

Charles VIII of France (1470–98) entering Naples.

changes going on in the world. As we have seen, the condottieri relapsed into medieval tactics and methods, in a terrain where it would have been greatly to their advantage to take to the new methods which many of them had already experienced first hand.

Nevertheless, Charles VII's introduction of a policy of separating his forces according to arms was a precedent which remained with us. It was picked up and used by an entirely new force that had come into being, the *Landsknecht*.

Infantry troops lay siege to a town with cannon.

Bill (fourteenth century).

as did their counterparts in England, Germany and Italy.

Naturally levies, whether feudal or civic, between the ninth and the thirteenth centuries displayed many of these adverse features, but they were part of a political, social and economic system which at that time could not be changed and within which all concerned had to operate. But once the socio-economic environment of the late Middle Ages had been trans-formed, and the cash-nexus replaced the value of land, the old military system could also be replaced by one which cor-responded with the new socio-economic realities. Paid military service based on general taxation replaced service based on the fief held by the vassal.

Other innovations of Charles VII stated that each company have its own banner, while its sub-units would carry pennants, and that each banner should be a different color so that it was easily distinguishable in the field, while the pennants carried numbers in the colors of the company banner. Furthermore, in place of the mixed fighting customary of medieval hosts, Charles divided his army into branches according to the wea-pons carried, and for this purpose issued regulations aimed at the combined operation of all branches in battle. These regulations sound very modern, and are doubtless the product of a highly fertile military brain, but in essence they were visionary rather than practical. One cannot transport man from one age into the next within a matter of weeks, months or years, let alone with the stroke of a pen. Centuries of ingrained habits and mental attitudes took a long time to accept and adapt themselves to the

PROFESSIONALISM

Battle of Cadore (Copy of painting by Titian, Uffizi, Florence).

The outgoing fourteenth century provided a new addition to the field of warfare: the first national army, or the first people's army, the Swiss. It was composed of the free peasants and the burghers of the towns. All Swiss males physically fit were subject to conscription and possessed the privilege to carry arms. In practice, though, only volunteers were called and the number of soldiers for each canton was determined according to the number of its inhabitants. In addition, particularly strong and able-bodied young men were conscripted for pikemen, since not everyone could handle the pike. It was also possible to provide a substitute for one's own person, though this custom does not seem to have become widespread before the middle of the fifteenth century.

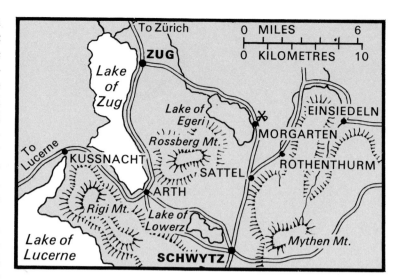

The principle of general conscription in a country with a population that lived almost exclusively on a subsistence agricultural basis, numbering hardly more than 500,000, was bound to have consequences affecting both strategy and tactics. Even to keep four or five percent of the male population under arms represented a burden which a country like Switzerland could hardly carry over a prolonged period of time. The soil had to be tilled, the livestock had to be taken care of. Therefore the men could serve only for relatively short periods. Consequently Swiss armies could never apply a strategy of attrition but had no other choice than that of annihilation. Their tactical body was the old Germanic square based on kinship and community, and when it entered battle the policy of defeating and dispersing the enemy was insufficient for the military requirements determined by the economic and social structure of the Swiss. An enemy, simply defeated, could fight again. To prevent him from so doing was the strategic objective of the Swiss levies. Taking of prisoners was strictly forbidden. A dead enemy was the only good enemy for he could no longer attack. Whoever fell into the hands of the Swiss was butchered in cold-blood. Although they were keenly interested in taking plunder, they had to swear an oath not to plunder the bodies of the fallen until the battle had been successfully concluded. To take prisoners and to plunder delayed the battle and whoever made himself guilty of such a delay was court-martialed, the most lenient sentence being to lose an arm by the sword. Hanging or de-

capitation for that offense was not uncommon. When, in the Burgundian War, a town offered only slight resistance to the Swiss, its population, men, women and children, were killed without mercy. The garrison of one castle were thrown alive from the castle tower. Those who had managed to hide were tied up in bundles and thrown into a nearby lake.

The core of the Swiss square consisted of lightly armed men equipped with long and short axes and short swords. They were surrounded by pikes several lines deep, whose task it was to break up the mounted attackers. Crossbows and later on firearms played only a minor role, because the Swiss aimed at engaging the enemy at close quarters as quickly as possible, where those equipped with swords, pikes and axes enjoyed a clear advantage. The excellent co-ordination of their close combat weapons gave to the Swiss foot troops on the battlefield, the strength and steadfastness which had been lacking in preceding centuries, when their role within the feudal army had never been considered a decisive one. Mounted attacks on a Swiss square came to a halt in front of the pikes, obstructing the

Below. *Note the square formations of the* Landsknechte *with the frontline apparently cut down.*

Left: *Battle of Mortgarten,
15 November, 1315. One of the
early Swiss battles.*

Right. *German engraving in the
style of a woodcut by Hans
Burgkmair 1577: Maximilian's
knights in triumphal procession
after a successful joust. These series
of woodcuts known as the*
Triumphs of Maximilian *form
one of the most accurate and
valuable sources of information
regarding the armor of the period.*

advance of those following behind, providing, of course, that
the pikes held their position. With the Swiss those who in the
early Middle Ages had been named the *fanti,* the 'boys,' as the
foot soldiers were contemptuously called by the knights,
became the full-fledged infantry, which from then on was
as decisive as any other branch of the armed forces on the
battlefields of Europe.

And more important for the Swiss themselves, they established their own independence. In 1231 and 1240 Emperor
Frederick exempted the cantons of Uri and Schwytz from all
feudal duties other than those owed to the Imperial Crown
directly. They were joined by Unterwalden and in 1291 signed
the 'Eternal Alliance,' which bound them to support each other.
After the end of the Hohenstaufen dynasty, followed by the
disorder of the Interregnum, Rudolf von Hapsburg was elected
German King and crowned Holy Roman Emperor. With the
rise of the House of Hapsburg a formidable threat began to face
the Swiss. Pursuing a policy of securing his own family domain
first, he endeavored to expand the Hapsburg crown lands as
widely as possible, and since he held possessions close to the
Swiss, they were naturally anxious that the Swiss cantons not
round off his possessions in the southwest. To stave off the
Hapsburgs was the cardinal point of Swiss policy. In 1315
Duke Leopold of Hapsburg was ambushed by the Swiss at
Mortgarten near the Lake of Egen, not very far from Lake
Lucerne. Caught with his feudal host on a narrow road dominated on either side by rock faces, the Swiss unleashed avalanches
of rocks upon the Hapsburg forces. Leopold had been careless
enough not to send a vanguard ahead and rode firmly into
the trap. Once the stone avalanches had taken their toll the
Swiss descended from the heights and slew whoever was left.
Mortgarten was a successful ambush, although not a full-fledged
field battle, but it was sufficient for Zürich, Zug, Glatus and
Bern to join the Swiss cause. Systematically they set about

expelling the Hapsburgs from their positions in Switzerland.

Another Leopold, the nephew of the one defeated at Mortgarten, took it upon himself to bring about a reversal. With an
army of about 4000 men he took the offensive against the Swiss
forces numbering approximately 6000 men. Instead of moving
as had been expected against Zürich or Lucerne he turned
towards the town of Sempach two miles north of Lucerne,
which had once been in the possession of his family but like
Lucerne had joined the Swiss Confederation. He gathered his
forces near the Sursee, at the southeastern corner of which is
Sempach. After laying siege to the town he turned east to meet
the Swiss, who had gathered by a bridge crossing the River
Reuss at Gislikon. Neither the Austrians nor the Swiss were
quite sure about each other's whereabouts. But less than half-
way to the Reuss the Austrians met the Swiss. The ground
steeply rising in the east was held by the Swiss, and the knights
dismounted when they arrived and tried to storm the heights on
foot. Their crossbowmen gave the Swiss considerable trouble.
Duke Leopold himself took part in the fighting at that point,
believing he had engaged the main force, but it was only the
Swiss vanguard. Unexpectedly for the Austrians the Swiss formations appeared from the north, their squares cutting like red-
hot knives into the flanks of Leopold's forces. The attack was so
powerful that the knights fighting on foot were simply swept
away. Leopold and a great many of his knights were clubbed to
death on the field of battle. What Courtrai had signaled, Sempach completed. The Swiss had demonstrated that they could
vanquish feudal chivalry by ambush at Mortgarten, that their
squares could defeat the mounted knights at Laupen and that on
the open field they could take offensive action against the
knights. The days of the medieval knight were running out. A
new age was dawning, but few seemed to have realized it.

The Swiss now took the offensive against Swabia, showing
time and again that their infantry was seemingly invincible.

Below.Landsknechte *council of war outside a besieged town.*

Right. *Georg von Frundsberg (1475–1523). The most prominent leader of the* Landsknechte *(Painting by Amberger).*

This was the turning point in military history of the Middle Ages. Considering their reputation, it is not surprising that it did not take very long before offers reached the Swiss to make their troops available to other warlords. The first conscription that took place in Switzerland in response to an outside request came from Florence in 1424, which was prepared to pay the Swiss 8000 Rhenish guilders for 10,000 men to serve for three months. By the end of that century such offers increased so greatly that it became a very profitable business for the Swiss cantons, and transformed the Swiss people's army into a mercenary force. However, the difference was that Swiss contingents were not made up of soldiers of fortune. They came from their own cantons and from their local communities. The long-term consequence of this was that the loss of blood was too severe for the Swiss to sustain for an extended period.

However, the Swiss had retained their supremacy on the battlefields of northern Italy and Burgundy for over a century. From the moment that the cantons began hiring their troops to foreign magnates the seeds of decay in the Swiss military system had been sown. Jealousies and rivalries weakened the cantons and destroyed the reputation of their levies. They ignored new developments in weapons and methods of fighting, for example, the advent of light cavalry, improved musketry and the increasing mobility of field artillery went almost unnoticed by the Swiss. With 10–15,000 pikemen the Swiss were prepared to take on any number of horsemen and were successful until they met their match in the *Landsknechte*, who had synthesized Swiss techniques with the latest developments which the Swiss had ignored. The *Landsknechte* did not object to the strategy of attrition practiced by their commanders. In the struggles be-

tween Emperor Charles V and Francis I of France over the possession of Lombardy, the Swiss contingent had simply left the battlefield because they were tired of the continuous marching maneuvers; according to their tradition, they expected a decisive engagement and were anxious to finish it.

In 1522 when the French commander Marshal Lautrec recruited another 16,000 Swiss, the Swiss demanded that the enemy be defeated by a massed attack with pikes and swords. The army of Charles V was commanded by the Italian Field Captain Prosper Colonna. It consisted of 19,000 men made up of Spanish infantry commanded by Pescara and German *Landsknechte* under Georg von Frundsberg. In April the imperial forces had established their position at a small hunting *château*, Bicocca, northeast of Milan. Colonna had built an intricate network of field fortifications, interconnecting trenches and earthwalls and an assault, though not impossible, was a risky undertaking. Lautrec had no intention of doing so. He was superior in numbers, with 32,000 men and intended to maneuver Colonna out of his position. This caused open mutiny among the Swiss: if the command was not given to attack, they would return home. Warned by his experience of the preceding year Lautrec gave in. He had another cause for concern, the rivalry between the leaders of the Swiss: Albrecht von Stein and Arnold von Winkelried. They had never liked each other, and they transferred the rivalries of the cantons they came from, between Bern and the original three cantons, to the battlefield. Winkelried had an international reputation and was instrumental in the Swiss attempt to overthrow the duchy of Milan in order to annex that territory to the Swiss confederation. At the battle of Marignano in which the Swiss were defeated Winkelried had blamed Stein for leaving the battle prematurely thus causing the Swiss defeat. He could not prove it and had to withdraw the charge. At Bicocca the two Swiss captains gave an appearance of unity, although Stein was the driving force behind the attempt to have the attack carried out. Lautrec drew up his plan of battle accordingly; 16,000 Swiss were to attack frontally, the other half, the Venetians and French, were to take Colonna's forces in the flanks. The two flank movements were to begin first, and once the enemy was engaged on his flank the Swiss were to make their frontal attack. The Swiss foiled this plan. They had been for weeks in a mutinous condition anyway and fearful that victory would be attributed to the forces who engaged the enemy first , they did not wait for the order to attack but stormed onto the battlefield on their own initiative. Suffering heavy losses they took the first trench and stormed part of the earth wall but then met a forest of the German *Landsknechte*'s pikes while Spanish musketeers took them under fire. The Swiss fought bravely, Winkelried on top of the wall challenged Frundsberg to come and fight it out with him. Frundsberg, sure of his success, ignored the challenge. Winkelried lunged into the phalanx of pikes and was killed outright. A terrible slaughter ensued in which the Swiss were thrown back leaving 3000 men killed including Stein. After the battle the ascendency of the Swiss confederation forces was over and, that of the German *Landsknecht* was about to begin.

The Hussite wars and the humiliating defeats which the Imperial German forces had sustained in them had made a reform of the existing military system absolutely necessary, all

Emperor Maximilian's (1459–1519) armory at Innsbruck.

the more so since the reforms in France did not escape notice. The turning point was the Battle of Guingate on the 7 August 1479 in which a Burgundian army consisting of Flemish foot soldiers defeated the French. The Burgundian army was led by Archduke Maximilian of Hapsburg, son-in-law of the Duke of Burgundy who had been killed in battle at Nancy two years before. Maximilian, the future Emperor Maximilian I, under the impact of that event recruited Flemings and trained them in the tactics of the Swiss and thus, two years later, achieved victory. He had placed great emphasis in his recruitment campaign on the fact that the recruits came from the same districts, another adaptation of the Swiss system which ensured common social origin, thus social homogeneity and community feeling. The victory at Guingate had neither strategic nor political consequences because Maximilian could not pursue the enemy

Right. *German mercenary helmet, 1550–1560.*

Below. *Halberd, 1488.*

Artillery of Maximilian I.

to impose his conditions. Moreover he was short of cash—the troops he had hired left for home. So he moved to other territories to recruit men and their contemporaries and called them *Landsknechte*.

There is no English equivalent for this term. To apply the term mercenary to them is misleading because they differed in their original composition and constitution in several important respects. As Maximilian's original instructions made quite clear, the troops hired were to originate from the same region. They were soldiers from a common region, serving as a unit, though not always under the same masters. They can be traced back to the popular levies of the Merovingian period, which since Charlemagne and the rise of the feudal system had been pushed into the background by the feudal host and had decayed. There are occasions when one sees this levy recurring, foot soldiers from the same region ready for action under a common leader to whom they had sworn obedience, or under a leader whom they had elected themselves. They had their own courts and were all freemen. A forerunner of the *Landsknecht* unit fought in 1276 for Rudolf von Hapsburg. After the battle the knights decapitated prisoners the unit had made without asking its permission, and its members refused further service. A hundred years later the city of Ulm and the League of the Swabian cities recruited a unit of free *Knechte*, who called themselves the Federation of Liberty. Since then these troops had played an important part in most feuds in Germany, under different names and with varying successes. In Holstein they were known as the Black Guards, and were the 'marine infantry' of the vassals of the Hanse. By that time of course their composition was very mixed, as can be expected, and included the dregs of society including murderers, but according to their code of discipline, marauders found harsh justice from their fellows, punishment ranging from being suspended by the limbs on chains to being burnt.

Battle of Laupen, 21 June, 1339.

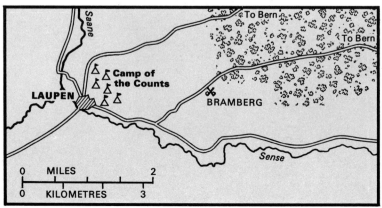

On those rare occasions when a city of the Reich did send its contingents to the emperor they were clothed in colorful garments, for purposes of recognition as well as demonstrating the city's status. *Landsknecht* was a convenient term for Maximilian to use. The estates of the empire were as anxious to rid themselves of the plague of mercenaries, as were those of France and other countries. Maximilian's recruiting drive immediately provoked suspicion; after all it was peace, whereupon Maximilian retorted that they were servants of the land, the proper meaning of *Landsknecht*, and this was shown by the method of recruitment, their origins and the rigid discipline imposed on them.

Between 1482 and 1486 he recruited them in the Rhineland and in the regions of the lower Rhine and trained them in the same way, or according to the Swiss model as he had done with Flemish troops. By 1486 *Landsknecht* had become a generally accepted term. Needless to say it required time to bring them up to the standard of the Swiss, but once this was achieved the Swiss contingents and *Landsknechte* viewed one another with deep hostility. The Swiss, conscious of their superiority, jeered at them, while the *Landsknechte* leaders would tell their men that they were every bit as good. Under Duke Sigismund of Tyrol, led by their captain Friedrich Kappler they defeated the Venetian condottieri in the Battle of Calliano in 1487. A year later, as part of the army of the Empire on their way to the Netherlands, they took quarters in Cologne. When Swiss troops also appeared at the gates of the city the Archbishop of Cologne refused them entry to avoid clashes between them and the *Landsknechte*. In 1490 when Maximilian campaigned against the Hungarians, the *Landsknechte* stormed Stuhlweissenburg, and their European reputation as equals to the Swiss was established. By that time Maximilian had two regiments of *Landsknechte*, each comprising 3000 to 4000 men.

They were devoted to Maximilian which was precisely what he had sorely lacked. He made sure that those contingents coming from the cities were conscious of representing a military elite. Nevertheless, from the start they proved to be a peculiar political institution, difficult to handle. They were a professional fraternity and war was their life's profession, often defiant and obstinate, but in battle unsurpassable in their bravery, and able to suffer hardship.

Maximilian recognized that the feudal military system, especially its economic aspects, needed replacing. The recruitment of a *Landsknecht* was organized on a completely new basis. A colonel, usually a warrior of some repute, was given an imperial patent to recruit men and for that purpose received a lump sum in advance. Often however, he kept a considerable part of the money for himself, relying instead on promises of the large booty. Many *Landsknechte* had to finance themselves, as far as their equipment was concerned. The colonel was in fact a military entrepreneur. Unlike Charles VII of France who managed to raise his small standing army by means of taxation granted by his estates, Maximilian and his successors could never persuade the Reichstag to do likewise. Hence to empower a colonel to raise the force was an expedient of a rather fragile nature. Cash was always short, and the only chance *Landsknechte* had of getting their money was from the booty they made on each campaign. Moreover, the Reichstag also put geographic limitations on the Emperor's power to conduct his recruitment campaigns. The Reichstag or the diet at Worms of 1495 granted him the right to recruit throughout the empire but only for the imminent campaign in Italy. Otherwise he was restricted to his own crown lands.

There is ample evidence that in their early recruitment campaigns, the recruiting officers accepted only men of good character and once they had taken their *Handgeld* they were recruited. The weapons had to be supplied by the recruit himself. Dishonesty among the recruiters was frequent and developed into a large-scale enterprise. Money was demanded for more *Landsknechte* than had actually been recruited. Weapons of those who received double pay, usually men of considerable experience who fought in the front echelons, were given to simple *Landsknechte* who received only the normal pay, and the recruiters kept the extra pay. On the regimental roll, however, the individual was listed as receiving double pay. In that way both the Emperor and the recruits were cheated.

The colonel upon receiving his patent appointed his captains who in turn appointed their lieutenants, ensigns, sergeants, supply masters and corporals. The latter post was also elective. The banner was to the medieval host what the *Fähnlein* was to the *Landsknechte*. About 400 men served under their flag and between ten to 18 *Fähnleins* made up a regiment, but both regiment and *Fähnlein* were administrative and not tactical units. The tactical unit was, as among the Swiss, the square, also called the battalion.

The major strength of the *Landsknechte* was their inner structure and the order that reigned within it. The *Landsknecht*, like any other profession, formed their corporation, similar to the guilds of the crafts and trades. Prior to battle the captain of each unit had to consult with the unit's council, called the 'ring' and inform it of his plans and listen to its opinion. Each unit elected its own representative who was to act as its spokesman before the captain. Jurisdictional and disciplinary powers lay with the supreme field captain, who exercised power with the aid of a magistrate and his assistants. The assistants came from the *Fähnlein* and were thus *Landsknechte* themselves, but in special cases the *Landsknechte* had the right to judge and carry out punishment over one of their members themselves. The accused was arraigned before the 'ring' first and had to answer for his action and defend himself as well as he could. If found guilty the *Landsknechte* immediately carried out the sentence, running the gauntlet of the pikes. All this was designed to give the *Landsknechte* the inner cohesion with which the Swiss had excelled themselves. They had their own constitution, the *Artikelbrief*, the letter of articles, upon which each recruit had to swear. In themselves these were not new, similar devices had been used by Emperor Frederick Barbarossa and by the Swiss, but the Germans had adapted them to their own needs. Georg von Frunds-

The Emperor Maximilian I (Painting by P Rubens, 1577–1640)

berg, renowned as the 'Father of the *Landsknechte*' advised the swearing in to take place in small groups, because 'when they come together in one great assembly not sworn in, they will not swear on the letter of articles and instead will put forth their own demands according to their liking, to which you will have to accede and thereafter you are no longer safe. One cannot force warring people all the time, therefore one has to have the law upon which they have sworn to show them.'

The content and form of these articles varied greatly, but the basic ingredient was the same; a contractual obligation between the *Landsknecht* and whoever pays him. They swore to undertake their duties, and the Emperor, to meet his side of the bargain, had to pay them as agreed, as a faithful lord to his men.

Square formations of militiamen engage in battle (Drawing by Albrecht Dürer, 1471–1528).

They swore to be obedient to all orders received; the principle of obedience was unequivocal and it was explicitly stated that it applied to all, irrespective of rank. In the sixteenth century the monthly pay of a *Landsknecht* amounted to four guilders. Often, however, arguments arose over this and the *Landsknechte* demanded that the month should begin or end with every battle or storming of a town. King Francis I of France once had to agree to keep the *Landsknechte* in his service for ten months and on the day before that battle to give them a month's extra pay. Phillip of Hesse, the German prince who became famous because his bigamy was sanctioned both by Melanchthon and Luther, advised his sons to conduct only defensive wars because otherwise the demands of the *Landsknechte* could not be met.

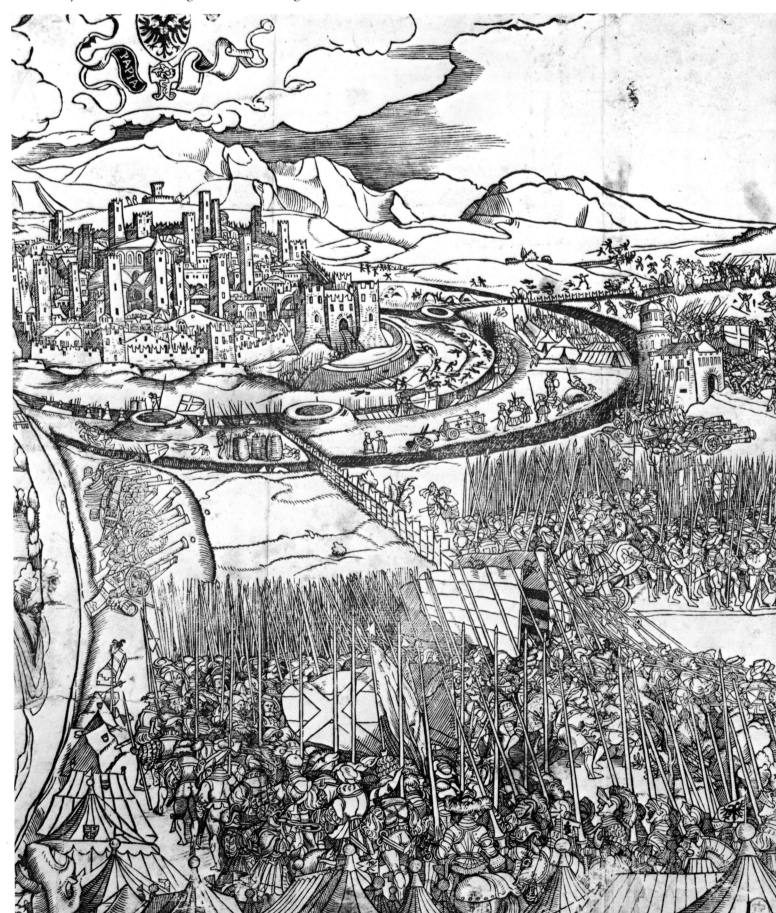

Right. *Battle of Sempach, 9 July 1386.*

Bottom. *Note the prominence of the infantry militiamen in the Battle of Pavia, 1525, in which Francis I of France is captured by Charles V. This marks the eclipse of the House of Hapsburg and its dominance in Europe.*

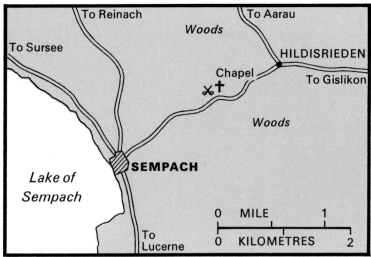

Furthermore the *Landsknechte* had to refrain from forming their own 'trade unions.' Complaints could be taken up by their own representative, or in other cases a *Landsknecht* in double pay, whom they would elect to bring the complaint before the captain. The feudal age did not end abruptly, and traces of it are to be found in the Letter of Articles. Horsemen were not recruited individually but in small units, the knight with his mounted aides, and they enjoyed special privileges as did other specialists such as artillerymen, engineers and sappers.

Every man was ordered to look after his own weapons, clothes and, wherever it applied, his own horse, which all had to be bought from quartermasters. They had also to buy their own food sold by the sutler-women which each *Fähnlein* had in its train. Since they could hardly carry the supplies needed for such a large army, inevitably the *Landsknechte* supplied themselves from the land, and in that respect were as much a plague as the mercenaries they replaced. In some Letters of Articles specific

Below. *Swiss forces confronting the Hapsburg feudal host in 1499.*

reference was made that fodder for horses, bread, vegetables and other foodstuffs were the only commodities allowed to be taken in friendly or neutral lands, while the taking of livestock and household goods and the breaking into of cupboards and chests was strictly forbidden. Some letters limit the demand of complete obedience only to the captain of the *Landsknechte*'s *Fähnlein*, others extend it to all captains.

Once a town or a city had been captured the orders of the colonel had to be obeyed strictly by all *Landsknechte*, even if pay was still outstanding. The occupying force was compelled to carry out fortification work, a stipulation which on many occasions caused difficulties, because the *Landsknechte* declared it was beneath their dignity to carry out manual labor. In case of fighting among the *Landsknechte* themselves it was expressly forbidden to call upon the 'nation' because if the fellow countrymen, in most cases men from the same province, came to help a full-scale battle would develop. Such fights were not infrequent, especially over women, supplies and booty. Duelling was not forbidden, but had to be fought with blunt weapons far from the main camp. Whatever booty the *Landsknecht* could make was his; only gunpowder and artillery pieces had to be handed over to the field captain.

The Letters of Articles were therefore a constitution as well as a rudimentary code of discipline with which to operate mass armies—at least by the yardstick of the late Middle Ages. They supplied part of the cohesion within which the effort of weaker individuals was maximized within the framework of the large unit. And large it had to be, for whoever led the greatest contingent into battle won. No state in the Middle Ages was economically strong enough to operate such mass armies, but this changed with the emergence of the French national state,

Above. *Battle of Novara, 6 June 1513. Victorious Swiss pit their forces against a French-Coalition Army.*

Below. *Battle of Pavia, 1525. Frundsberg defends the forces of Francis I.*

Emperor Maximilian visits a gun workshop.

the consolidation of the English Crown under the Tudors, the emergence of Spain, and the territorial aggrandizement of the Hapsburg dynasty. It changed not in the sense that the funds which had previously been lacking were now suddenly available, they were more accessible, but never in sufficient quantity to carry out the campaigns conducted in the fifteenth and sixteenth century. Therefore, as far as the *Landsknechte* were concerned the financial problem was an endemic one. Maximilian had tried to create an elite troop loyal to him, but how could he and his successors maintain that loyalty if they could not meet their own part of the contract? In Central Europe the answer to this fundamental problem was supplied only in the seventeenth century by Wallenstein.

Shortage of pay was made up by booty, and to obtain it excesses were unavoidable. The songs of the *Landsknechte* at the time tell in drastic terms of the woe they brought to the territories in which they fought. However excessive cruelty was not a characteristic peculiar to the *Landsknechte* or to the mercenaries (the so-called Age of Chivalry abounds with examples); the difference is one of proportion. Much larger numbers were now involved, and when a city was stormed by masses of *Landsknechte*, a few thousand of them raped and pillaged and not a few hundred knights as before. Often after a city had capitulated, having been promised that life and property would not be violated, the gates would open and the looting would start

immediately. A field captain or a colonel might have been able to deal with individual offenders, but how could he put his entire force on trial? And if he tried to punish selected individuals to set an example, the individual concerned would count on the support of his comrades. The provost coming to arrest one of them would find himself confronted by the entire unit. Quite apart from that, the *Landsknechte* knew very well that their superiors were as interested as they were in taking booty, that they were making their profits at the expense of their men, and to a large extent were compelled to do so by their ultimate employer's shortage of funds.

In their campaigns the *Landsknechte* carried with them an extensive train. Each of them wanted to have his women with him, or at least a boy servant. Women of course were indispensable to care for the sick and wounded. But that was not their only purpose. In 1567 when the Duke of Alba marched from Italy to Flanders, his army was accompanied by 400 courtesans. Such luxuries encumbered the movement of the troops. Among the German *Landsknechte* women were used to carry the men's baggage and other belongings; the average weight carried by any woman in the train has been estimated to have been about 50 to 60 pounds. One has to consider the dead weight which such a train represents when looking at their tactics.

Their main weapon was the pike. Upon receiving the order to form a snake, the command was given to level the pikes. The

II

snake was the ordered movement by which a marching column forms into an attacking square. This movement required considerable exercise to carry it out successfully and it seems to have been achieved with greater exactitude in the late fifteenth century than later, when the *Landsknechte* were burdened with their entire train. They functioned well in set battles, but when the *Landsknechte* came upon the enemy unexpectedly it was rather more difficult.

Nor was the handling of the pike easy. As one contemporary writes:

'The most unpleasant feature was the vibration of the shaft. I have myself experienced when fighting with the long pike that it is almost impossible to hit the target, because the point vibrates so much,

particularly in a hefty thrust, but mostly when the full length is used with the right arm fully stretched. It requires a sure slow thrust, carried out with thought and waiting for the right opportunity, to hit in combat an armored *Doppelsöldner* at the most favored points at the neck or abdomen and catch precisely the joints of his armor.'

Superior masses beat inferior masses, but often the forces were equally matched. To solve the problem posed by equal masses one had to cut a breach in the other. Before the advent of musketry and artillery, this task fell to a very select group. Firstly they had to be particularly strong because they had to wield a double-edged sword larger than themselves with both hands. This sword was so heavy that it allowed only one stroke which had to hit its target on the first attempt; if that failed its

Francis I taken prisoner at Pavia. Note the elaborate armor protecting the horses and particularly the 'crinet' which runs down the back of its neck.

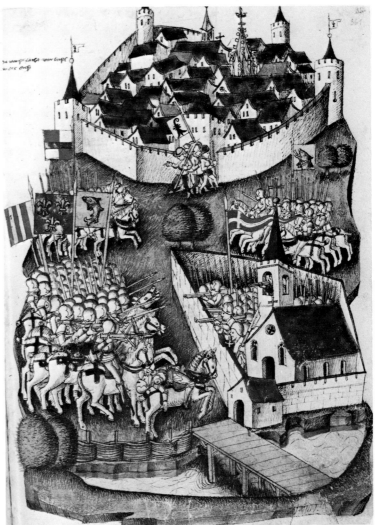

Landsknechte *maneuvers. The cavalry armed with pikes and crossbows prepares to attack the occupiers of the city.*

carrier would be pierced by the pikes of the enemy. In such engagements shortly before the armies met, this select group would step out of the second row, slightly ahead of the first; this constituted its surprise element. Because of the risk involved, strength alone was not sufficient. Even special monetary incentives were not enough so therefore more often than not, men who stood under sentence of death were given a chance to redeem themselves. These men of the greatest courage or deepest despair were those belonging to that group which

the *Landsknechte* called the *Verlorener Haufe*, the lost company. They had to hack their way into a square a hundred wide, a hundred deep.

They were no longer needed once musketry was widely used by the *Landsknechte*. The crossbow had already been abandoned by Emperor Maximilian in 1507. The Swiss and German examples found their imitations throughout the European mainland but with varying results. In France Louis XI after his defeat at Guingate, tried to form his infantry along the same principles but never managed to equal it except in 1507 outside Genoa. Francis I tried, equally unsuccessfully. His infantry was renowned for deserting in masses, as in 1543 when French infantry, meant to defend Luxemburg deserted, leaving the fortress to the Germans. In Spain it is claimed that King Ferdinand of Aragon called in a Swiss force to use as a model for his own infantry. Whether this is true or not, the Spanish infantry when it emerged and began to fight in Italy did so in exactly the same way and with the same tactics as the Swiss and the *Landsknechte*. At the Battle of Ravenna in 1512 the Spanish infantry acquired a high reputation which it was to maintain for a century and a half. What is unique about the Spanish is that they displayed and maintained their own national character from the start. The time had not yet come when the Spanish empire had the resources of the New World behind it. Castile and Aragon were too poor to hire mercenaries; necessity obliged them to draw on their own people for military resources. They and the *Landsknechte* remained the dominant fighting force on the battlefields of Europe until the middle of the seventeenth century.

CANNONS AND ARTILLERY

Left. *Siege of Arras by King of France (*Chroniques d'E de Monstrelet, *fifteenth century).*

Right. *Attackers bombard moated city with siege artillery using early firearms (*Chroniques de Alexandre le Grand, *fifteenth century).*

The origin of the cannon is obscure; one reason for this is the unfortunate application of the word, artillery, by early writers to denote any form of missile-throwing device. The word was in general use to cover mechanical engines such as ballistae and catapults, and it appears to have been carried over to describe the new invention of the cannon, leading to confusion. There is, for example, the note in Grafton's *Chronicles* that in 1267, during the rebellion of the Duke of Gloucester, Henry III approached London with his army 'making daily assaults when guns and other ordnance were shot into the city.' There is no other evidence to support the statement, and it is undoubtedly due to a misapprehension on Grafton's part over the meaning of artillery.

The first reliable reference is in 1326, when the manufacture of brass cannons and iron balls for the defense of the commune and camps and territory of Florence was authorized. An earlier,

Above. *Early wheel-mounted cannon employed against stronghold, c 1450.*

Right. *Medieval mortar for firing missiles at an angle (Bellifortis by Conrad Kyeser, c 1405).*

Far right. *Hand cannon.*

much quoted, reference in the archives of Ghent to the effect that in 1313 'The use of [cannon] was discovered in Germany by a monk' has since been demonstrated to be a forgery added several years after the alleged date. And in 1340 the accounts of the city of Lille show payment to *Jehan Piet de Fur, pour III tuaiux de tonnaire et pour cent garros, VI livres XVI sous . . .* 'for three tubes of thunder and 100 arrows. . . .'

The earliest cannons appear to have been cast (probably using techniques already mastered in the founding of bells) and of no great size. Fortunately a contemporary drawing of an early cannon exists in a manuscript written in 1325 by Walter de Millimete, which shows it to be in vase-like form with a bulbous breech-end and a flared muzzle, indicating an early appreciation of the need to apply more metal to those parts requiring reinforcement against the effect of the explosion within. The weapon was muzzle-loaded, the projectile being an

arrow bearing a binding of leather around the shaft to fit closely in the bore of the gun. Ignition was accomplished by holding a hot iron to a train of powder at the vent over the gun's chamber through which the flash passed to ignite the powder charge within the gun. From the illustration it would appear that the gun was about three feet long and probably of about two inches caliber. The most remarkable thing about it, at least to present-day eyes, is the absence of any form of carriage or mounting; it appears to have been laid on a trestle bench, with no means of controlling elevation or recoil.

At this stage of the gun's development, such omissions might be excused; it was enough that the gun fired at all, and discharged a missile and made a satisfactory noise. If the missile actually succeeded in doing damage, so much the better.

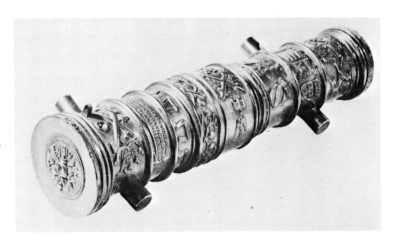

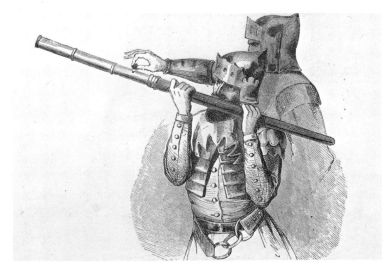

Above. *Note whicker baskets as a protective device for the artillery crew. The right hand cannons are sighted to demolish the city walls.*

Top. *German siege gun from 1507.*

Mezeray's account of the Battle of Crécy observes that King Edward 'struck terror into the French Army with five or six pieces of cannon, it being the first time they had seen such thundering machines.'

These early cannons known variously as *pots-de-fer*, *vasili*, or *sclopi*, were soon superseded, largely because the casting process was an involved and difficult one which demanded highly skilled artisans and also because the soft bell-bronze was quickly worn away by the heat and force of the explosion. A simpler and cheaper form, more easily manufactured and more durable in action, was needed and, in view of the exterior form being close to that of the workaday tun or barrel, the cooper's tech-

Above. *German artillery.*

Left. *Bombarding a city under attack.*

nique of building up a hollow cylinder by arranging strips of metal side by side and binding them with hoops was soon adopted.

In March 1375 Jehan le Mercier, one of the Counselors to the King of France was instructed to organize the manufacture of *un grand canon de fer*; an excellent record was kept of the whole operation and is one of the earliest descriptions of cannon manufacture. Three master smiths, one common smith, eight assistants and one laborer erected three forges in the market place of Caen and set about forging 2300 pounds of iron. The

Below. *New cannons.*

gun's tube was built up from longitudinal strips of iron forged to shape and then welded together with heat and hammering. Wrought-iron hooped rings were then heated and passed over the tube to hold it in shape. Finally the whole cannon was tightly bound with 90 pounds of rope and then covered in tightly-sewn hides to protect the ironwork from rain and damp.

Once this system was mastered, the guns began to increase in size. At the Siege of Odruik by the Duke of Burgundy in 1377, cannons which threw 200-pound stone balls were recorded, and in the same year the Duke ordered a cannon built to fire a 450-pound ball, which equates roughly to a caliber of 22 inches. This use of stone shot is attributable to the system of gun construction and to the qualities of the gunpowder then in use. An iron shot of 22-inch caliber would have weighed about 1400 pounds; the force needed to accelerate such a mass would have been so great that, without doubt, a gun constructed of strip iron bound by hoops would have burst asunder before the shot had even moved.

The gunpowder of the day was composed of 41 percent saltpeter, 29.5 percent sulfur and 29.5 percent charcoal; the proportions used today are 75:10:15. Moreover the ingredients used in the fourteenth century were unlikely to have been refined to any great degree of purity. These three substances were compounded by grinding them separately into fine powders and then mixing them in proportion by hand. The result was a fine powder which, when rammed into the cannon, consolidated so that it was impossible for the igniting flame to pass into the heart of the mass. This led to irregular ignition; the surface of the charge ignited, which led to the splitting up of the mass, which in turn led to flame entering and more ignition. The end result was that much of the powder was wasted, since it was still burning when the shot left the muzzle, and this was a serious defect, since the gunpowder was the most expensive component of the whole system. When iron, in 1375, cost 2.5 pence a pound (at modern equivalent prices) and lead 5 pence, gunpowder was 60 pence a pound, largely because of the scarcity of saltpeter.

Although the first cannons were loaded from the muzzle, attempts at breech-loading were made very quickly. The 1342 accounts of the Bailiffs of St Omer show an inventory of the castle of Rihoult in Artois, in which cannons are listed with separate chamber-pieces. The top rear end of the barrel was cut away leaving a trough-like section behind the breech-end. Into this trough a chamberpiece, resembling a tankard or mug complete with handle and pre-loaded with the powder and shot was dropped so that it lined up with the barrel. It was then secured by wedges and fired. Reloading was accomplished by knocking out the wedges, removing the chamber-piece, and dropping in a freshly loaded one. Attractive as the idea was, it had to be abandoned since the accurate fitting of breech to chamber-piece was beyond the manufacturing skills of the day, and the consequent leakage of flame and gas at the joint was extremely dangerous and also wore away the surfaces of the joint, making the leakage worse after every shot.

The first major technical advance came with the adoption of *corned powder*. The original fine powder, known as *serpentine*, had a tendency to separate out into its constituent parts when being transported in barrels, the heavier saltpeter and sulfur falling to the bottom leaving the charcoal on top. This meant that it had to be re-mixed on arrival at the gun, a dangerous practice due to its susceptibility to ignition by friction. The

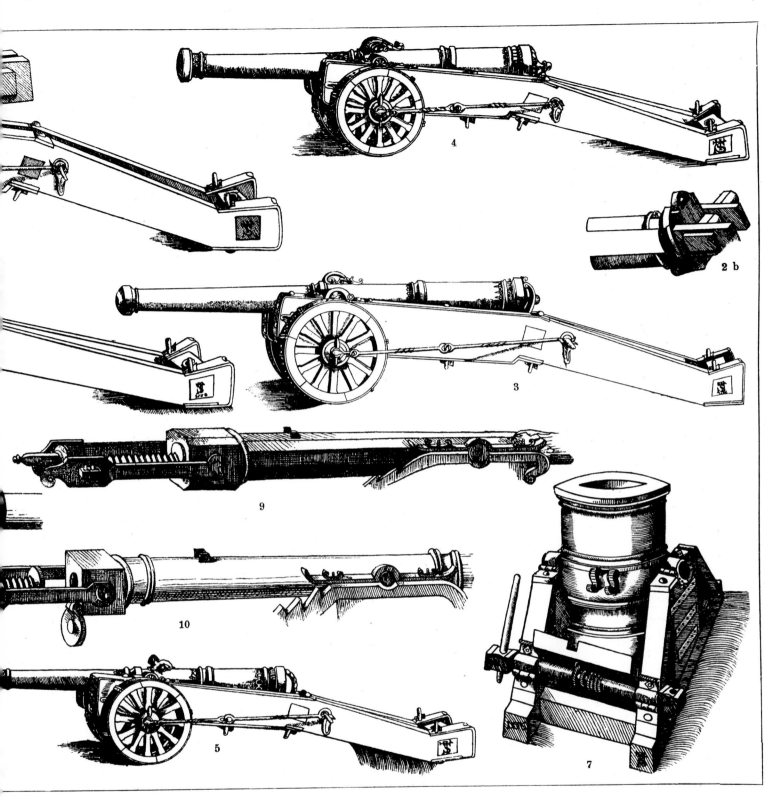

4

2 b

3

9

10

7

5

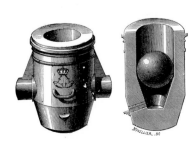

improvement known as *corning* appears to have originated in France in the early fifteenth century; the three ingredients were mixed together while in a wet state and the resulting paste was then spread thinly and allowed to dry into a cake. This was then broken up and crumbled into granular form in which each grain contained the correct proportion of ingredients. This form of powder had great advantages over serpentine; it would not separate in transit, it was less sensitive to damp, and because of the irregular granular form it packed less tightly when loaded, allowing the ignition flame to penetrate more easily and give more certain ignition and a faster explosion. Indeed, it was so much more efficient that it was estimated to require one-third less powder than serpentine.

The only drawback was that the increased power and violence of corned powder was often too much for the cannon. But since the powder was too good to be foregone, it hastened the next major technical step, a return to casting and the abandonment of the stave-and-hoop system of construction. By the middle of the fifteenth century cannons were again being cast in bronze in France, and as cast-iron became a more common material it was also adopted.

The final necessity was to add mobility to firepower by mounting the cannons on some form of wheeled carriage to allow them to be transported in and out of battle. The relative immobility of the early cannons severely limited their tactical use. They were simply carried to the field in a convenient wagon or cart, removed, and laid on beds of timber or even on the bare ground. As a result their employment was limited to firing one or two shots at the start of the engagement before the tide of battle rolled past them, leaving them either well-behind their own lines and impotent, or captive inside the enemy's lines. Towards the end of the fourteenth century the first wheeled artillery appeared, light two-wheeled carts known as *ribauldequins* which carried a number of small-caliber cannons which had numerous iron spikes projecting beyond the muzzles for protection against enemy horsemen.

It can be seen, therefore, that at the end of the Middle Ages the basic requirements of artillery had been met: cast guns, wheeled carriages, and a reliable and powerful propellant. For the next four centuries the improvements which appeared were ones of degree rather than of innovation, and there was little significant difference between the cannons at the siege of Constantinople and those which fired at Waterloo.

Above. *Sixteenth-century German siege artillery.*

Right. *A wrought iron field-gun.*

Above. *Sighting a cannon.*

A royal tapestry of Spain depicting Spanish galleys off Tunis.

nueue et Emperador desde Rada ala Gole ta y alli manda allentar el exercito enla parte do...
del Emperador y sus successores enel Reyno de España. Manda el Emperador fortificar la...
el exercito Casi mediado el mes de Agosto. Bueluese el infante don Luys conla armada de Po...
con las galeras de España. Los Alemanes e Italianos enotras naues se boluieron a sus tierras.
que lleuan los soldados viejos Spañoles se parte con determinacion de combatir la ciudad de B...

VT REPETIT CAESAR GOLETTAM ET PRISTINA CA...
HANC MVNIRE IVBENS CVSTODI TRADIT IBERO...
INQVE FIDEM RECIPIT PERCVSSO FOEDERE POEN...
REGIBVS HISPANIS QVID VECTIGALIS IN ANNOS

RENAISSANCE TRENDS

After Constantinople fell into the hands of the Turks in 1453, the Byzantine Empire, which had lasted for a thousand years, disintegrated. In a short siege 250,000 Turks with a formidable artillery force had overcome the seemingly impregnable walls of the city and its 9000 defenders. The second Rome had collapsed. On its debris arose the Ottoman Empire, significant for Central and Western Europe because of its expansionist policy, which in the span of two centuries would lead it to the gates of Vienna. As a power factor it began to play a serious role in the struggle between Emperor Charles V and Louis XII and his son Francis I of France. Francis created a precedent which was to become a cardinal point in French foreign policy for centuries to come, of trying to keep Central Europe in check by alliance with the strongest powers on its eastern frontier.

The fall of Constantinople caused an exodus of artists, scientists and artisans, from which both the West as well as the East benefited. In Russia Ivan III initiated the consolidation and the expansion of Muscovy. Byzantine architects made important contributions to the building of the ducal palace in the Kremlin, symbolizing the Muscovites' claim that the Kremlin was the rightful successor of Constantinople, the Third Rome.

In the struggles between Charles V and Francis I, the Emperor remained supreme, but his victory was as hollow as was his claim to the continuance of the universalism of the Holy Roman Empire. His was the last rearguard action of the Medieval Empire. It was beyond his strength to rule an empire over which the sun never set, from the newly discovered Americas to the Balkans, from the shores of the North Sea and the Baltic to those of the Mediterranean. He admitted this by the resignation of his crowns to his son and brother. Retiring to the abbey of St Juste he died after having caught a cold while rehearsing his own funeral. He had been carried in an open coffin by the monks through the abbey and exposed to draft.

In his wake stepped forth the national and territorial states of modern Europe. National states consolidated themselves quickly in the West, from Spain and Portugal to France and England. The center of Europe, however, was the crater of the explosion called the Reformation. The scattered fragments which this event, the German Revolution, left behind developed either new life of their own, growing into strong territorial states, or became mere pawns in the power game

Philip II of Spain (1527–98) and Mary I. His marriage to the ill-fated Mary Tudor took place in 1554. (Engraving by Joseph Brown).

of states stronger and more consolidated than themselves.

By the end of the fifteenth century, the medieval mounted host ceased to play its role. The infantry and the tactics of the Swiss, the *Landsknechte* and the Spaniards had replaced it, and throughout the sixteenth century fire weapons developed and increased at such a pace that within the span of 150 years they reduced the pike to a merely decorative weapon. The invention of gunpowder had not immediately been followed by that of the fire weapons. The transformation of explosion into powers of penetration was yet to take place. To bring about an explosion was easy. Gunpowder was often encased and used when mining a fortification under siege, but it was another matter to convert the energy thus released into a concentrated direct propellant for a missile, to transform the explosive force operating in all directions into a force operating in one direction only.

Who invented the first fire weapon transforming explosives into power to penetrate is not known. Whoever hit upon the ideas of using a tubular instrument, of providing it with a hole for ignition, of cleaning the saltpeter, and of loading such an instrument, remains equally unknown. Reports of such early artillery pieces being employed came first from Italy, then from France and England, Spain and Germany, all during the first half of the fourteenth century. The first report of such fire weapons being actually deployed in fighting comes from two German knights in 1331. What evidence there is seems to

Mid-sixteenth century Muscovy warriors.

indicate that during their early use they were loaded only once, because the crew consisted of one man to two artillery pieces.

Gunpowder itself was still in need of considerable refinement because ordinary saltpeter ignited only with difficulty. Therefore the problem was to find the right mixture of saltpeter, sulphur and carbon substance, a problem which preoccupied the military chemists until well into the nineteenth century. In any event, the first literary evidence refers to the 'infernal' noise these machines of war were making. When Luther condemned weapons of war he explicitly listed the fire weapon. The example of what the Venetians did with their Bolognese prisoners who had used firearms has already been cited. In 1467 when the condottieri fought against Florence using fire weapons, the Florentines ordered that no quarter should be given to them if captured. Thirty years later the condottiere Paolo Vitelli ordered that all musketeers among his prisoners should have their hands hacked off, because it was undignified that noble knights should meet their end in that way at the hands of common foot soldiers. He said this in spite of the fact that he used fire weapons himself. Among the risks a gunner took, apart from the fact that his infernal machine might blow up in his face, was that upon capture he would be put into the barrel of his artillery piece and shot out himself.

The time and method of warfare which this new weapon was about to replace had its lamentors:

'Hardly a man and bravery in matters of war are of use any longer because guile, betrayal, treachery together with the gruesome artillery pieces have taken over so much that fencing, fighting, hitting and armor, weapons, physical strength or courage are not of much use any more. Because it happens often and frequently that a virile brave hero is killed by some foresaken knave with the gun . . .'

The oldest guns appear to have been relatively small. Large pieces used specifically for siege operations, however, were in evidence from the latter part of the fourteenth century. The city of Nuremberg had one such piece, christened 'Chriemhilde'; the barrel weighed 275 kilos and was pulled by 12 horses. Its wooden base, or cradle, in which it was put for operation needed 16 horses. This was followed by four wagons carrying 11 stone balls each for ammunition and another five wagons

Pedro of Castille (1334–69).

with the rest of the equipment. The greatest artillery piece still in existence in Vienna is over eight feet long. The stone ball it fired weighed 600 kilos.

The earliest specimens were made of wood held together by metal rings, then out of iron and fourteenth-century gun barrels were cast from bronze, but technology in that respect did not advance very quickly. Even by the end of the fifteenth century exact cylindrical barrels were a very rare achievement, and

Right. *Conquest of Granada, 1481–1492.*

The siege of Constantinople, 1453.

required two men to service it, one man to aim and the other to ignite the gunpowder with a slow match. As on the artillery piece the hole for ignition was on top of the barrel. Once that hole had been drilled in the side and a small pan holding the powder had been attached it was possible for a musket to be fired by one man, aiming and firing it at the same time. From that primitive base began the technical development culminating in the wheel lock. Cartridges too were soon in evidence contained in uniform, small wooden cases. The early musketeer carried about a dozen of these with him as well as his powder horn. The gun sight came up in the early fifteenth century. The recoil of the gun provided difficulty until it was overcome by various devices culminating in the wooden shaft and butt.

The early musket or arquebus, as it was immediately called, demonstrated its advantages over the crossbow with an effective range of approximately 250 feet compared with the crossbow's maximum of 130 feet. The musket came into use during the first two decades of the sixteenth century. It was less clumsy and therefore easier to handle. The barrel rested on a fork to insure steadiness of aim. Light enough to be carried, its bullet had a velocity strong enough to penetrate even the heaviest armor and mail, something which could not be achieved by the muskets' early forerunners. Nevertheless the handfire weapons were still crude and not always easy to operate.

Inevitably handfire weapons became the subject of public

proper lafettes did not exist until the late seventeenth century, at least one that was adequate for the size of gun carried and quickly movable. When during the fifteenth century metallurgical technology had advanced to make iron casting possible, the stone ball was replaced by the metal ball, and they were able to reduce the walls of fortifications into rubble very quickly. The first to have used them appear to have been the French in northern Italy in 1494.

With the appearance of the gun, gunsmithery became a recognized profession of considerable repute. Almost like the chemists gunsmiths treasured their knowledge dearly, keeping its secrets to themselves and handing it on only to their pupils. One such gunsmith wrote a treatise concerning the entire technology of gun and gunpowder manufacture as well as on loading, aiming and firing a gun. Written originally in 1420 it circulated only in very close circles and was not seen in its printed version until 1529. How effective the early siege guns were is difficult to assess. But the fact they must have rated highly is shown by the numerous examples of requests by those who lacked such instruments. Nuremberg lent its Chriemhilde to various borrowers. Frederick of Brandenburg in 1414 asked the Teutonic Knights to loan him their gun to bring his unruly Brandenburg nobility, entrenched in their castles, to heel. In open battle the effect of the big guns was at first minimal. How to aim was an art in itself which had to be acquired first. Often the first salvo was too high, and since loading was not easy, the opposing infantry had enough time to advance to an area within its range. It seems that initially the affect their noise had on morale was greater than the result achieved by the projectile.

Handfire weapons made their first appearance almost simultaneously with that of the artillery piece. The earliest specimen

Right. *Maneuvers (Military treatise by Wolf von Senftenberg, 1570).*

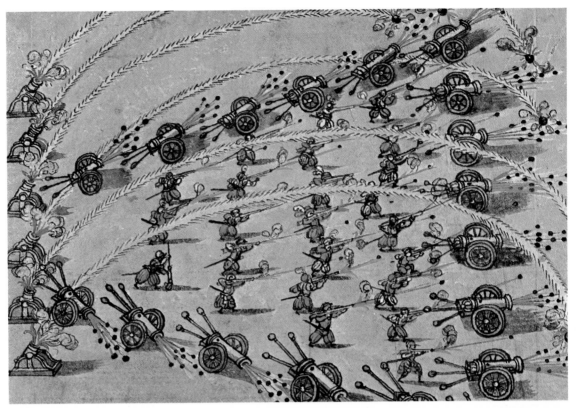

Below. *Battle of Lepanto, 1571.*

controversy. A French writer recommended the re-introduction of the crossbow, since they were not so vulnerable to rain as was the powder of the musket. This controversy was also carried on in England where one writer praised all the advantages of the longbow, pointing out that in wet weather the musket would be useless, whereupon the reply was made that wetness equally affected the bow. Furthermore expert longbow shooters were rare, and the musket was a weapon on which everyone could be trained fairly easily. Still, as late as 1627 at the siege of La Rochelle, the English longbowman was very much in evidence.

The French armies in Upper Italy carried handfire weapons in 1495. The Swiss used them in 1499, and the use of them by the *Landsknechte* of Frundsberg is recorded in 1526. But the first major encounter in which both sides used handfire weapons extensively was in 1503 between the French and Spaniards in southern Italy. The French, led by the Duke of Nemours, tried to dislodge the Spaniards from their fortified position in Barletta. When the French did not succeed and withdrew, the Spaniards, under the leadership of Gonsalvos of Cordova, made a sally from their position with light cavalry and two detachments of arquebusiers. French detachments turned to attack the Spanish cavalry which, pretending to flee, led them in front of the muzzles of their fire weapons which brought the French

Top. *King Louis XI of France, a descendant of the Viscontis of Milan reinstates his claim to the Duchy of Milan and captures Ludovico Moros, Duke of Milan, in 1500.*

Above. *The reconquista of Spain: entry of Ferdinand and Isabella into Granada 1492.*

Right. Landsknechte *transported by boat down the Upper Rhine.*

Below. *Philip IV the Fair of Castille who married Joanna daughter of Ferdinand and Isabella.*

Right. *Renaissance statue of Theodoric the Great.*

attack to a halt while the Spanish cavalry regrouped, renewing its attack which the French were no longer able to resist. This encounter was repeated on a much larger scale in the same year at Cerignola where, as Fabricio Colonna said, it was no longer the valor of the general and his troops which decided the issue but the wall and the trench occupied by Spanish musketry, who beating off the French massed attack counterattacked with muskets and cavalry and decided the battle in favor of the Spaniards.

Spain had once again entered the military scene and was assuming the part of a major European power. In 1479 Ferdinand of Aragon and Isabella of Castile assumed their joint rule of the two kingdoms. Spain was not unified, but a beginning had been made. The issues which cemented the ties between them firmly were religion and external threat. With the onset of the age of heresy and the Council of Constance, Pope Sixtus IV established the Inquisition in 1478. The fall of Constantinople had re-awakened the fear of another major Muslim invasion on the Iberian peninsula. Muslims still ruled in southern Spain. These factors together produced the last phase of the Spanish *reconquista.* A local incident, the capture by a Spanish nobleman of Alhama southwest of Granada, inspired Ferdinand and Isabella to support him and extend this to a crusade against the entire Moorish community in Spain. The Muslims under Abu Hassan tried to recapture Alhama, but in their hurry they had forgotten their siege train in Granada. He had to return to fetch it, but by then news was received that Ferdinand was advancing with an army of 4000 horsemen and 12,000 foot soldiers. Abu Hassan laid a highly successful ambush which might have ended Ferdinand's venture had not Hassan been dethroned by his son Boabdil through an intrigue in his own camp. Hassan could not pursue his success and sought refuge at the court of his brother Abdullah at Malaga. A year later, in 1483, the victor of Alhama, the Marquis of Cadiz, set out to raid the Malaga region but was completely routed by the Muslims under Abdullah. Boabdil, anxious not to leave all the glory in the hands of his uncle, decided to capture the town of Lucana, but instead was captured by the Count of Cabra.

Boabdil was a rare catch and Ferdinand decided to release him on submitting to conditions which would bind him and Granada to the Spanish Crown. Boabdil accepted a two-year truce and the condition that Spanish troops could cross his kingdom to the territories of his father and uncle. Pope Sixtus IV was elated by the Spanish success, in view of the fears entertained after the Muslims under Mohammed II had captured Ortranto in 1482. He sent a standard and a silver cross to the Spanish King and Queen for the crusade against the Muslims on their own soil. This crusade now became the great common denominator for the Spanish nobility (eliminating their customary factiousness) and for the soldiers who were to be part in the struggle of the Cross against that of the Crescent.

As in the rest of Europe, feudal levies in Spain were no longer a force to be relied upon. Therefore Isabella, resourceful as she was, used the recently created constabulary, which in Spain was the seed bed of its national army. In addition Swiss mercenaries, German *Landsknechte* and many other volunteers from France and England were recruited. With that army she hoped to capture the Arab castles. But for that artillery was required. Gun founders and gunsmiths were invited from Germany, France and Italy, forges were built and guns were cast. A supply train of 80,000 mules kept the siege forces supplied. Distinct novelties in the Spanish forces were the creation of a corps of field messengers to keep the flow of communications, information and orders moving throughout the theater of war, and a field medical service for the wounded, the first recorded case of a modern field hospital.

The Spanish army assembled at Cordova numbered 80,000 troops, 10,000 horses, and over 35,000 infantry. The rest were specialists such as gunners, engineers and miners. Nor was the element of sea power ignored in a country surrounded on three sides by the sea. The Castilian fleet was to cut the lines of communication between the Muslims in Spain and their brethren in Africa. In this they succeeded, while on land a series of sieges reduced the Muslim castles systematically. Towns and castles which surrendered were treated leniently; those which

Battle of Ravenna, 2 April 1512: the victorious French against the papal – Spanish army.

Arquebus from a fifteenth-century German ms.

resisted were reduced to rubble, and in one case where a town had been taken, but whose garrison subsequently revolted, over a hundred of its inhabitants were hanged on the walls. In 1487 Malaga was captured, and by 1489 the whole of Granada was Ferdinand's. All he had to do was to occupy it. The last center of resistance was the city of Granada itself. It held out until 1492 while Ferdinand devastated its immediate environs. When it finally surrendered on the 2 January 1492, the last Muslim stronghold in Europe had ceased to exist.

Spain, with the exception of Navarre, had been united; situated between the Atlantic on the one side and the Mediterranean on the other, protected in the north by the Pyrenees, Spain was in an impressively strong position since the New World had been discovered and Spain began to exercise its mastery over it. What the Hundred Years' War had achieved in France and in England, the *reconquista* achieved in Spain. A tide of Spanish nationalism surged forward which would not tolerate the alien elements within it any longer. Jews had the choice between baptism and expulsion, but the Moors were systemati-

cally decimated. In the same year as the surrender of Granada Spain formally became a united country.

Militarily its infantry had shown its strength and steadfastness which were increasingly to be displayed all over Europe during the next century and a half. Now the Spanish forces marched for the Spanish Empire, an Empire which for a short time was to include most of civilized Europe. In 1520 Charles, the grandson of Ferdinand, was elected Emperor of the Holy Roman Empire of the German nation.

The battle for supremacy between the Empire and France, fought out in northern Italy, dominated the first quarter of the sixteenth century. It ended with Charles' forces victorious but incapable of securing a worldwide empire. On the other hand, while the kings of Christendom quarreled, the Turks advanced in the Mediterranean and into the Balkan countries, and met almost no resistance until in 1529 they were stopped at the gates of Vienna. (Towards the end of the next century that spectacle was to be repeated.)

However, the most important war for the future political development of Europe occurred in the second half of the sixteenth century and arose from the rebellion of the Netherlands against Spain. Charles had inherited them and added them to his Spanish possessions. Under his son Philip this over-lordship came to be violently resented in the northern provinces of the Netherlands for religious and economic reasons. The prosperous Flemish cities had been early converts to the cause of the Reformation, and when Philip II ascended to the Spanish throne in 1556, envisaging himself as the counter-reformer *par excellence* and insisting upon the principle of religious uniformity, according to the principle *cuius regio eio religio*, war was inevitable. The first signs of trouble appeared in 1559 when Philip's regent, Margaret of Parma, introduced reforms designed to end the privileges of the Flemish patricians such as patronage and preferment and to curb their powers generally. The nobility of the Netherlands bound itself together by a document called the 'Compromise.'

Riches hitherto unknown streamed into Spain from the New World, without doing Spain much good, for the bullion received was spent mainly on war, and went into the hands of the bankers of Genoa, Antwerp and Augsburg. The Spanish Netherlands had developed into Europe's most prosperous region. The vessels of the Dutch merchants reigned supreme on the trade routes between Europe, America and Southeast Asia. Economic power was available to sustain a rebellion against the Spanish. The Dutch Protestants under the influence of Calvinism, whose principles corresponded more with their own economic realities and future aims, saw in that rebellion not only a means of repelling the onslaught of the Counter Reformation, but at the same time the opportunity through which they could wrest maritime supremacy from Spain and transfer it to their own cities. In a struggle lasting many years the battle-hardened Spaniards failed to subdue the Dutch. Philip's axis which ran from Flanders to Milan was beginning to disintegrate. In essence it was a conflict between the powers of commerce and the powers of an almost purely military state. The Dutch had developed their native industries, their wool mills at Leiden, their bleaching processes at Haarlem, their shipbuilding industry and those indirectly associated with it,

Above right. *The rulers of Europe: Emperor Frederick III, Maximilian, as Roman King, Ferdinand II, King of Spain, Henry VII King of England, Philip the Fair as representative of Burgundy, and Charles VII King of France.*

Bottom right. *Fifteenth-century German armor-smith. During that period the city of Augsburg was particularly renowned in Europe for the quality of its armor.*

Below. *Walnut pistol with engraved inlay.*

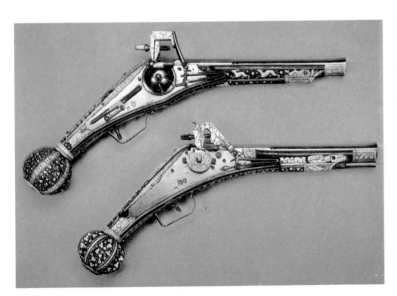

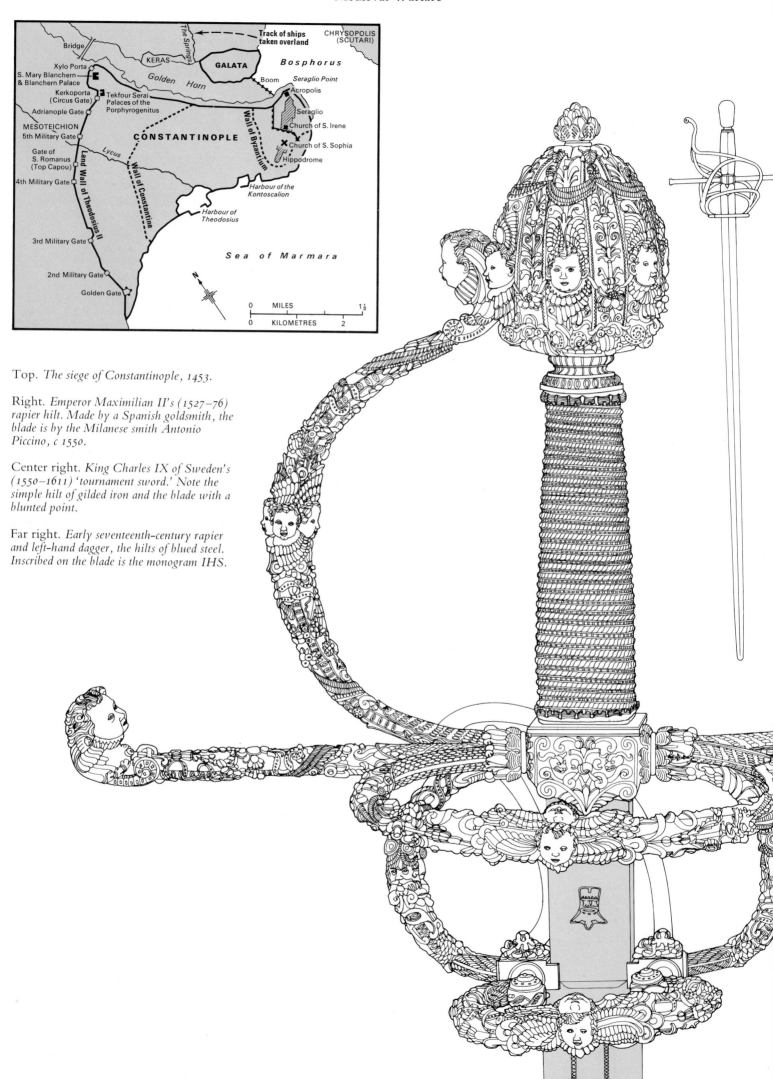

Top. *The siege of Constantinople, 1453.*

Right. *Emperor Maximilian II's (1527–76) rapier hilt. Made by a Spanish goldsmith, the blade is by the Milanese smith Antonio Piccino, c 1550.*

Center right. *King Charles IX of Sweden's (1550–1611) 'tournament sword.' Note the simple hilt of gilded iron and the blade with a blunted point.*

Far right. *Early seventeenth-century rapier and left-hand dagger, the hilts of blued steel. Inscribed on the blade is the monogram IHS.*

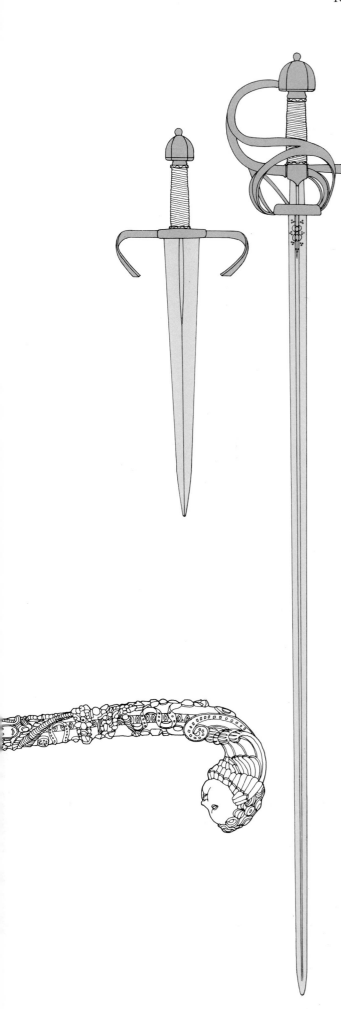

Armor of King Ferdinand of Portugal.

and the processing of imports which came from overseas, sugar, tobacco and diamonds. It was a Jesuit who coined the phrase that heresy furthers the spirit of commerce.

In 1567 the Duke of Alba, entered the Netherlands at the head of a Spanish army made up mainly of Spanish contingents but also Walloon, Italian and German mercenaries. He was opposed by a force that did not have a united core such as the Spaniards did. The German, English, Scottish and French mercenaries, lacked that bond which united Philip's army, the hatred of heretics. However, they did have an efficient army. Their first weapon of defense derived from their geography; by opening the sluices of their dykes, they put up a defensive barrier which was difficult to overcome.

But it cannot be said that the Dutch won that conflict because of their superior patriotism, let alone because their forces were militarily superior to those of the Spanish. Indeed, on occasions resistance in the Netherlands was often impeded by merchants who were inclined towards peace. Rich cities like Amsterdam delayed their break with Spain for many years. Military supremacy undoubtedly lay on the side of the Spanish, and this did not change when Elizabeth I of England aided the Netherlands, first surreptitiously and then openly. Nor did the defeat of the Armada in the English Channel affect the issue so profoundly as to tip the scales against the Spanish in the Netherlands. What made all the difference was that the Estates General could pay its mercenary forces regularly, while the Spanish were short of cash even to pay their own men, let alone their mercenaries. Without the economic means to conduct war, corruption among the Spanish captains became rife; mutinies of increasing

Left. *Advancing infantry squares.*

Right. *Besieging a fortified city (Swiss ms, mid-fifteenth century).*

Far right. *Siege of the fortress in Fillech in Upper Hungary illustrating the direct bombardment of interior of the fortress. Notice the main siege base on the far upper left.*

Below. *Attack on the Spanish Armada by fireship, 1588.*

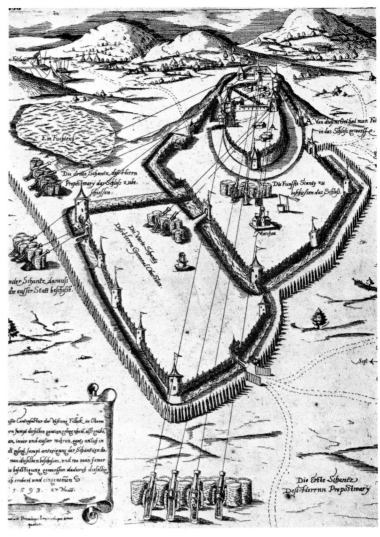

frequency destroyed the military effectiveness of the Spanish army. On 4 November 1576 when the mercenaries could not be paid, the town hall of Antwerp and several hundred houses were ravaged by the *furia espagnola*, and 10,000 of its inhabitants were killed.

The army of the Estates General faced considerable difficulties. Their commanders were the Princes of Orange of the House of Nassau, but they were under the permanent and minute scrutiny of the merchants. Members of the Estates General participated in the decision-making process at military headquarters. Moreover each commander had only those troops for which his province paid. The merchants were at the beginning unwilling to part with the sums required to keep an army in the field. But in their own interests they had to pay punctually, and that punctuality kept their army in being, while the superior power of their opponents was eroded because the enemy lacked economic substance. Great emphasis was placed on the training of men and officers, and since the Dutch contingents were small and numerous which increased their tactical mobility, the demands on men and officers were correspondingly higher. The Dutch could keep the Spaniards at bay on land; they could not conquer them. Where the Spanish Empire could be conquered by the Dutch was on the High Seas, which was really the least of their offensive operations. When in the end the Spanish gave the Dutch their independence, it was because they had been successfully repelled on land for 80 years; on the High Seas they had to yield completely to the Dutch. In the course of the struggle between the Netherlands and Spain a new military theory was developed which broke the remnants of military practice of the Middle Ages which had been left.

Pike exercises.

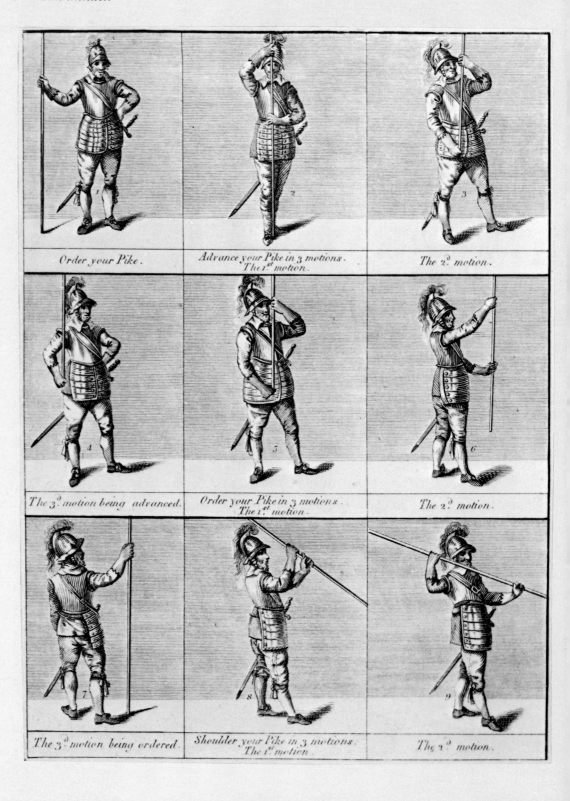

Order your Pike.

Advance your Pike in 3 motions.
The 1st motion.

The 2^d motion.

The 3^d motion being advanced.

Order your Pike in 3 motions.
The 1st motion.

The 2^d motion.

The 3^d motion being ordered.

Shoulder your Pike in 3 motions.
The 1st motion.

The 2^d motion.

THE PEASANT AT WAR

The 3d. motion being Shouldred.

Port your Pike in 3 motions. The 1st. motion.

The 2d. motion.

The 3d. motion being Ported.

Charge your Pike.

Advance your Pike.

Shoulder your Pike in 3 motions. The 1st. motion.

The 2d. motion.

The 3d. motion being Shouldred.

During the early Middle Ages peasants had been part of the popular levies until the military system of the feudal society established the clear differentiation between the caste that made war its profession and those who tilled the soil. However, this did not exclude peasants altogether; as servants of knights and as foot soldiery of the mounted feudal hosts, men of peasant origin were the most numerous. As an independent military force, however, they did not exist except on two occasions: the peasants' rebellion in England in the fourteenth century and the peasants' rebellion in Germany in the sixteenth.

Of these two rebellions the last is the most important, because the German Peasant Rebellion and the resulting Peasant War represented the first revolutionary rising in modern European history, whose militant expression also showed signs of military organization. The feudal nobility, itself seriously affected by stagnating feudal revenues, squeezed the peasants as hard as they could to extract the maximum. Upon the peasantry rested the burden of the nobility—the princes, the urban patricians and the Church. Of course, the peasants were not alone in feeling the pressures exerted by those above. On several occasions we have had cause to refer to the impoverishment of the lower nobility and the consequences that resulted from it. The urban communities increasingly began to feel the heavy hands of the vassals against which they defended themselves as well as they could. This resulted, once Luther had opened his struggle against the Papacy and for the Reformation of the Church in 1517, in a coalition of interests whose major cause was the abolition of the abuses of the Church. In an age in which all levels of society were deeply permeated with the Christian faith, it is no surprise that the religious issue stood before any other. Luther, in fact, divided the Germans and mobilized his supporters against the ecclesiastical and economic pressure of his opponents. But within a matter of a few years this opposition expanded into a general rebellion against all lords, secular and spiritual, and therefore against the entire feudal system. At that point the popular movement overtook Luther himself, who, well aware of the need of support of the secular powers, stopped short and came out in their favor against the popular movement. Within that movement Thomas Müntzer, once a fervent supporter of Luther, became the intellectual and political driving force who rejected Luther's claim that reforms should and could be initiated only from above. Müntzer was the son of prosperous artisans, had studied theology and become a priest. Access to the records of the Council of Constance had opened his eyes about the way in which Hus had been tried and after Luther had taken the initial step in 1517, he became his supporter until, among other differences of opinion, the realization that change and reform could only be brought about by revolution from below finally divorced him from Luther. From then on he traveled through the German and Bohemian lands as a radical agitator, who, like Luther, could rely on an invention which by that time was barely more than fifty years old for the spread of his message: Gutenberg's printing press. For the first time in history the printing press had become a mass medium which published the numerous tracts of the parties involved in the struggle in large editions.

Luther's refusal to support the revolutionary cause, which by 1521 was carried not only by the peasants but also by numerous burghers and the lower nobility was the first sign of the disintegration of the anti-Rome movement. One member of the lower nobility, Franz von Sickingen, had begun to recruit troops against the Archbishop of Trier in the spring of 1522, hoping that neighboring secular lords would give him their support. When he attacked Trier he was beaten by the princes of

The siege of Gotta, 1567.

the Palatinate and Hesse. Sickingen, who died of a wound obtained in the battle, had acted unwisely. Instead of driving a wedge between the faction of the upper nobility among whom he had a great number of supporters, his premature action had united them in fear of a general uprising of the lower nobility. It demonstrated that the lower nobility was no longer a political factor which could affect issues in any way. It ignored the economic aspects underlying the entire upheaval and remained politically impotent, while in fact the opportunity existed to lead a widespread popular movement throughout Germany. The cities also began to fear the rural mobs more than those forces of oppression against which they had complained so often. They had considered the peasants as their striking arm in battle, but once it displayed its potential power, they disowned it.

The broad coalition of interests that had existed between 1517 and 1521 broke asunder; Sickingen's attempt, representing the interests of the lower nobility as well as the attempt by Thuringian cities between 1522 and 1524 to replace the influence of the landed lords by their own, proved abortive. This led directly to the final phase in which the peasants played the major role.

Southwestern Germany was the point of origin of the Peasants' War, and Swabia, Württemberg, Baden and Alsace were

mildly, because it was very likely that otherwise they might make common cause with the unruly peasants of the upper Rhine against the clergy and the nobility, which would only be a disadvantage to the Reich.

The stronger and larger the rural community, the stronger was its military potential, and this was particularly the case in southwest Germany, the Tyrol and in the territory of the Archbishopric of Salzburg. Particularly in southwest Germany, including Alsace, the peasants had frequent occasion since the middle of the fourteenth century to use their arms against the marauding bands of mercenaries which Charles VII had tried to push east. Apparently the standing feudal levy proved a complete failure against them and it was left to the peasants to attack these bands, first by means of guerrilla warfare, and then in open battle in 1444, when they forced the mercenaries to abandon their route down the Rhine and pushed them back across the frontier into France. These peasant forces operated sometimes with and sometimes without the support of the towns in their area. The patricians of Colmar expressed great anxiety about the peasant forces because they might get together and rise against 'the pious people.'

On the whole no general assessment of the military potency of the peasant forces on the eve of the Peasant War is possible, except to say that the Alpine regions were more advanced than the others. Nor can it be said that any of the previous rebellions in the fifteenth century had a common denominator linking one with the other. In the sixteenth century that common denominator was supplied by the Reformation, the religious and ideological content of which was spread throughout the Ger-

The German Peasants' Rising: title page of the Twelve Articles, 1525.

its early centers. But what military experience did those peasants have to draw upon? Of course they were all members of popular levies, but their experience and effectiveness differed very widely in extent and quality. The levies in the Alpine regions bordering on the Swiss Confederation had drawn on the Swiss experience; they were well equipped with arms in their personal possession. Muskets were in evidence among them from the first decade of the sixteenth century. On the whole, however, the burgher levies of the cities were better equipped, and their mobilization could be carried out very quickly over the guild organization. The city of Ulm and others maintained their own artillery which was kept in the arsenal or in other cities, in the towers of the town wall.

Very important from the point of view of military experience was the mercenary system or *Landsknecht* recruitment. Response to recruitment campaigns in southwestern Germany and in the Tyrol had always been strong, and service in these armies must have been attractive to many young men who stood to inherit nothing from the soil other than its toil. In their military service they acquired qualities which the peasants lacked, and above all military experience, such as how to stand fast against the enemy's cavalry, as well as how to handle and resist shooting weapons. Emperor Maximilian realized this at an early stage. When *Landsknechte* had served with the French, which he had strictly prohibited, he ordered that they be punished only

man lands by wandering preachers and floods of tracts from which the lower strata gained the conviction that Luther's and Müntzer's cause against the lords was a just one.

The first signs of the Peasant War were the uprising of the Stühlingen peasants just north of the Swiss border and similar uprisings in northern Switzerland, in the Black Forest and in the Bishopric of Bamberg in the early summer of 1524. It reached its crest in the late fall of 1524 and paused between December 1524 and January 1525, to resume in February and reach its full force in the Alsace, the Palatinate, Württemberg, Franconia and Thuringia. The Tyrol, Salzburg and other Hapsburg crown lands followed suit in May.

The rising of 1525 caused considerable anxiety among the patricians of the cities in these regions. Yet the peasants offered a widely differing picture. Some groups formed themselves very rapidly and went into action against the nobility of the neighborhood and tried to win over the lower nobility and the burghers to their cause. Other peasant units with little military strength rallied but undertook little or nothing to gain supremacy in their region. They were also the first to be beaten and dispersed. Hence only those peasant formations which possessed great strength in numbers and arms were effective and then only if they were prepared to use these strengths immediately.

But the spontaneous nature of the rising of the Stühlingen peasants set the pace in the early months. They refused all feudal services and then they laid siege to Stühlingen Castle. Realizing that to operate successfully militarily they needed a proper command structure, they elected their own captains, sergeants

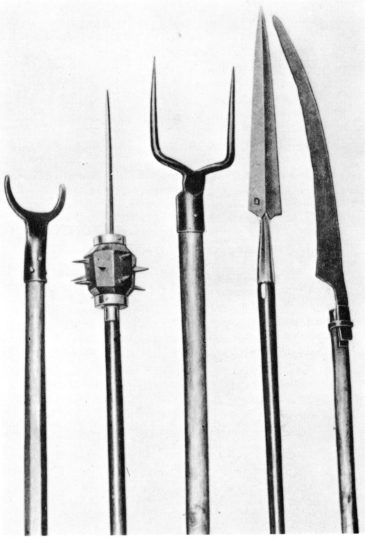

Left. *Fourteenth-century peasants: Italian gardener and woodman.*

Right. *Weapons of the sixteenth-century Peasants' Rising.*

Below. *Swabian peasants at war in 1525.*

and corporals. Their leader, Hans Müller from Bulgenbach, was characteristically a former *Landsknecht* in Imperial service. While laying siege they tried to find support from the Swiss south of them and concluded an alliance with the burghers of the town of Waldshut. The feudal lords appeared to be slow in reacting, for only by September did Frundsberg have his plans ready to raise an army against the peasants. The peasants profited from the lack of money of the Hapsburgs. However, they were unable to achieve *all* their military objectives, especially the conquest of the castles of the region. In that situation both sides were ready for negotiation. The Stühlingen peasants were asked to give up their arms and ask their lord for forgiveness. That was rather too much for them and they took to the field without reaching a military decision. Although the Hapsburgs were still at a disadvantage, their forces were engaged in upper Italy in their war against France. The bulk of the peasants desired to return home to bring in the harvest later in the season. What remained was a hard core under Müller who moved into the Black Forest from which throughout the winter months of 1524–25 they could not be dislodged. While Archduke Ferdinand of Hapsburg demanded drastic punishment of the peasants the nobility, divided and uncertain, did little.

The demands of the Stühlingen peasants and of the other peasant risings were moderate, demanding little more than the abolition of their feudal services. New trends, probably under Müntzer's influence, towards a greater radicalization can be observed from the early months of 1525 onwards when the complete removal of feudal lordship was demanded, based upon the claim of the equality of all men before God.

Then in February 1525 the great peasant assault began, launched by six main peasant formations in southwestern Germany. The strongest of them contained over 10,000 peasants. Their center was the free Imperial city of Memmingen, one of the few German cities which supported the peasants from the very beginning. In March 1525 it freed all its peasants from serfdom and feudal dues and granted them the right to elect their own chaplains and the use of the public land. From Memmingen spread the 'Twelve Articles,' containing the peasants' demands, the programatic foundation of the entire rebellion in 1525 throughout Germany. By the middle of March the rising spread from Swabia into Franconia and from there into Nuremberg followed by the rising of the region of the Odenwald Forest and the entire Neckar Valley. By the middle of April the rising had spread from Lake Constance to the Upper Werra in the north: 40,000 men in Swabia and about 25,000 in Franconia, against whom the nobility could at first put no equivalent force into the field. The sheer size of the rising

The Wars of Religion: Left. *Protestants forces besiege the town of Poitiers 1569.* Above. *Engagement of the French forces during the Battle of Jarnac, 13 March 1569.*

precluded a unified body of peasantry and a common strategy forming, but its absence did not count as long as the nobility itself was unable to agree on a common plan of action.

One of the reasons for the absence of a common strategy was the existence of different aims among the peasant groups; moderates wished no more than amelioration of the feudal burdens, and radicals designed the overthrow of the entire feudal system.

Absence of military organization was not a reason. On the contrary, the peasant formations organized themselves along the military principles of the time; that is to say, they copied the organization and structure of the *Landsknechte*. Each unit comprised several *Fähnleins*, each of which was about 500 men strong. The *Fähnlein* itself was subdivided into *Rotten* or groups of from 15 to 20 men. The commander was the Supreme Field Captain elected by the entire peasant formation. He appointed quartermasters, supply masters, wagon castle masters, judges and provost marshals. Each *Fähnlein* was commanded by a captain whose immediate subordinates were the ensign and

the members of the war-council. All of these officers were elected by the *Fähnlein*, while the captain would appoint a supply master in charge of booty, and a sergeant. The *Rotte* also elected its own leader.

A rather more difficult problem than that of setting up a military form of organization was that of equipping it. The peasants at first had only those weapons which they themselves possessed—simple pikes, short swords and perhaps armor. Added to these came a great number of agricultural implements converted into weapons, such as flails and scythes. Therefore one of the first endeavors of the peasants was to obtain fire

Landsknechte *camping.*

weapons, musketry and artillery. Peasants from the Alps and the urban contingents were better equipped with muskets than the rest. But artillery had to be captured first, and artillery could only be obtained from the cities.

There were bound to be differences between those peasant formations who had rallied together spontaneously and those whose formation had been carefully planned by their leaders. The former were generally badly equipped in comparison with the latter. The systematically planned capture of Marktdorf and Meersdorf by the peasant formation of Lake Constance gained them six heavy and several light pieces of artillery and 16 tons of gunpowder. At Dinkelsbühl and Göppingen the peasants took the contingents of musketry they needed and some artillery. A considerable arsenal of weapons of all kinds was held in Nuremberg, but the peasants were aware that that city would be too hard a nut for them to crack at that early stage. Other cities, although not siding with the peasants, but wishing to avoid the inconvenience of having to fight with them and the devastation of their surrounding countryside, handed over weapons voluntarily. Some even loaned artillery to them. Rothenburg, which at first sided with the peasants, handed its two heavy artillery pieces, gunpowder and ammunition together with crews to a prominent leader of the peasantry, Florian Geyer, a Frankish knight of the lower nobility.

These supplies were forthcoming as long as the insurrection spread, but after it had suffered its first reverses, such as at Frankenhausen and Böblingen, the cities of the area were rather more reluctant, and gradually all supplies were throttled. Possessing artillery does not mean having the capacity to use it effectively. It seems that among the peasants skilled artillery crews were very scarce. Badly equipped peasant formations in the Salzburg region received their first modern weapons only after they had beaten an army of the Styrian nobility in July 1525 capturing its entire artillery and ammunition, but sub-

sequently could make very little use of it for lack of experienced crews. From April 1525 onwards an order was given by the Supreme Captains of all the peasant formations to train artillery crews. Peasant artillery was successful in the siege of individual feudal castles, but not against cities or in battle in the open field.

Next to armament the problem of securing enough supplies for the peasants was most important. Both 1523 and 1524 had been years with bad harvests and the supplies held in villages, towns and cities were below the normal level. The larger the peasant formation the more difficult the problem of feeding it. In the end the solution was the same as that taken by any other military formation of the time; they lived off the land; preferably that of the enemy, but if need be their own as well. Many of the attacks upon castles and abbeys of the time had their origin not in the strategic importance of this or that point or in their hatred of priests and nobility, but simply because large amounts of supplies could be expected to be stored there. After the storm and capture of the castle of the Counts von Gleichen, the peasants requisitioned 200 buckets of wine, dried meat of 35 cattle, meat of 70 pigs, 200 barrels of beer and all the bread available. The Counts later complained in a list of the damage they had suffered that the peasants had also fished their pond to the point of exhaustion. In other instances, as in the case of fire weapons, towns, estates and abbeys were forced into regular supply deliveries, lest the peasants would put the red cock on their roofs, that is to say set their buildings on fire. In regions under their control traversed by important trade routes such as Rothenburg, merchant convoys were supplied with special letters of protection in return for contributions in money or in kind. To plunder and to ravage at will was against their principles and contrary to their aims. To replace an old order by aimlessly devastating entire territories would have been self-contradictory.

Right. *Artillery pieces of the army of Maximilian I.*

Below right. Landsknechte *in combat (Painting by H. Holbein the Younger, 1531).*

Bottom. Left and right. *Musket excercises.*

Guard blow and open your Pan.   Present.   Give Fire.

Dismount your Musket.   Unlock your Match.   Return your Match.

Clear your Pan.   Prime your Pan.   Shut your Pan.

Other areas under peasant control were systematically divided up by their commanders, the supplies each was capable of delivering were assessed and it was then up to the captain of the *Fähnlein* to insure these deliveries, bringing them together at the headquarters of the supreme field captain who then made his allocations for the *Fähnleins* under his command. But as soon as deliveries of these supplies were disturbed, supply difficulties or shortages made themselves felt immediately. When the city of Nördlingen stopped its deliveries because its population began to be seriously affected by them, the peasant army felt the pinch at once. Supplies were best regulated where the insurrection had been carefully planned and where a large region had been brought under control. If one sees democratic principles at work in the organization of the peasant forces, the issue of supplies shows that some formations were not as democratically handled as one might be led to assume. The peasant army of

Maximilian I (left) in a knightly tournament.

Lake Constance had to pay five guilders per 100 men for the support of their captain. Also special taxation was levied in some areas solely for the commanders.

As the insurrection wore on through 1525 mercenaries also found employment in the peasant armies, and their increase inevitably introduced in some formations the barbaric habits of their profession. To counteract this the mercenaries, instead of being distributed over the entire force, were concentrated in a special company or companies. For one thing this insured that the habits of a few would not affect the entire body of the peasantry. For another, military expertise was concentrated in one troop, a warrior elite that could be entrusted with special tasks for which military experience was essential and, of course, their activities could be kept under better control.

To insure discipline among their ranks the peasant leaders drew up special regulations, or Letters of Articles, which insofar as military discipline was concerned, were closely modeled on those of the *Landsknechte*. The Frankish peasants of the Rothenburg area were the first to do so. In them they first insisted on the equality of all men before the Lord and then went into more

Artillery pieces used by the armies of Maximilian I.

detailed provisions which are said to have been drafted by Florian Geyer. They insisted on unquestioning obedience to the orders issued by their captains in the field and strictly prohibited independent raids for booty. Offences against these commands were punishable by death. To aid the provost in his policing duties it was forbidden to insult or obstruct him. But the captain and other officers were responsible to the entire formation and had to give account of their conduct to the massed assembly if they were asked to do so. This, of course, is a novelty not to be found in any of the Letters of Articles of the *Landsknechte*. In administrative matters the captain was dependent on the advice

Henry II of France is mortally wounded in a tournament in 1559. This spelt the end of the tournament as a popular spectacle in France.

of his councillors, but not in the military sphere. He was to send out no letters personally or receive any, other than those passed or read by the council. The purpose of this rule was to prevent the captains of mercenaries and *Landsknechte* from entering into negotiations with the enemy to strike a better bargain, often behind the back of their men. In matters concerning general discipline the peasant articles were even more explicit and stricter than those of the *Landsknechte*. Blasphemy, swearing, gambling, excessive drinking and the keeping of prostitutes in the camp were forbidden. So were fights; if one should break out then it was the task of those coming to the fray to put an end to it immediately. Whoever broke the peace of the camp could be killed forthwith. One disciplinary code even prohibited envy, hatred, anger and ill will, though one wonders how such an offence could be proven let alone prosecuted. No one was to leave the camp without permission. The first thing Florian Geyer did when entering Rothenburg with his formation was to erect gallows 'to punish the wicked and to protect the good from the bad.' On the march or in action the peasants were ordered to protect women, maidens, widows, young children, the old and the sick. Millers seem to have enjoyed a special protection; they were explicitly named because of their usefulness. Cities, towns, villages, churches and abbeys could not be attacked except on explicit orders from the captain. Within the camp the officers were always to put up their abode at a central point, accessible to all men.

When on the march, the peasant formation was preceded by a vanguard of two *Fähnlein*, followed by the mass. These were

Trained militiamen and nobles preparing to attack a city. Note here the disciplined cavalry formation and the guns lined up on the distant right sighted ready to fire on the town (Watercolor by an unknown artist, sixteenth century).

Right. *The taking of Marseilles, 1596.*

followed by the train and artillery, if they had any, and again by a rearguard of two *Fähnlein*. No reference to cavalry is ever made because the peasants had none. This was to prove a serious deficiency, because the men who lacked the experience of the *Landsknechte* in withstanding mounted attacks were prone to give up their position.

Generally speaking the peasants were well-equipped with muskets and artillery by the middle of 1525; what they lacked was both training and experience. Their pike was not the long pike carried by the *Landsknechte* but the short one, which deprived them of a vital weapon essential to withstand cavalry attacks. In open field combat they displayed uncertainty and fared better against isolated castles. Having no cavalry of their own, their weakness was the weakness of their infantry which in open battle tended instinctively towards the defensive rather than the offensive.

Once the nobility and the cities rallied against the peasants, their fighting discipline was relatively low. It was not difficult to cut a breach into their square and in the face of a mounted attack the peasants tended to leave rank and look for a more protected position, the worst possible thing they could do. Religious and social fervor alone could not match years and decades of military experience. But once in firm positions they displayed an astonishing degree of bravery. The peasants of the Upper Allgäu in southern Germany withstood a concentrated cannonade and defended their positions to the last. The peasants of Salzburg defended that city for almost three weeks against the massed

attacks of Frundsberg and his *Landsknechte*. Even when the square was scattered, they put up ferocious resistance time and again.

During the short era in which peasant armies operated they could hardly have achieved total military victory. Political competition between peasant armies and their internal differences based on religious sectarianism coupled with their growing disunity over the course to be pursued and aims to be

achieved was opposed by their enemies' unity of will to put an end to the insurrection despite their differences. By the summer of 1525 most of them were defeated by forces in the employ of the League of Swabian cities and by Imperial forces. Only in the Tyrol did the struggle spill over into 1526. After that the peasant army came to an end; members, when caught, were butchered like vermin. Peace had been re-established; the peace of the gallows, the sword, the wheel and the fire.

The Thirty Years' War: the forces of Jan Tserklaes, Count of Tilly (1559–1632), cross the River Lech.

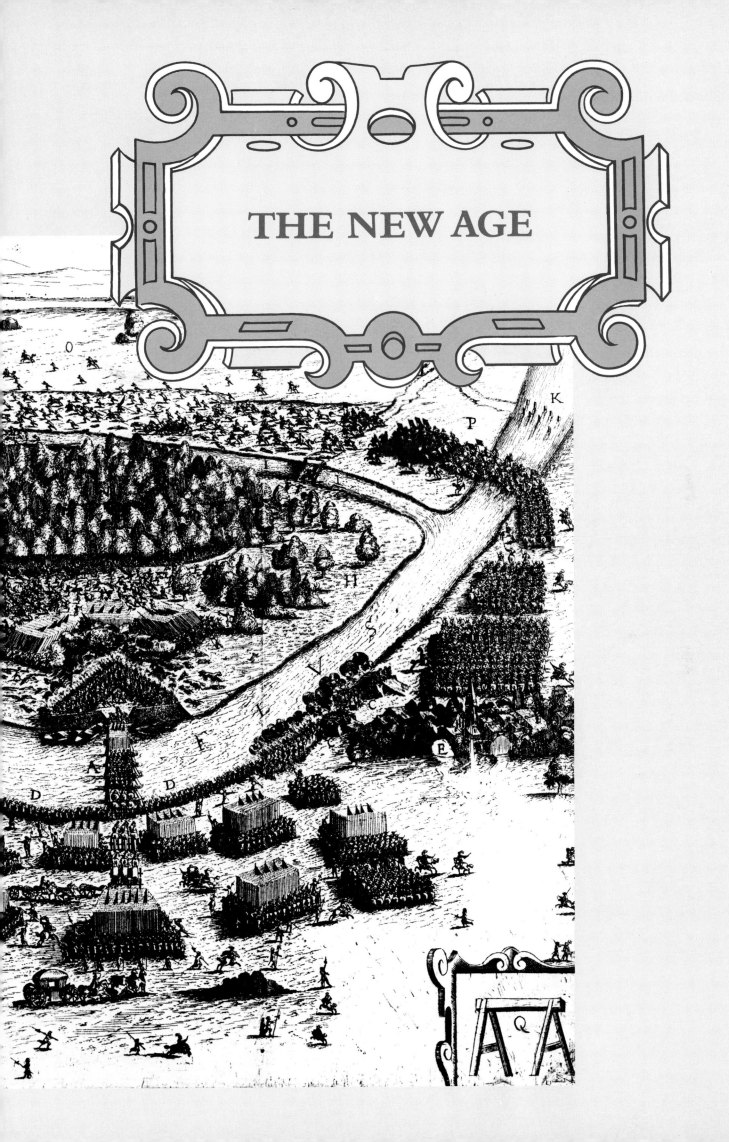

THE NEW AGE

Until the end of the fifteenth century military theory had been a rather under-developed area of discussion and investigation. The various writers who concerned themselves with it were in the main not soldiers themselves but were clericals or laymen and their writings consisted of excerpts from Xenophon and Vegetius. The latter had emphasized the need for physical strength for Roman soldiers and drawn up some exercises for them. The Archbishop of Bourges, Cardinal Aegidius Romanus, in addition to taking extractions from Vegetius, invented tactical formations which had no relevance to the military practice of the Middle Ages or any other age.

Only the transformation of warfare produced a theoretician of outstanding quality, Niccolo Machiavelli, the prophet of the army of the future. Born in 1469, he witnessed in his youth with his own eyes how the once powerful cavalry was replaced by the infantry as the decisive arm in all battles. In his writings on military affairs he argued the case in favor of an efficient citizens' militia to replace the horror of the mercenaries. As Chancellor of Florence, he advised the city to organize a militia recruited by districts and led by a captain experienced in warfare. The militia were, in the main, composed of infantry soldiers and its tactics

The Thirty Years' War, 1618–1648.

copied the infantry tactics of the Swiss and the *Landsknechte*. But the political realities of Florence imposed their own limitations. Such a militia could become potentially dangerous to the Republic as within the militia were supporters of the expelled Medici Family. The politics of Florence were full of mutual suspicion. Therefore the powers of the captain over the militia had to be severely limited which seriously impeded his contact with his troops.

Machiavelli's militia existed for seven years; with its aid Pisa was reconquered by Florence. But when in 1512 the Medici Family supported by Spanish troops crossed the frontier, it was the end of the Florentine Republic. Its militia could not withstand the Spaniards. Machiavelli's own studies were based on a thorough knowledge of the warfare of the Romans. One of the aspects of Roman expertise which seems to have eluded him, however, was Roman discipline. Nor did he formulate clear strategic concepts. When the medieval host was replaced by infantry and by fire weapons which in a short span of time had developed a degree of sophistication not matched by the weapons of old, new tactical formations were possible. Masses of troops now entered the field. Since these troops were costly they were valuable, and the strategy of attrition began to take the upper hand over that of annihilation. Machiavelli, in spite of the

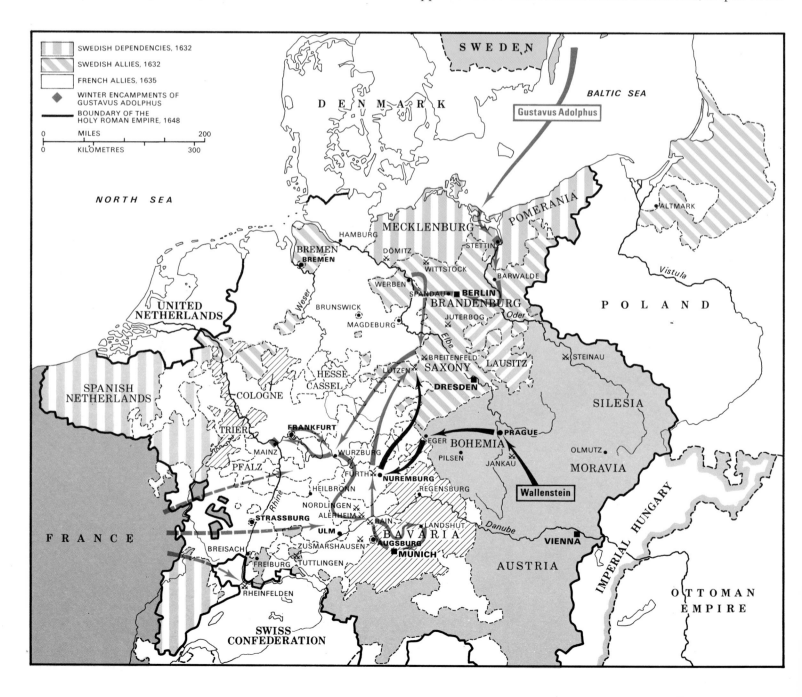

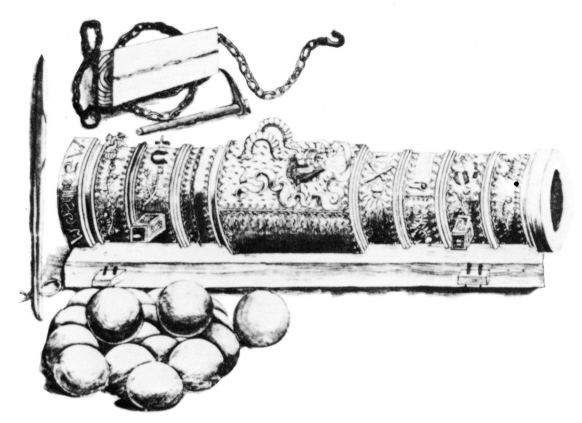

Below. *Infantry techniques c 1616.*

realities around him, still advocated the latter, although at one point he said that good generals give battle only when necessity forces them to it or when they have a favorable opportunity. In other words, Machiavelli failed to differentiate clearly between these two strategic alternatives, nor did he realize the complementary nature of the economic forces which imposed attrition in place of annihilation upon the generals of the period.

'He who knows to deliver a decisive battle well, in spite of any other mistakes committed in the conduct of a campaign, would find approval. He who lacks that ability, however able in other branches of warfare, would never bring a war to an honorable end. Because a major battle which you win eliminates the error you may have committed previously.'

If battles had been fought like that, there might well have been soldiers left to fight them, but no money to pay them. The tactics of the Swiss may have influenced him. The recognition that mercenaries consist of the dregs of society was a lesson driven home to him by personal experience. The alternative which he suggested, that an army should consist of one's own subjects infused with patriotic spirit, remained a prophecy to be turned into reality only centuries later.

Indeed, on a smaller scale and with numerous qualifications Machiavelli's prophecy was first practiced by the Spanish, but the extent of their operations was such that Spanish manpower alone no longer sufficed. They too had to take recourse to recruiting foreign contingents. But the Spanish army, refining and sifting through the filter of their own experiences and those of the Swiss and the *Landsknechte*, was the first in the history of modern Europe to develop anything resembling modern infantry tactics. The infantry usually massed in the center of the order of battle with the field artillery before them and cavalry protecting the rear and the wings. Battles were fought in parallel order, but in view of the essentially static battle order and the presence of excessive baggage trains, it was rarely possible to follow up a victory on the battlefield by a swift pursuit of the enemy. Nevertheless, in spite of their unwieldly nature, Spanish tactics were superior to the less well-trained armies of the time.

However, as the cost of firearms in general, or a train of artillery in particular, was beyond the resources of a mercenary

Military dress showing definite Spanish influence.

captain, the tendency pointed towards control of the armed forces by the monarchy, the one power able to raise the funds necessary for modern equipment. Hence it has been rightly argued that the introduction of firearms and their growing pre-eminence brought about further concentration of power in secular hands. It raised the monarchy above the Church and turned war from a moral trial into a political instrument.

The Spanish military system brought forth the first large scale standing army and was copied by most European powers. Military service gradually ceased to be a function of caste and developed into a 'national' profession. But while still in the process of being copied by the armies of the European continent, the Spanish system was challenged by that of the Dutch who brought forth one of the important military innovators in the person of Prince Maurice of Orange, the son of William the Silent. His main innovation was the 'reform of the rabble' which constituted his infantry. Realizing that the fundamental weakness of the Spanish army lay in its relative immobility, a considerable impediment considering the geography of the Spanish Netherlands, Maurice placed a premium on mobility, a policy well-suited to a terrain crisscrossed with a network of canals and dykes. (He himself would hardly have claimed the reputation of an innovator, since he based his system on the example provided by the Roman infantry, or at least on how the writers of antiquity like Livy had described it.)

Externally the novelty was uniform drill; internally it was

Defense of Cadiz (Painting by F. Zurbaran, The Prado, Madrid).

discipline. Proceeding from the premise that the United Netherlands would have to mobilize its forces at very short notice, it was necessary to transform civilians by means of a few signals into a militarily useful instrument. Infantry drill achieved just that. True, a certain amount of drill was practised by the Spanish infantry squares. But Maurice brought mobility into his infantry by introducing specific commands and uniform movements. Units were sub-divided into platoons, and at a signal given either by drums or bugles they could dissolve and re-form, every man knowing his place in the unit. The Dutch were renowned for being able to assemble 2000 men in an hour and a quarter.

In addition to creating and maintaining order, Maurice's innovations gave each infantry unit an extraordinary degree of mobility, so that even during the excitement of battle the commander had his men under firm control and was always in a position to direct them uniformly and purposefully. Wherever reinforcements were needed they could attack at several different points simultaneously if necessary.

Prince Maurice and his cousin Prince William Louis of the Netherlands went so far as to build up vast formations of lead soldiers to perform on table tops the exercises that they intended to apply in the field. The Dutch army was subjected to severe drill and field exercises which if forced upon a unit of mercenaries would have caused rebellion. On the other hand, their soldiers accepted this, if for no other reason than that they were generously and punctually paid. Compared with their Dutch opponents, units of the Spanish army often went as long as three years without pay; looting and disorder became a general feature associated with them. Maurice also established regular ranks within each company (about 130 strong) from captain to lieutenant downwards. They were officers

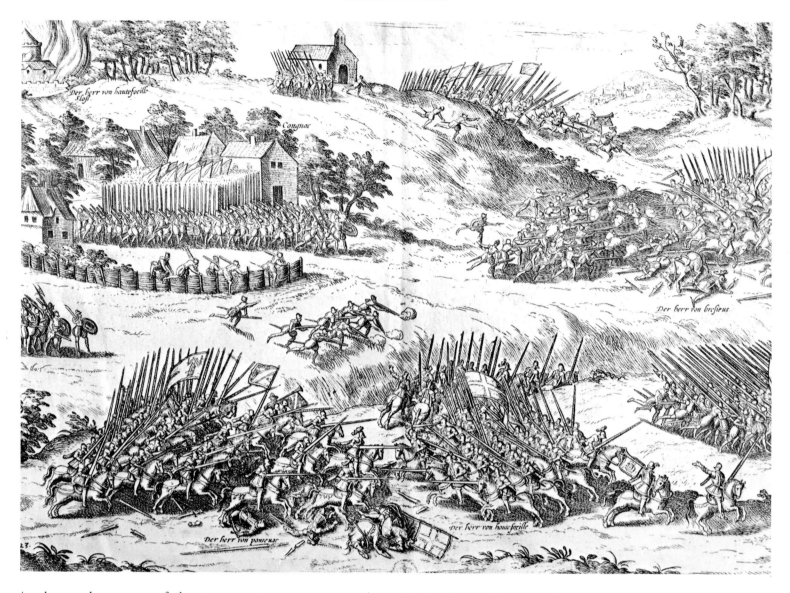

Battle of Cognac, 6 January 1568.

in the modern sense of the term, not mercenary captains.

Well-paid, well-officered troops could also be ordered to build their own earthworks, a type of work which mercenaries had always considered to be below their dignity. Internal discipline was strictly enforced. Maurice had two men hanged because one had stolen a hat, the other a dagger. One man was shot for robbing a woman.

The lessons taught by Maurice found their emulators in the conflict that dominated seventeenth century warfare in Europe: the Thirty Years' War. The problems present since the decay of the feudal system as well as their solutions were dramatically highlighted for the last time in the warfare of Gustavus Adolphus and much more so in that of Wallenstein.

Gustavus Adolphus refined the tactics of the Dutch. From the age of seventeen he had constant experience of war and was determined to learn from each experience whatever lessons were to be learned. Accepting Maurice's maxim that mobility is based on thorough drill and discipline, and discipline upon sound administration, he saw to it that all were at a high point of efficiency during his time as a military commander. Drunkenness and low speech were severely punished, though in an army of 70,000 successful enforcement of discipline, such as Cromwell was later to impose upon the New Model Army, must have been difficult if not impossible.

The areas in which he excelled 'were tactics, organization and arms.' Gustavus refined the Dutch example of army drill to a fine art. The highest tactical unit was the brigade, arranged in a linear pattern six deep, alternating with musketeer and pike units. The musketeers moved behind the pikes to cover them-

selves against a cavalry charge, while the reserve pike units would fill the gaps in the line left by them. Apart from perfecting infantry tactics and those of the cavalry, now equipped with light swords and pistols, Gustavus Adolphus made his own unique contribution. He realized and put to full use the potential inherent in the artillery. He was the first great field gunner who, in order to increase the mobility of his forces, reduced the vast range of artillery types and calibers, designed lighter types of gun carriages, and standardized his artillery into three main types. First, there were the siege pieces weighing 60, 30, and 15 cwt; second, the field pieces of 24, 12 and six pounders; and third, regimental pieces, two to a regiment, which were light four-pounders. Gunnery drill, especially for the regimental gunners, was stepped up to a pace which enabled them to fire eight rounds to the musketeer's six shots. In contrast to the Spaniards and the Spanish system as practiced by his opponent Tilly, Gustavus was able to reduce his baggage trains to an absolute minimum. For supplies he depended on well-fortified supply depots which were set up along the army's line of advance.

Having entered the Thirty Years' War in 1630 Gustavus Adolphus fought the decisive battle at Breitenfeld near Leipzig on 17 September 1631. His opponent, Marshal Tilly, was described by a contemporary as 'short in stature . . . meager and terrible in aspect; his cheeks were sunken, his nose long, his eyes fierce and dark.' Apart from Wallenstein, Tilly was the most able commander on the Imperial side and a master of Spanish tactics. At Breitenfeld he commanded an army of approximately 40,000 men, a quarter of whom were cavalry. Drawn up in seventeen great squares they waited for the Swedish attack. The Swedes attacked in a way which insured that the musketeers were covered by pikemen and could file between their ranks, discharge their muskets and retire to reload. Instead of Tilly's immovable squares the Swedish army was divided up into smaller units, 'each unit like a little movable fortress with its curtains and javelins, and each part would come to the assistance of the other.'

Assisted by a barrage of artillery which fired at a ratio of 3:1 to the Imperial guns, the Swedes caused havoc among Tilly's

troops and precipitated an abortive cavalry attack which left Tilly's flanks unprotected. Gustavus Adolphus immediately exploited the much greater mobility of his forces and rolled up the Imperial front. All this took place while the Swedish artillery was still pounding away at the immobile Imperial squares. Not drilled effectively enough to retire systematically and in order, the squares, once broken up, disintegrated and stampeded. The Swedes won the day. A year later, still reaping the rewards of valor and fame, Gustavus Adolphus was killed.

An opponent of a different caliber was Wallenstein, probably the greatest commander of the Thirty Years' War. Wallenstein was a superb general with a political head and historical perspective. Aware of the fragility of the Empire, he endeavored to limit and contain the centrifugal forces of the territorial princes

Below. Cavalry exercises. A Guiding a flask. B Loading a pistol. C Drawing a rammer. D Loading with a bullet and ramming home.

A foot soldier prepares to release an arrow-charge from his longbow while holding his pike at the ready to defend himself against possible cavalry attack (after The Double Armed Man *by William Neade, 1625. The book proposed that the British Army continued to use the longbow in conjunction with the pike as illustrated.*

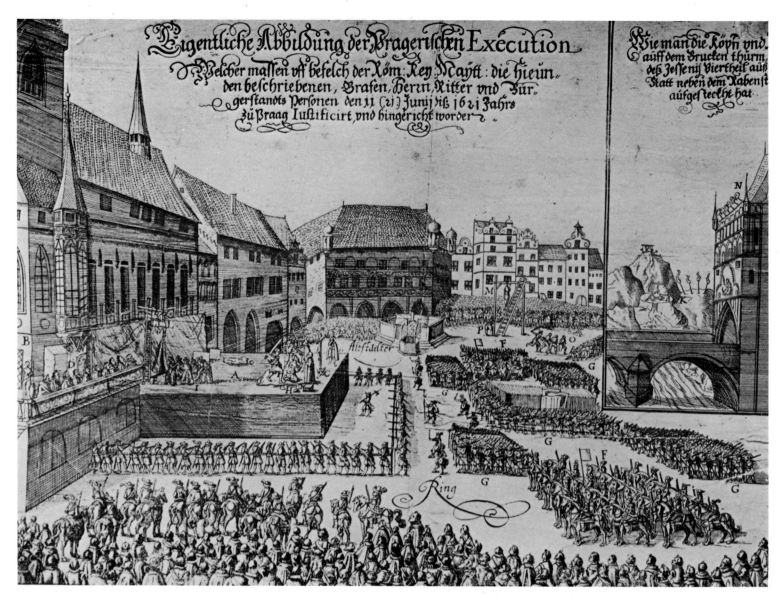

and thus gave the Empire the opportunity to enter, under the direction of the Imperial Crown, that avenue which its neighbors to the west had entered some time ago—a centralized unitary state. That he failed does not reduce the quality of his powers of analysis and vision, qualities in which he was rivaled by only one man in his time, Cardinal Richelieu. Wallenstein, at times, tried to make Imperial policy when his master vacillated, sometimes even against his master's will, but always in the interest of the Empire. However, even he was not strong enough to overcome entrenched feudal prejudices.

In addition to military and political sense, Wallenstein also had a sound economic sense. Not only did he aquire a vast territory, he administered and developed it so profitably that he was able to lend money to the Emperor. Money to Wallenstein was a force which could make or unmake things, armies included. The problem of how to finance armies had been almost 500 years old. The Imperial Court and its councilors were well aware that raising an army required money. To maintain order and discipline within it required even more. Yet in 1621 the Imperial coffers were nearly empty. Of course there was always the Imperial Diet, the Reichstag, which could grant money and supplies but this was not always feasible nor desirable as witnessed in the Hussite wars. When the Reformation divided the nation and, more important, the princes, no funds were to be had. Moreover, the territorial princes of Germany at their western frontier were able to see for themselves how a dynasty based on a centralized administration could gradually erode the powers and privileges of the lesser princes and lords. Spain

Above. *Frederick V (1596–1632), Elector Palatine, became King of Bohemia in 1619. After his defeat at the Battle of the White Mountain in 1620, he was forced to give up his crown and flee the Holy Roman Empire. Noblemen and citizens who helped him were executed in Prague in 1621.*

Above right. *Maurice of Nassau (1567–1625) attacking a dam held by Spanish forces supported by English naval forces on the river.*

Right. *The miseries of war: soldiers enlisting for battle.*

provided another such example, as did Europe's offshore island in the north-west, England. Any attempt to introduce a permanent system of taxation was bound to fail if put to the German princes. The Empire was to be strong, but not stronger than its princes. Among the Imperial forces mutinies were frequent between 1619 and 1625, all caused because pay was not forthcoming.

It was during this time that Wallenstein offered to raise an army at his own expense. That is to say, he would initially raise the forces, their initial pay, their clothes, weapons, ammunition, their wagons and tents. As the cost of this army was bound to exceed the resources of even the richest private person, Wallenstein suggested that the principle of finance should be changed. Contributions levied on the districts should no longer be one token payment, a kind of punitive measure levied in enemy territory, but should become a regular standard tax during wartime to be paid by every territory and city throughout the Catholic part of the Empire, and throughout the Hapsburg

Crown lands. The Emperor and his councilors agreed. Whether they realized the full consequences of this decision upon the constitutional practice of the Empire is unknown. Probably they did, but operating on the principle that the morrow will take care of itself, they were interested first and foremost in having an army capable of defeating the threat from the Protestant north. The Emperor empowered Wallenstein to levy and collect the contributions, which he did promptly and successfully, and as long as Wallenstein stood at the head of the Imperial army, the discrepancy between what an army required for its maintenance and pay and the financial resources available disappeared.

But once the system was put into practice in November 1625, the Imperial Chancellery was flooded by protests against the practice. Wallenstein, it was alleged, was bleeding the community dry, yet the very quarters which complained and pleaded that they were near the point of exhaustion, year after year managed to raise the contributions levied by Wallenstein. The army was no longer an instrument assembled to meet a particular emergency. It developed into a permanent institution, into an instrument of the Emperor, and thus a potential danger for the territorial princes. But that was not how the princes, in particular the Elector of Bavaria, Maximilian, put it to the Emperor. An army which by 1626 exceeded 50,000 in the hands of a man, the Bohemian noble Wallenstein, could become a danger to the Emperor himself. However, this argument initially was ignored; the Emperor was more afraid of military ineffectiveness and the marauding mobs into

De Sweedsche Armade.

Above. *Gustavus Adolphus (1594–1632) at the Battle of Leipzig, 1631.*

Right. *Cavalry excercises.*

which an army degenerates if it is not fed and paid properly.

Wallenstein's method of levying contributions was not arbitrary, a fact which further upset the citizenry. Of each area he demanded just so much that the economic basis of its population remained secure enough to exist and to allow the creation of such surpluses as would enable the area to have sufficient funds to meet the contribution of the following year. The first contributions were levied on the Hapsburg Crown lands, followed by the territories of the Reich. Suddenly, the Emperor was in the possession of power which he had not had for centuries; his army was not that of the princes but his own.

Under Wallenstein a standing army of a significant size

Below. *Preparing to fire an early mortar.*

1. *To Horse.*   2. *Uncap your Pistol.*   5. *Span your Pistol.*   6. *Prime your Pistol.*

3. *Draw your Pistol.*   4. *Order your Pistol.*   7. *Shut your Pan.*   8. *Cast about your Pistol.*

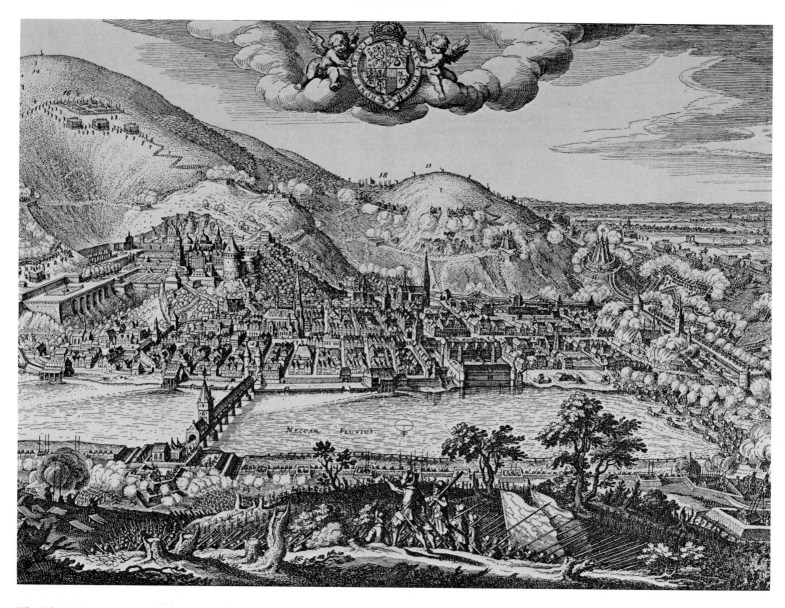

The Thirty Years' War: Tilly besieges Heidelberg.

appeared in Europe. Adherents of the Spanish system, like Tilly, maintained that any army over 40,000 men would be impossible to lead and contradicted all existing tactical and strategic doctrine. When Tilly made that remark Wallenstein's army numbered 125,000 men, an army too large for the Catholic Electoral princes of Germany. From the moment of the army's inception, the princes opposed him by means of intrigue, and finally in 1630 they succeeded in having Wallenstein replaced.

But with Gustavus Adolphus' invasion of Germany the picture changed completely. Having beaten Tilly at Breitenfeld he rapidly moved to southern Germany and Wallenstein was recalled. When Gustavus reached Munich in July 1632, Wallenstein moved from Bohemia across into Germany, threatening to cut the lines of communication of the Swedes. Gustavus was forced to return and entrenched himself behind the fortifications of Nuremberg, awaiting Wallenstein's attack. Wallenstein was one of the few generals who never fought an offensive battle. Instead of doing as Gustavus expected, Wallenstein built a fortification of earthwalls on a long ridge overlooking the River Regnitz less than five miles from the city and waited. Every corner was covered by his artillery and he waited there for six weeks. Wallenstein had only 27,000 men in this expedition and while he waited Gustavus gained further reinforcements until his army totaled 57,000 men. But reinforcements also have to be fed, and it was this factor which forced

Gustavus to leave the city and attack Wallenstein on 1 September 1632. For four days the Swedes attacked. After losing 7000 men in this battle, Gustavus gave up. On Wallenstein's part the battle was a masterly, classic demonstration of the strategy of attrition. Gustavus Adolphus's reputation as 'Master of Germany' was shattered.

Two months later, after Wallenstein invaded Saxony, they met again on the plain of Lützen. Gustavus had intended to head him off from his Leipzig supply base. The battle began on 16 November 1632. From morning to night the Swedes attacked Wallenstein's forces and overcame some of his formations, but not the hard core. Only the onset of darkness put an end to the battle. Both armies were totally exhausted and Wallenstein marched his troops to Leipzig in the darkness. It was a battle that had neither victor nor vanquished. Its significance lies in the fact that among the fatal casualties of the Swedes was their own King, Gustavus Adolphus.

The confrontations between Gustavus Adolphus and Wallenstein established a new age of warfare. Major armies trained and drilled according to maxims and tactics profoundly different from those of preceding centuries. The age of modern warfare, whose outlines had been visible on the horizon for a long time, had stepped to the fore. Medieval warfare, whose principal aspects had long been in decline, had disappeared in the last great religious conflict in Europe, the Thirty Years' War. The cannonades of the artillery, and the volleys of the muskets and rifles, were to reverberate throughout the world from that day forward.

How to lay siege to a city
(Military treatise by
Wolf von Senftenberg, 1570).

PICTURE CREDITS

AB Nordbok: 208, 209 (top), 245 (right).
Author's collection: 12 (bottom), 13 (both), 14 (both), 15 (bottom), 16, 18,
27, 28, 35, 104, 106 (bottom), 107, 135 (left), 147 (bottom), 149 (top), 151
(bottom right), 185 (top), 190 (both), 191 (top), 192 (both), 195 (bottom),
196 (bottom), 221, 227 (bottom), 229 (top), 233 (bottom and top), 234
(both), 241 (top).
Badische Laandesbibliothek, Karlsruhe: 31.
Bibliothèque de Cambrai: 69 (bottom).
Bibliothèque Municipale, Boulogne: 179 (top).
Bibliothèque Nationale, Paris, 2, 4, 19 (bottom), 20, 51 (bottom), 59, 64–65,
66 (bottom), 69 (top two), 72 (top right, bottom left), 73 (top), 74, 75, 80,
81 (bottom), 87, 88 (bottom), 90, 91, 96 (bottom), 97 (all three), 98
(bottom), 100 (bottom), 101 (top right), 112 (two bottom right), 104–105,
119 (both), 121, 122–123, 136 (both), 137 (top), 141 (both), 142 (bottom
left) 143, 144 (top two), 146, 147 (top), 148 (top), 150 (both), 200, 214 (top),
251.
Bodleian Library, Oxford: 138–139, 144 (bottom), 145 (above), 149
(bottom left), 151 (bottom left), 172–173, 182 (bottom).
British Crown Copyright reserved (Tower of London): 67 (all three), 70,
71, 134 (bottom), 149 (bottom right), 152 (top left and bottom), 162–3, 166
(both), 167, 175 (top left), 185 (right), 191 (bottom left).
British Museum Library Board: 8, 29, 46 (top), 51 (top), 68 (top left), 82
(bottom), 88 (top), 101 (left and bottom), 108 (right), 120, 124 (left), 125
(bottom right), 126 (bottom), 134 (top), 142 (top left, bottom right), 145,

148 (bottom), 152 (top right), 153 (bottom), 154, 168 (bottom left), 171,
181, 183 (top).
British Tourist Association: 157 (bottom).
Burgerbibliothek, Bern: 174 (bottom), 179 (right), 180 (bottom), 182 (top),
183 (bottom), 223 (left).
Burstlid Waldbergen Zeilsches Gesamlarchiv: 229 (bottom).
Cambridge University Library: 56–57.
Cathedral of Oviedo: 40.
Central Library of Ghent: 109 (top right), 165 (both), 168 (top and bottom
left).
Courtauld Institute of Art: 98.
Danish National Museum: 22.
Dean and Chapter of Westminster Abbey: 135 (left).
Eric Lessing: 45 (center), 58 (left), 62 (both), 63, 78, 85 (bottom), 108
(bottom left), 109 (top left), 112 (left), 155 (bottom), 168 (bottom right),
168 (right), 191 (bottom), 218.
Fotomas Index: 174 (top), 224, 245 (left), 249 (bottom).
Germanisches Nationalmuseum, Nuremburg: 157 (top), 188 (bottom), 226,
232 (bottom), 233 (bottom), 238–39, 242, 245 (left), 247 (above).
Heidelburg University Library: 44–45.
Ian Hogg 10–11, 46 (bottom right), 47 (bottom), 49 (both), 50 (all three), 54
(top), 55 (right two), 111, 113.
John Freeman: 174 (top), 224, 245 (left), 249 (bottom).
Jordan Ministry of Tourism and Antiquities: 93 (bottom).
Lauros-Giraudon, Paris: 69 (bottom), 176, 179 (bottom).
Mansell Collection: 34, 92 (both), 176, 177 (both).
Mary Evans Picture Library: 1, 29, 33 (top), 89 (bottom), 93 (top), 98 (top),
103, 110, 184, 189, 203 (bottom left), 205 (top right), 209 (bottom) 228, 241
(bottom), 249 (top), 250.
Master and Fellows of Corpus Christi College, Cambridge: 98, 100 (top).
Master and Fellows of Trinity College, Cambridge: 38, 39.
Ministère des Armes, Paris: 204, 215 (top).
Museum Arquol Madrid: 11 (bottom).
National Museum of Iceland: 26.
National Maritime Museum: 22 (bottom), 215 (bottom).
Niedersächsiche Stats und Universitätsbibliothek, Göttingen: 45 (far right),
47 (far right), 202 (bottom).
National Gallery: 31 (top).
Offetliche Kulturbesik, Basle: 233 (bottom right).
Osterrshisde Nationalbibliotek, Vienna: 196 (top), 217 (bottom).
Patrimonic Nacional, Madrid: 211.
Percy Hennell: 60.
Petit Palais, Paris: 6.
Phaidon Press Ltd: 60.
Photo Bulloz, Paris: 6, 76–77, 112 (top), 194, 198, 230–31, 235, 236–237,
244, 246.
Photo KLM Aerocarte: 140.
Pierpont Morgan Library: 66 (top).
Prado Museum, Madrid: 243.
Public Record Office: 58 (right).
Radio Time Hulton Picture Library: 7, 32 (bottom), 85, 164 (bottom), 170
(bottom), 175 (bottom), 180 (bottom right), 246, 248.
Thames and Hudson: 151 (right).
Trustees of the British Museum: 33, 37–38, 89 (top), 108 (bottom), 137
(bottom), 180 (top), 213 (top), 219 (top), 225.
Scala: 188, 243.
Universitäts Bibliothek, Göttingen: (top) 155.
Viking Ship Museum; Oslo: 25.
Victoria and Albert Museum: 60, 170 (top), 156 (bottom), 170 (top), 236
(left).
Uffizi Museum, Florence: 188.

The author and publishers extend their grateful thanks to Mrs Stuart Rose
of Illustration Research Service and to Kate Lewin for extensive help with
picture research; to Richard Natkiel for the provision of maps; to P L
Gwynn-Jones for the section on Heraldry – and to Ian Hogg for his section
on Siege Techniques, Castle Building Techniques and Cannon and
Artillery.

Extract on page 93 from Sir Charles Oman's *Art of War in the Middle Ages
A.D. 378–1515*, Cornell University Press, 1960.
Extract on page 78 from Henri Pirenne's *History of Europe*, Allen and
Unwin, London, 1939.

The Publishers have tried to acknowledge all copyright material where this
has been possible, nevertheless apologies are made for any errors or
omissions.